GW00862593

Edexcel GCSE

Applied
Business

Written by

Carol Carysforth, Rob Dransfield,
Mike Neild and Catherine Richards

Series editor: Andrew Ashwin

A PEARSON COMPANY

Published by Pearson Education Limited, a company incorporated in England and Wales, having its registered office at Edinburgh Gate, Harlow, Essex, CM20 2JE. Registered company number: 872828

www.heinemann.co.uk

Edexcel is a registered trade mark of Edexcel Limited

Text © Pearson Education Limited 2009

First published 2009

13 12 11 10 09
10 9 8 7 6 5 4 3 2 1

British Library Cataloguing in Publication Data
A catalogue record for this book is available from the British Library.

ISBN 978 1 846903 77 9

Copyright notice
All rights reserved. No part of this publication may be reproduced in any form or by any means (including photocopying or storing it in any medium by electronic means and whether or not transiently or incidentally to some other use of this publication) without the written permission of the copyright owner, except in accordance with the provisions of the Copyright, Designs and Patents Act 1988 or under the terms of a licence issued by the Copyright Licensing Agency, Saffron House, 6–10 Kirby Street, London EC1N 8TS (www.cla.co.uk). Applications for the copyright owner's written permission should be addressed to the publisher.

Edited by Rachael Williams and Alyson Jones
Designed by Tek-Art
Typeset by Tek-Art, Crawley Down, West Sussex
Original illustrations © Pearson Education Limited 2009
Illustrated by Tek-Art
Picture research by Susie Prescott
Cover photo © MBI/Alamy
Printed in the UK by Scotprint

Every effort has been made to contact copyright holders of material reproduced in this book. Any omissions will be rectified in subsequent printings if notice is given to the publishers.

p172 Extract from 'Public Expenditure Statistics Analyses 2008', Chapter 4 © Crown copyright 2008. Reproduced under the terms of the Click-Use Licence.

There are links to relevant websites in this book. In order to ensure that the links are up to date, that the links work, and that the sites are not inadvertently linked to sites that could be considered offensive, we have made the links available on the Heinemann website at www.heinemann.co.uk/hotlinks. When you access the site, the express code is 4011P.

Disclaimer
This Edexcel publication offers high-quality support for the delivery of Edexcel qualifications. Edexcel endorsement does not mean that this material is essential to achieve any Edexcel qualification, nor does it mean that this is the only suitable material available to support any Edexcel qualification. No endorsed material will be used verbatim in setting any Edexcel assessment and any resource lists produced by Edexcel shall include this and other appropriate texts.

Copies of official specifications for all Edexcel qualifications may be found on the Edexcel website – www.edexcel.com

Contents

Dedication

This book is dedicated to Sophie Anne Carysforth – may you enjoy a life full of love, laughter and friendship and have the determination, confidence and good fortune to make all your dreams come true.

Author acknowledgements

Our grateful thanks are due to the following people and organisations who helped and assisted us during the writing of this book: Chris Reid and Louise Mack, two young entrepreneurs who willingly provided insights into the challenges they face running their own businesses; Karsten-Peter Grummitt at Dodona Research and Lucy Jones at Neilsen EDI Limited for helping us with information on cinema market share; David Robinson at Richer Sounds plc, Bill Bailey at Bowland Wild Boar Park and James Moorhouse at Cummins Turbo Technologies for providing invaluable information for case studies on their respective organisations.

Especial thanks are also due to everyone at Pearson who was involved in this project. In particular, our publisher Lewis Birchon for his ongoing help, encouragement and support; Maura Moran for her expertise with macros; Rachael Williams, our managing editor for masterminding the entire metamorphosis from typescript to completed textbook so efficiently, and finally, Alyson Jones and Susan Ross for their careful and expert editing.

Carol Carysforth
Rob Dransfield
Mike Neild
Catherine Richards

Introduction

Welcome to the Edexcel GCSE Applied Business qualification, which enables you to learn about the business world in an interesting and practical way. This book has been specially written to help you do this, so that you will quickly understand what business organisations actually do and how they work. You will do this by applying what you learn to real businesses to see what happens in practice. This is why your award is called 'Applied' Business. We very much hope you enjoy finding out how businesses operate today, as well as discovering how the actions of different businesses can affect us in our everyday lives. Many students who have successfully achieved GCSE Applied Business have been so interested, they have gone on to learn more by studying business at a higher level, such as GCE Applied Business or BTEC National Diploma. Others, who wanted to work in business as soon as possible, have started apprenticeships in areas such as finance or administration.

This introduction has been written to help you understand more about the qualification and how you will be assessed. You will find tips on how to use this book, as well as a description of the different features it contains for quick and easy reference. These include Make the Grade sections that follow each unit, which have been designed to help you prepare effectively for your assessment.

About the qualification

The GCSE Applied Business qualification can be studied as a Single Award or as a Double Award.

- The Single Award means you achieve one GCSE. You will do this if you successfully complete Units 1 and 2.
- The Double Award is equivalent to two GCSEs. You obtain this if you also complete Units 3 and 4.

All the units are covered in this book, so you will find everything you need whether you are taking the Single Award or the Double Award.

Remember it

GCSE Applied Business is a **vocational** qualification. The word 'vocational' simply means it is related to the world of work, in this case the world of business.

Take it further

Talk to your tutor and find out whether you are taking the Single Award or the Double Award. Then find out the order in which you will study the units.

What you will learn

In each unit you will learn about different aspects of business.

- Unit 1 introduces you to the world of business and business enterprise. You will find out about the activities businesses carry out, how businesses are organised and the tasks that are carried out by the people who work there. You will learn how many businesses today aim to operate ethically, in addition to finding out about the importance of customers and the rights and responsibilities of employers and employees.

- Unit 2 focuses on financial transactions. These are crucial as all businesses must keep financial records as well as make payments for goods and services they buy. You will find out how businesses work out whether or not they are financially successful and how to understand the main documents – balance sheets and the profit and loss account – that tell them this.

- Unit 3 enables you to learn more about customers and customer protection, building on the basic information you learned in Unit 1. It will also help you learn about recruitment and training as well as how to apply for a job. All businesses are affected by external factors which are outside their control. You will find out how the actions of their competitors and the economic climate influence the way in which businesses operate.

- Unit 4 concentrates on how businesses use financial planning, building on the topics you covered in Unit 2. You will find out about the importance of cash flow, break-even and budgeting, as well as the ways in which businesses can obtain additional finance if they need it.

Introduction to assessment

You will be assessed for every unit you study. Two units are **internally assessed** and two units are **externally assessed.**

- Units 1 and 3 are based on coursework and are internally assessed. For these units you will investigate two chosen businesses. One will be a local business and the other will be a national or international business. Your tutor will help you to select appropriate businesses and you will know in advance exactly what aspects of the business you must find out about.

You will use your information to compile a research folder and use this to complete a series of tasks that have been written by Edexcel. Again you will see these in advance so you will know exactly what to expect. You will carry out these tasks under controlled conditions. This means that you do the work in school or college, not at home, and a tutor is present when you are doing it. You will also leave any partially completed work and your research folder with your tutor until the next controlled assessment session.

Your completed work is marked by your tutor and then sent to Edexcel for checking.

Describe it

Internal (controlled) assessment takes place in your school or college and your work is marked by your tutors.

External assessment means your work is sent to Edexcel to be marked.

Remember it

The time you have to complete your research is limited to a maximum of 24 hours and the time you have to write up your work is limited to 12 hours. This means you must use your time wisely. You will find helpful guidance in the Make the Grade sections for Units 1 and 3.

- Units 2 and 4 are externally assessed. After you have completed one of these units you will take a 60-minute external examination. This is based on a business scenario which is followed by a series of questions. These may be multiple choice or require a short or extended answer. You will gain practice answering questions to similar scenarios before you take the assessment.

Remember it

If you are worried about your ability to achieve a good grade at your first attempt, there is usually the opportunity to re-sit an assessment if you need to improve your grade.

How to use this book

This book includes lots of different types of activities to help you apply the knowledge you have gained. Throughout the book, a specific topic is covered either over two pages or four. You may prefer to work through each topic methodically. If you prefer to see the full picture, then skim through the whole topic first to see what it is about before you start to read any of the details. You will find plenty of photos, diagrams and illustrations to help you. There are also activities to carry out in groups or as a class, as well as discussion topics.

At the end of each unit you will find a Make the Grade section. This has been specially written to help you to prepare for your assessment. For Units 1 and 3, Make the Grade gives you guidance on the type of information you need to collect for your internal assessment, as well as sample marked answers so you can see the type of responses that are good and not so good! For Units 2 and 4, Make the Grade focuses on the types of question you will have to answer in your external assessment, and again gives you examples of excellent responses and those which need some improvement.

Features of this book

This book contains several features to help you find the information you need quickly and easily.

- **Describe it** Key words or concepts that you need to understand are highlighted.
- **Assessment tips** Helpful information for your assessments.
- **Talk about it** The opportunity to discuss and debate relevant topics in class.
- **Research it** The opportunity to investigate certain topics further.
- **Hotlinks** Website details of relevant businesses. You can find links to all the websites mentioned in this book at www.heinemann.co.uk/hotlinks. Just enter the express code 4011P.
- **Remember it** Key concepts that you need to know for your assessments are highlighted.

- **Case studies** These show how the information you have learned applies to actual businesses. There are often questions and activities to complete.
- **Apply it** These features enable you to apply what you have learned.
- **Take it further** These activities are designed to stretch you. You can work on these on your own or in small groups in order to understand even more about a topic.
- **Just checking** Questions to check that you understand a topic.

Case study

Research it

Describe it

Remember it

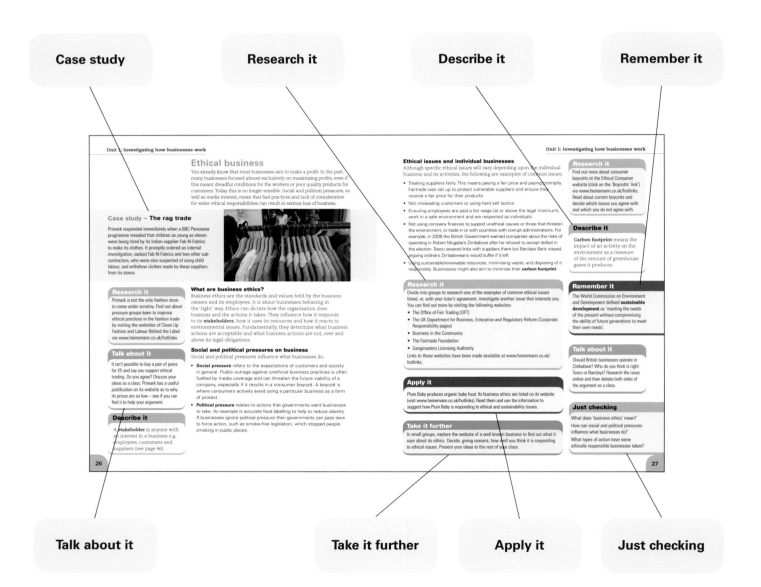

Talk about it

Take it further

Apply it

Just checking

And finally...

This book has been written to help you enjoy studying business, as well as get the maximum benefit out of your course and the best possible grades for your assessments. We hope you enjoy using it and find the information it contains both interesting and easy to understand. We also hope it inspires you to keep learning about businesses, what they do and the possible effects of their actions on all of us.

Carol Carysforth
Rob Dransfield
Mike Neild
Catherine Richards

Unit 1 Investigating How Businesses Work

There are many different types of business organisations. You see examples every day; when you are on your way to school or college, out shopping, searching on the Internet or watching television. They include offices, shops, banks, factories, solicitors, estate agents, garages and football clubs. A farm, a local council, a charity and even your school or college can be described as business organisations.

If you walk past a large business and look through the windows it may seem quite mysterious, scary or fascinating – depending upon your point of view! You may wonder, what is going on in there? What do the people who work there do all day? How are things organised so that they work together productively and don't get in each other's way? How do they know what each other is doing? What are they trying to achieve – and why?

This unit answers all these questions by looking at real businesses and seeing how they work. You will find lots of practical examples and activities to help you relate the information you are reading to the real world of business. By the time you have completed the unit you will know about business enterprise, about the activities businesses carry out, how they decide what **aims** they want to achieve, how they set **objectives** or targets, and then measure their success by checking how well they meet these.

Describe it

Aims are the goals businesses want to achieve.

Objectives are specific steps taken to achieve a goal.

Apply it

On your own, write down the names of ten different business organisations. Include both local and national examples. Try to make them as varied as possible, both in terms of size and what they do.

In small groups, compare your lists. Decide on a final list of 30 different businesses that illustrate a wide range of business activities. Present this list to the rest of the class.

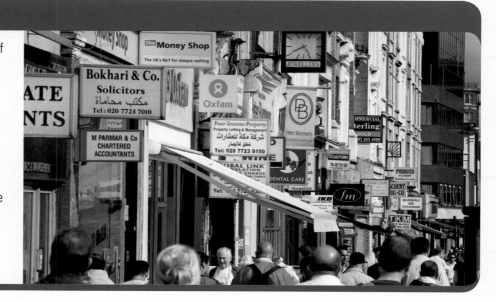

You will probably already know that not all businesses are successful. You will find out more about the risks that business owners take as well as the rewards they can achieve. You will learn about different types of business ownership and also find out about the pressures on businesses today to be **ethical** as well as **profitable**.

To achieve its aims and objectives, a business has to perform certain functions. You will find out how businesses organise or structure these functions and how the people who work in different **functional areas** communicate with each other.

Finally, you will learn about **stakeholders** – all those people who have an interest in, or influence on, a particular business. As a student, you are a stakeholder in your school or college. As employees, your tutors are also stakeholders. As customers, you are all important stakeholders in businesses you use regularly, such as a local taxi firm or takeaway. You will find out how businesses try to meet the needs of their customers and their employees. You will also find out how the law protects all employees and employers and what happens when a disagreement or dispute occurs.

This unit covers the following topics:

1.1 What is a business and what do businesses do?
1.2 How are businesses organised?
1.3 Why are stakeholders so important?

Describe it

Ethical businesses do not take unfair advantage of vulnerable groups of people or lie or cheat to increase their profits.

Profitable businesses are those that earn more than they spend.

Functional areas are those into which business activities can be organised, e.g. sales or finance.

Stakeholders are groups of people with an interest in a business.

How you will be assessed

This unit is one of two compulsory units that you will need to study for the Single Award in Applied Business and one of four compulsory units that you will need to study for the Double Award in Applied Business. Your learning for this unit will be assessed through a controlled assessment task (internal assessment). The task is set by Edexcel and requires you to research two selected businesses and then, using your research, to write your answers to the task during a series of supervised lessons. Your tutor will give you guidance about appropriate businesses to investigate and you will find lots of useful hints and tips in the Make the Grade section at the end of this Unit on pages 62–7.

1.1 What is a business and what do businesses do?

Enterprise

What does it mean if someone is 'enterprising'? In everyday life, it means that they have the ability to use their wits and resources to achieve a positive result.

People who run successful businesses are usually enterprising. The word used to describe them is **entrepreneurs**. To be 'entrepreneurial' is the same as being enterprising – it involves having a variety of skills and using them to achieve business goals.

Remember it

The word **entrepreneur** is a French word, which means 'to undertake'. In the past tense it becomes 'entrepris', which is the same as our word 'enterprise'!

Case study – Two entrepreneurs

Chris Reid and Louise Mack are both young, successful entrepreneurs. When Chris left school he worked in sales before helping someone else to set up a new business. Today he runs Connect Software Solutions Ltd, which provides management software for childcare providers, such as nurseries, and employs nine members of staff.

Louise started a modern apprenticeship in hairdressing in 1998 and worked in a town centre salon. Five years after gaining her NVQ3 she became salon manager. Two years later she set up her own business on the outskirts of town and now employs six members of staff.

Chris says: 'I wanted to be in control and be my own boss. It helped that I'd worked in sales and already developed a business. I needed to learn time management plus how to plan for the future. My biggest problem has been cash flow and also losing my driving licence for six months, so I couldn't visit customers. To get around this I developed online demo software, which has also saved us money in the long term. I work about 70 hours a week but think it's worth it. I think it's important to grasp opportunities and be willing to take a risk. Also, to be a limited company if credit levels could be high.' (*You will learn more about what Chris means by this later in this unit on page 20* .)

Louise says: 'I wanted to use my experience to run my own salon. Although I had no business training or advice, I already knew how to run a successful salon. My biggest problem has been finding good, experienced, responsible and reliable hair stylists. I enjoy putting my own ideas into practice, such as my loyalty scheme for regular clients. I work 42 hours a week in the salon, as well as planning future developments and promotions at home. I think it's important to do a thorough business plan, research the area well, choose the right location and also market and advertise the business wisely.'

Apply it

1 In groups, list the skills Louise and Chris possess that help them run their businesses. Compare your ideas as a class.

2 What other skills do you think entrepreneurs need to be able to run a business successfully? Discuss your ideas with your tutor.

Take it further

What are the benefits and drawbacks of being your own boss? Discuss your ideas with your tutor.

Research it

Charles Dunstone, Larry Page, Steve Jobs, Perween Warsi and Linda Bennett are all entrepreneurs. Find out which businesses they started or helped start and add five more entrepreneurs of your own to the list.

What is business enterprise?

Business is about providing goods and services to enough customers who are willing to pay a price higher than the cost of making the goods and services. The main features of business enterprise are financial, commercial and industrial.

- Financial relates to the money to start and run a business.
- Commercial means having customers (a market) to sell your product or service to.
- Industrial, because some businesses are concerned with creating or manufacturing a product.

Why do some businesses fail?

The reasons businesses fail usually fall into one of the following categories.

- The owner – may be incompetent at business or selling, give up too quickly, be unwilling to work hard, not make necessary changes or expand the business too quickly.
- Competitors – may offer cheaper/better/more innovative products or services and/or provide better customer service.
- Finance – there may be insufficient money to run the business or existing funds may be spent unwisely.

Talk about it

In January 2009, after 99 years of doing business, Woolworths stores finally closed their doors and 27,000 staff lost their jobs. What went wrong? Critics claimed the stores were messy, out of date and sold only cheap tacky goods. Were these the reasons? Find out more about what happened and then suggest why Woolworths failed at a time when many discount stores were thriving.

Just checking

What is an entrepreneur?

Identify four reasons why businesses sometimes fail.

Business activity

All businesses exist to carry out one or more business activities. These are grouped into three main categories, called industrial sectors.

- The **primary sector** includes all businesses that produce or obtain raw materials or natural products from land or sea, for example farming, fishing, mining and quarrying.
- The **secondary sector** comprises businesses that manufacture, process or construct goods, for example oil refineries, house builders, steel producers, mobile phone manufacturers and car makers.
- The **tertiary sector** includes businesses that supply goods and/or provide a service to customers, for example retailers, banks, transport companies, insurance firms, legal businesses and restaurants.

Some businesses carry out more than one activity and may operate in more than one sector.

- They may produce *and* supply goods, such as farmers who have farm shops.
- They may supply goods and services, such as garages, which sell and service cars.
- They may manufacture *and* sell goods and offer additional services to customers. Apple produces computers, iPods and iPhones and sells them in its Apple stores and online. It also operates iTunes and provides support to customers who have bought its products. Check out the full range of Apple products and services on their website. A link has been provided at www.heinemann.co.uk/hotlinks. Just enter the express code 4011P.
- They may be involved in activities relating to every sector, such as oil companies like BP, which extract oil from the ground, refine it and then supply fuel to motorists.

Apple is an example of a business that carries out more than one activity and operates in more than one sector

Remember it

The **core business activity** is the one that is most important or where the business has the most experience, and is usually the most profitable for the business.

Research it

1 Working in groups, identify which activities are carried out by each of these businesses by referring to their websites. Say which sector(s) each one operates in. Compare your ideas as a class.

   (a) Amazon (b) HSBC (c) BAE Systems (d) Stagecoach (e) Dell (f) Thomson Reuters (g) Rolls Royce (h) Red Vision (i) Farrington Oils (j) Whitbread (k) BUPA (l) Balfour Beatty

2 Add four businesses of your own, preferably one from each sector and one that carries out more than one activity.

Competition in business

Almost all businesses have to cope with competition. This benefits customers because it gives them more choice. It also helps to keep prices low.

The growth of businesses trading online has increased competition for many established firms. Customers can now choose from a wider range of products and prices in the comfort of their own home and are helped by price comparison websites such as Money Supermarket™ and Kelkoo, and websites where customers give reviews of their experiences, such as TripAdvisor. To remain competitive, some businesses have had to change their approach or even **diversify** from their original core activity.

Examples of companies that have diversified include:

- Dixons, which has replaced its town centre stores with an online store to sell electrical and electronic goods more cheaply.
- Boots, which stopped offering beauty treatments to focus on improving its core retail business in order to compete with firms such as Superdrug.
- HMV (which also owns Waterstones), which has introduced new technology products, boosted sales of computer games and converted stores to include social hubs and entertainment areas to meet competitive challenges from supermarkets and Amazon, which offer discounted CDs, DVDs and books.

Describe it

To **diversify** means to do new and different business activities.

Hotlink

Visit the websites Money Supermarket™, Kelkoo and TripAdvisor by going to www. heinemann.co.uk/hotlinks.

Talk about it

View 1: Supermarkets are great because they offer huge choice at low prices.

View 2: Supermarkets reduce choice because local businesses, like butchers and fishmongers, cannot compete and so have to close.

What do you think? In teams, make a list of five main points supporting each argument. Can you arrive at a 'right' answer? Explain your response.

Just checking

Name the three industrial sectors. What business activities does each carry out?

How do businesses cope with competition? How has the growth of e-business affected this?

Case study – **Wild boars make for a different livelihood**

According to Defra (the Department for Environment, Food and Rural Affairs) half of farms in the UK supplement their income by carrying out additional activities to their core business activity of farming. Many offer holiday accommodation or operate a farm shop. Bill Bailey went one step further. In 2000, he converted his farm into Bowland Wild Boar Park that breeds wild boars and sells related products in a farm shop. It also offers a range of facilities for young children, including lamb feeding, chick stroking and barrel rides.

1 **Check out the advice given to farmers about diversification on the Defra website by clicking on the 'Farming' link, then the 'Working in farming' link, and finally the 'Diversification' link (via www.heinemann. co.uk/hotlinks). Identify three other activities farmers might carry out to supplement their income.**

2 **Suggest two reasons why farmers may need to diversify to make a living.**

3 **Check out the Bowland Wild Boar Park facilities by visiting the website via www.heinemann.co.uk/hotlinks. Suggest four reasons why the park is so successful.**

4 **Identify one business in your own area that has had to change its activities or diversify to remain competitive. Find out why this occurred and whether the change has been a good idea or not.**

Compare all your ideas as a class.

Describe it

Profit means that there is money left over when all the business costs are deducted from the sales revenue.

Business aims

All businesses have aims or goals they want to achieve. Most importantly they want to survive and to be successful. To do this, privately owned businesses must make a **profit**. This means that they earn more from their sales than they spend on buying (or making) stock and running the business. Most businesses have other aims too, although it is important not to have too many!

Case study – Not all joy for Starbucks

Starbucks opened 100 new coffee shops in the UK between 2007 and 2008. These included new drive-through stores, with environmental patrols to check throwaway cups are not just dumped, and more shops in airports and train stations. Some think that Starbucks should improve its products and service to compete better with Costa and Caffé Nero. In Australia, Starbucks closed 61 out of 85 stores because Australians preferred their local cafes.

Research it

Find out what you would pay and what you would get for your money if you stayed at one of London's most expensive hotels, The Lanesborough, by visiting its website via www.heinemann.co.uk/hotlinks. Then perform an Internet search to find out which is the most expensive hotel suite in the world!

Understanding business aims

In business, the main aims are usually concerned with one or more of the following:

- **Making a profit** This is essential for most privately owned businesses and is the amount the business owner can keep or reinvest in the business each year after all the costs have been paid. Publicly owned businesses, such as NHS hospitals and the police, aim to make a profit if possible and have strict financial targets to meet. Some privately owned businesses, called social enterprises, use the term 'surplus' rather than profit (see page 22).
- **Providing goods and services to the local or wider community** All businesses make goods, provide goods or provide services. Some focus just on the local community, such as a newsagent or a convenience store. Others concentrate on the wider community, such as the Royal Mail, which delivers post all over the country.
- **Surviving as a business or expanding** If sales are poor and profits are low or non-existent the business will try to cut costs so it can keep going until the situation improves. When times are good, an ambitious business owner may want to expand and open new branches or sell on a wider basis, for example nationally or internationally. Primark, the budget retailer, plans to open new stores in both the UK and Europe, and Tesco is expanding into India.
- **Maximising sales or improving the quality of a product** Businesses that aim to maximise sales may reduce the price or make special offers to customers such as supermarket BOGOF deals (buy one get one free). Other businesses aim to improve quality. This is particularly true for luxury goods and services because these customers are less concerned with price.
- **Providing a highly competitive service** A highly competitive business will always try to find ways to capture customers from its rivals. This might be through offering better quality, lower prices, better after-sales service, higher technical specifications and so on. It will also try to out-think rivals by being more innovative or offering something new or different. Ryanair, the budget airline, is very competitive (see case study on page 19).

Describe it

Maximising sales means to sell as much as possible.

- **Providing charitable or voluntary services** All large charities and voluntary organisations, such as Oxfam or the Samaritans, operate like other business organisations. The difference is that they use the money raised to support a special cause or provide a service to people in need. In addition to paid staff they often recruit volunteers, such as sales staff in charity shops.
- **Being environmentally friendly** Most businesses today have green policies to cover issues such as pollution, waste disposal, packaging, recycling and energy use. Supermarkets, for example, have recycling banks and give away 'bags for life' to try to reduce the number of plastic bags used.

Achieving business aims

It is one thing to decide upon aims and quite another to achieve them. Primark wants to expand in Spain and open stores in Germany, Portugal and the Netherlands. To improve their chances of success, businesses need to stay focused upon their goals and work out the best way to achieve them. They do this in the following way:

- They first decide on the **aims** they want to achieve (for example, Primark wants to expand).
- Then they identify specific steps they must take to achieve these aims (for example, Primark decides to open new stores in Europe). Another word for these steps is **objectives**.
- They convert these objectives into **targets** so they can check progress. These targets are specific and measurable, so that it is easy to see if they are being met (for example, Primark's target included opening four new Spanish stores during 2009).

Talk about it

Starbucks changed its aims in late 2008 when sales fell during the economic downturn and profits plunged. It closed hundreds of US stores to cut costs. What should Starbucks do now? Improve its coffee, cut its prices, expand again? Discuss your ideas for its future aims and objectives as a group.

Describe it

Aims are the long term goals the business wants to achieve.

Objectives are steps then taken to achieve these goals.

Targets are set to check achievement. They are usually both specific and measurable.

Apply it

Bilal likes running and intends to make money for charity by entering the Great North Run. This will be his first half-marathon, although he has run 10K races before. The race is in October and it is now April. Bilal plans to join an athletics centre with a running track and review his clothing, footwear and nutrition. He has worked out a 16-week road running programme to build up his stamina and speed and calculated how far he must run each week and at what pace.

1 **What is Bilal's aim?**
2 **He has two objectives. What are they?**
3 **How will Bilal check he is meeting his target?**
4 **Is his target specific and measurable? Give a reason for your answer.**
5 **Rachel is going on holiday in July and needs to save £300 for spending money. In groups, identify Rachel's aim, two appropriate objectives and measurable targets she can achieve.**
6 **One of your aims is to achieve your GCSE in Applied Business. As a class, decide upon appropriate objectives and targets to measure your progress.**

Just checking

Describe at least five major possible business aims.

Why do businesses set targets that relate to their aims?

Business objectives

Businesses set objectives that link to their chosen aims. Some examples are shown in the table below.

Aim	Objectives
Maximise sales	Reduce prices
	Introduce new products
	Increase advertising
Be environmentally friendly	Reduce waste
	Reduce energy usage
	Increase recycling
Be highly competitive	Reduce prices
	Improve products/services
	Introduce new products/services

The business will then decide upon the specific targets individual staff need to achieve. These are linked to the job they do and their seniority.

- A sales manager is responsible for all sales targets set for the organisation.
- All staff are responsible for environmental targets, such as reducing energy by switching off lights and computers for example.
- Departmental staff are responsible for targets relating to their own area, for example sales staff have sales targets, whereas production staff have targets that relate to quality and output.

Research it

Talk to your tutor about the aims and objectives of your school or college. Then find out about the targets of the different staff who work there.

Apply it

1 Suggest two appropriate aims for each of the following types of business and one objective to link to each one.

(a) Private gym　　　(b) Taxi firm

(c) Ambulance service (d) Animal welfare charity

(e) Luxury hotel

2 In 2008, Asda announced plans to build a £1 billion online business by 2011. It now sells food, fashion and furniture online and through its Asda Direct catalogue.

(a) Why do you think Asda has made these plans?

(b) Suggest three objectives Asda's IT and marketing staff might now have. Use Asda's website via www.heinemann.co.uk/hotlinks to get ideas.

(c) How will Asda know if it has achieved its aims?

Evaluating whether aims and objectives have been met

Many business owners have a vision and set goals they want to achieve, but some fail because they become so involved with their day-to-day activities that they forget about them. Achieving aims and objectives means constantly checking to make sure targets are being met, and taking action if they are not.

Case study – Still aiming high!

Ryanair is Europe's largest low fares airline. Since it started in 1985 it has expanded its fleet of planes, its routes and its passenger numbers. It out-performs its competitors by keeping its operating costs to a minimum so that it can keep fares low. It charges for additional services like bag check-in to supplement its income. Visit the Ryanair website via www. heinemann.co.uk/hotlinks.

Ryanair wants to continue growing and in 2008 had more planes on order, despite predicting its first loss for 20 years because of increased fuel costs. In this position, many businesses would increase prices but Ryanair plans to lower theirs even more. Its aim is to make tickets so cheap it can still fill its planes.

The chief executive, Michael O'Leary, estimated this plan could result in a loss of £47 million in 2009, but thinks it is worth it to maximise his passenger numbers.

1 **Identify Ryanair's main aims.**

2 **What steps have been taken to achieve these?**

3 **Why is Ryanair now predicting a loss?**

4 **Richard Branson also owns an airline – Virgin Atlantic. Although he also aims to be profitable he intends to achieve this in a different way to Ryanair. Check out Virgin Atlantic's mission statement in the 'All About Us' section of their website (go to www.heinemann.co.uk/hotlinks). Identify the similarities and differences between Ryanair's main aims and objectives and those of Virgin Atlantic.**

5 **Suggest what evidence you would need to have to know whether both businesses are meeting their aims and objectives and how you would obtain this.**

6 **Michael O'Leary has said he would like to offer cheap transatlantic travel. Suggest how this could affect the future aims and objectives of both Ryanair and Virgin Atlantic.**

Take it further

The economic problems that started in 2008 affected the plans of lots of businesses. Many faced falling sales, such as estate agents, house builders and airlines. Others benefited, such as discount stores Primark, Aldi and Netto. Imagine you owned a small retail clothes store in 2007, when business was booming. What would have been your plans? How would you have changed these when things became tough a year later? Discuss your ideas as a group.

Just checking

What is the difference between a business aim, objective and target?

Why should objectives be measurable?

How can a business know if it has achieved its aims and objectives?

Business ownership

There are several different types of business ownership. In this section you will learn what these are, their main features, the responsibilities of the owners and how the type of ownership usually relates to the size and scale of the business.

Case study – The start of a Monsoon!

In 1972, Sri Lankan born Peter Simon was a sole trader, selling hippy clothes on a market stall on the Portobello Road. Today he is worth over £600 million as the founder and chairman of retail stores Monsoon and Accessorize. Along the way, with his ex-wife Kate, he formed a private company and floated it on the Stock Exchange, but then took it private again by buying out other shareholders at a cost of £185 million. He also founded the Monsoon Accessorize Trust in 1994 to help improve the lives of women and children in Asia. Find out more by visiting the Monsoon Accessorize and Monsoon Accessorize Trust websites via www. heinemann.co.uk/hotlinks.

Remember it

Sole traders are personally responsible for all the debts of the business, so risk having to sell their own possessions if the business owes money to banks, suppliers and so on. This is called **unlimited liability**. It means that the responsibility of the owner for the debts of the business is unlimited.

Remember it

The shareholders of a limited company have **limited liability**. This means they are only liable (responsible) for the amount they agreed to invest in the business. If the business had to close and owed money to suppliers or the bank, for example, the personal possessions of the shareholders could not be claimed to help pay those debts.

The private sector

Most businesses in Britain are owned by private individuals like Peter Simon. They range from small enterprises such as a local taxi firm to large organisations such as British Airways. Businesses can be owned in the following ways:

- **A sole trader** is generally the smallest type of business. As its name suggests, it has one single owner, but may have several employees. The owner has complete control over every aspect of the business from cleaning up to paying wages. Young entrepreneur Louise Mack (see page 12) is a sole trader. Other examples of sole traders are plumbers, florists, decorators and market traders.

- A **partnership** is owned by two or more people who are jointly responsible for the business. Many professional people, such as architects, accountants, doctors and solicitors, form partnerships. Most partnerships are small in size and scale but there are some exceptions where all the employees become partners when they join the business, such as the John Lewis Partnership. Most partnerships also have unlimited liability but there is now a provision to set up a limited liability partnership (LLP). In this type of business, the owners' responsibility for their debts is limited to the amount they have invested in the business.

- A **private limited company** is the type of business owned by young entrepreneur Chris Reid (see page 12). You can tell because the name of the business ends in 'Ltd'. The owner(s) are also the shareholders because they each own a 'share' in the business. They often run the business too, so are also the directors. Many family businesses are private companies.

- A **public limited company** is generally the largest type of private enterprise. In this case the company name ends with the letters 'plc'. The shares are usually traded on the Stock Exchange and can be owned by members of the public as well as institutional investors, such as banks and insurance companies. The directors are paid a salary and can decide whether to own shares or not. Selling shares publicly means that large amounts of money can be raised to expand or develop the enterprise. All shareholders have limited liability.

- A **franchise** is different from the usual type of business. In this case an established business (the franchisor) appoints franchisees to run outlets or enterprises. The franchisees pay a fee to use the business name and are usually provided with help, support and training. Examples include The Body Shop, Domino's Pizza and McDonald's. The main benefit of this for someone wanting to run their own business is that it gives them the experience of running a business themselves but helps reduce the risk of failure.

- **Workers' cooperatives** are another variation of business ownership. In this case the business is jointly owned and run by the workers who share the profits. They decide between them how the business should be run. Workers' co-ops are usually quite small and are different from the Cooperative Retail Society which is operated nationally and owned by its customers.

The public sector

The public sector is the part of the UK economy that is owned, financed and controlled by the government. It includes:

- **Government departments**, which are responsible for the provision of services on a national basis, such as education, health, defence, environmental issues, the police, parts of the prison service, national transport and tax collection.

- **Local authorities**, which provide local services, such as refuse collection and recycling, libraries, road maintenance, social services and environmental health.

- **Health trusts**, which exist to deliver health care in a local area.

- **Public corporations**, which are state-owned businesses, such as the BBC and the Royal Mail service. These businesses are expected to be profitable, just like private firms.

Research it

1 In 2007, the British government took control of Northern Rock bank. See if you can find out why.

2 Check you know the name of your local authority and look on its website to see the services it provides.

Just checking

Describe the main features of the different types of business ownership.

Why do many business owners prefer to have limited liability?

Remember it

Peter Simon **floated** his business on the Stock Exchange. This means that ownership is transferred from a sole trader, partnership or private limited company to plc status. This process is often referred to as 'going public'.

Talk about it

Why is Louise happy to be a sole trader whereas Chris thinks it's important to have limited liability (see page 12)? Discuss your ideas as a group.

Research it

The features of different types of ownership are given at startups. co.uk, an online resource for starting up a business. You can find out about cooperatives on the Co-operatives UK website and franchises at the British Franchise Association website via www. heinemann.co.uk/hotlinks.

Divide your class into five groups. Each group should investigate how to start up a different type of business. Your tutor will decide whether your group will research starting up as a sole trader, in partnership, as a private limited company, a workers' cooperative or a franchise. Produce a brief factsheet and present your findings to the class.

Assessment tip

You need to know how the ownership of businesses you investigate affect its legal liability if it is made bankrupt or goes into liquidation. Make sure you understand these terms now!

The voluntary sector

Charities and voluntary organisations are 'not for profit' businesses. They aim to raise money and make a surplus, after paying for essential expenses. They use this surplus to support a special cause or provide specific services to people in need. All charities in Britain must abide by several regulations and are overseen by the Charity Commission. Unpaid trustees are appointed to ensure that all the money is managed properly and that accurate accounts are kept.

Social enterprises also aim to make a surplus, rather than a profit for shareholders. These are businesses set up to achieve a specific social or environmental goal and any surplus is used to further this aim. A well-known example is Jamie Oliver's restaurant Fifteen, which he set up to provide training and employment for unskilled and unemployed young people.

Research it

1 Working in small groups, choose a different charity for each group. Use its website to find out what cause it aims to support, how it carries out its work, what its main aims are and how much it raises each year. Then compare your findings as a class.

2 The Big Issue is a social enterprise. Investigate its social aims and how it achieves these by visiting its website via www.heinemann.co.uk/hotlinks. Next, search the Internet to find two examples of social enterprises in your own area and compare your findings with the rest of your class.

Size and scale

The size of a business

A very small business may consist only of the owner. In some cases, sole traders may employ one or two staff. Small businesses are the most common type of business organisation in the UK but it is large businesses that employ the most people. A large business organisation such as Tesco or the NHS may employ thousands of people.

The scale of a business

This relates to the size of the business's operations, rather than its physical size. A company producing 100 pairs of jeans a week operates on a smaller scale than one which produces 10,000 pairs a week. The second business usually needs more workers, more production facilities, more equipment and greater investment.

Economies of scale

Big businesses that operate on a large scale normally need more customers because they need to sell more goods. They can attract these customers because their massive size also allows them to gain advantages which small businesses cannot. These advantages allow them to be able to reduce their unit costs. Note that large businesses will almost always have higher costs than a small firm but it is the cost per unit produced that is crucial.

The benefits of being big are known as **economies of scale**. For example, Toys R Us buys very large amounts of toys from manufacturers. It is able to negotiate lower prices for the toys with manufacturers because it buys so many. It can pass on these lower prices to customers which makes it more competitive.

Eddie Stobart lorries are easily identifiable on British roads. Because it is a big firm it can afford to buy larger trailers that carry more goods on each journey. If they can carry twice as many goods, the lorries do not need twice as many drivers, twice as much fuel or have to pay twice as much insurance. As a result, the cost per unit carried is lower than other transport firms that cannot afford to buy such large trailers.

Size, scale and ownership

Normally there is a link between size, scale and ownership. Sole traders are usually small in size and scale, whereas public limited companies have the money and resources to be far larger and to operate on a wider scale. However, there are exceptions. Although Nike Inc is a huge global enterprise with over 30,000 employees and sales of $18 billion a year, it doesn't own any factories or manufacturing plants! Instead it contracts out the production of its footwear and clothing to 700 factories in 52 countries all over the world.

Describe it

Economies of scale are the financial benefits of operating on a large scale which lead to lower cost per unit produced.

Research it

Find out more about Nike and its operations by visiting their website via www.heinemann.co.uk/hotlinks.

Just checking

What is the difference between the private, public and not-for-profit sectors?

Explain the difference between the size and scale of a business and how these often relate to the type of ownership.

Talk about it

Many small businesses use the Internet to sell their products. The global nature of the Internet means that small firms might receive orders from anywhere in the world. In small groups, discuss the problems that might occur for a small business in such circumstances, then compare your ideas as a class.

Case study – **The grass *is* greener**

At 19, Stephen Waring ran his lawn care business called GreenThumb from the back of his car. His idea was popular and the business quickly grew but there was a limit to the scale of the operation that he could manage alone or with his staff. So, in 1996, Stephen set up a franchise operation. Franchisees pay around £26,500 plus VAT for the licence and start-up package, which includes training. His company now looks after over 270,000 lawns but is aiming to reach one million – so he is still looking for franchisees! Find out more about franchising by visiting the Business Link website (click on the 'Buy or sell a business' link) and about Stephen's GreenThumb business via www.heinemann.co.uk/hotlinks. Now answer the following questions.

1 **What is meant by the phrase 'scale of operation'?**
2 **Suggest three advantages to becoming a franchisee of GreenThumb rather than setting up in business alone to look after people's gardens.**
3 **Suggest three advantages for Stephen in being a franchisor rather than opening branches all over the country and employing his own staff.**
4 **Your friend Sarah is keen to become a franchisee with a firm you've never heard of. What checks should she do before she makes any commitment and why?**

Compare your answers as a class.

The risk-reward ratio

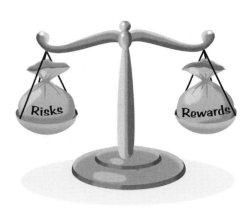

Businesses need to get the balance right

All business owners take a risk when they start their business – but the amount of risk varies. Some business ideas are more risky than others whilst others are positively foolhardy, such as trying to set up a global online distribution company from your bedroom or becoming a mobile cat walker! Other risks are involved once a business is up and running. Failing to cope with these can result in the business having to close.

The rewards are associated with the amount of profit that a successful business might be able to generate. For many entrepreneurs setting up businesses, the lure of profit is an important motivator and often an aim.

In business it is important to balance the risks against the potential rewards. This section looks at identifying risks and rewards and evaluating the balance between them.

Case study – **Wounded in battle**

Toshiba, the Japanese electronics firm, lost about $1 billion when its newly developed HD-DVD player lost out against Sony's Blu-ray player, which is now the established format for high definition (HD) recorders. The fate of Toshiba's player was sealed in 2008 when major film studios like Warner supported the Sony format. Sony will now gain substantially from the multibillion pound high definition DVD industry.

Toshiba was not the only loser. So too were any early purchasers of its HD-DVD recorders, who are now saddled with a pretty useless piece of kit.

Take it further

If you don't understand any of the technical terms used in the case study above, find out what they mean. Then suggest why Toshiba was prepared to spend so much developing its HD-DVD player with no guarantee that its format would be adopted. Was Toshiba wise or foolish? Compare your ideas with those of your class.

Talk about it

1 In groups, identify one more example of each type of risk. Then assume you were setting up a business. Assess your risks and decide what you could do to minimise them.

2 Discuss with your tutor the type of risk assessments that take place in your school or college.

What is risk?

The risk factor in business is the chance that the business will fail or will not do as well as expected. There are several different types of risks:

- **Personal**, for example a serious mistake could ruin your reputation, such as a professional photographer who fails to turn up at a wedding.
- **Economic**, for example unemployment levels rise, people have less to spend so demand for your product or service falls.
- **Financial**, for example a major customer does not pay you.
- **Technological**, for example your product is made obsolete by a competitor.
- **Commercial**, for example a major customer cancels an order.
- **Operational**, for example your computer system breaks down.
- **Legal**, for example you fail to comply with health and safety laws.

The degree of risk is the chance of it occurring. Risk assessment means identifying and ranking risks in relation to how likely they are to happen, their possible effect and taking action to minimise or eradicate them.

What are rewards?

These are the potential financial, social and personal benefits gained by the risk-taker if the venture is successful. They include being independent and in control, making their own decisions and earning more money than they would as an employee.

Risk/reward ratio

Risks vary from one type of venture to another, but one rule usually applies.

Low risk = low return   High risk = high return

This is why gamblers who bet on the favourite in a horse race get worse odds than those who back an outsider. In business, the risk/reward ratio indicates whether the business is a 'good bet' or not. The larger the ratio the better, so if you put £1000 into a business with a potential return of £2000 (1:2) this is not as good as if the potential return was £3000 (1:3). Anyone asked to invest in a business weighs up the risk/reward ratio using the factors shown below.

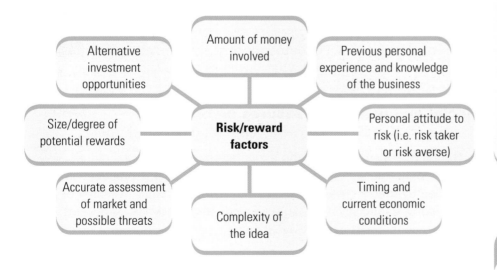

Research it

Interview one person you know who runs a business. Ask him or her to identify the rewards he or she has gained as a result of running their own business. Draw up a list as a class and assess which you think are the most and least important and why.

Research it

If you've ever tried to write neatly resting on a wobbly desk, then you may think Andrew Gordon is a genius. He invented the Stable Table wobble wedge, a small device that props up wobbly table legs. But when he appeared on the BBC television programme Dragons' Den, where entrepreneurs pitch for financial investment, the panel of Dragons thought his idea was ridiculous. Despite this, Stable Table has gone from strength to strength. Find out more about Andrew's business today at his website and suggest two reasons why it is successful.

Just checking

Identify the different types of risks that businesses take and the rewards they can achieve.

Explain the relationship between risks and rewards and how businesses balance one against the other.

Take it further

You can watch past clips from Dragons' Den by visiting the show's website via www.heinemann.co.uk/hotlinks. Select two or three business ideas that interest you and see if you agree with the panel's decision in each case.

Ethical business

You already know that most businesses aim to make a profit. In the past, many businesses focused almost exclusively on maximising profits, even if this meant dreadful conditions for the workers or poor quality products for customers. Today this is no longer sensible. Social and political pressures, as well as media interest, mean that bad practices and lack of consideration for wider ethical responsibilities can result in serious loss of business.

Case study – The rag trade

Primark responded immediately when a BBC Panorama programme revealed that children as young as eleven were being hired by its Indian supplier Fab-N-Fabrics to make its clothes. It promptly ordered an internal investigation, sacked Fab-N-Fabrics and two other sub-contractors, who were also suspected of using child labour, and withdrew clothes made by these suppliers from its stores.

Research it

Primark is not the only fashion store to come under scrutiny. Find out about pressure groups keen to improve ethical practices in the fashion trade by visiting the websites of Clean Up Fashion and Labour Behind the Label via www.heinemann.co.uk/hotlinks.

Talk about it

It isn't possible to buy a pair of jeans for £5 and say you support ethical trading. Do you agree? Discuss your ideas as a class. Primark has a useful justification on its website as to why its prices are so low – see if you can find it to help your argument.

Describe it

A **stakeholder** is anyone with an interest in a business e.g. employees, customers and suppliers (see page 46).

What are business ethics?

Business ethics are the standards and values held by the business owners and its employees. It is about businesses behaving in the 'right' way. Ethics can dictate how the organisation does business and the actions it takes. They influence how it responds to its **stakeholders**, how it uses its resources and how it reacts to environmental issues. Fundamentally, they determine what business actions are acceptable and what business actions are not, over and above its legal obligations.

Social and political pressures on business

Social and political pressures influence what businesses do.

- **Social pressure** refers to the expectations of customers and society in general. Public outrage against unethical business practices is often fuelled by media coverage and can threaten the future viability of a company, especially if it results in a consumer boycott. A boycott is where consumers actively avoid using a particular business as a form of protest.

- **Political pressure** relates to actions that governments want businesses to take. An example is accurate food labelling to help to reduce obesity. If businesses ignore political pressure then governments can pass laws to force action, such as smoke-free legislation, which stopped people smoking in public places.

Ethical issues and individual businesses

Although specific ethical issues will vary depending upon the individual business and its activities, the following are examples of common issues.

- Treating suppliers fairly. This means paying a fair price and paying promptly. Fairtrade was set up to protect vulnerable suppliers and ensure they receive a fair price for their products.
- Not misleading customers or using hard sell tactics.
- Ensuring employees are paid a fair wage (at or above the legal minimum), work in a safe environment and are respected as individuals.
- Not using company finances to support unethical causes or those that threaten the environment, or trade in or with countries with corrupt administrations. For example, in 2008 the British Government warned companies about the risks of operating in Robert Mugabe's Zimbabwe after he refused to accept defeat in the election. Tesco severed links with suppliers there but Barclays Bank stayed, arguing ordinary Zimbabweans would suffer if it left.
- Using sustainable/renewable resources, minimising waste, and disposing of it responsibly. Businesses might also aim to minimise their **carbon footprint**.

Research it

Divide into groups to research one of the examples of common ethical issues listed, or, with your tutor's agreement, investigate another issue that interests you. You can find out more by visiting the following websites:

- The Office of Fair Trading (OFT)
- The UK Department for Business, Enterprise and Regulatory Reform (Corporate Responsibility pages)
- Business in the Community
- The Fairtrade Foundation
- Gangmasters Licensing Authority

Links to these websites have been made available at www.heinemann.co.uk/hotlinks.

Apply it

Plum Baby produces organic baby food. Its business ethics are listed on its website (visit www.heinemann.co.uk/hotlinks). Read them and use the information to suggest how Plum Baby is responding to ethical and sustainability issues.

Take it further

In small groups, explore the website of a well known business to find out what it says about its ethics. Decide, giving reasons, how well you think it is responding to ethical issues. Present your ideas to the rest of your class.

Research it

Find out more about consumer boycotts at the Ethical Consumer website (click on the 'Boycotts' link') via www.heinemann.co.uk/hotlinks. Read about current boycotts and decide which issues you agree with and which you do not agree with.

Describe it

Carbon footprint means the impact of an activity on the environment as a measure of the amount of greenhouse gases it produces.

Remember it

The World Commission on Environment and Development defined **sustainable development** as 'meeting the needs of the present without compromising the ability of future generations to meet their own needs'.

Talk about it

Should British businesses operate in Zimbabwe? Who do you think is right: Tesco or Barclays? Research the issue online and then debate both sides of the argument as a class.

Just checking

What does 'business ethics' mean?

How can social and political pressures influence what businesses do?

What types of action have some ethically responsible businesses taken?

1.2 How are businesses organised?

Organisation structures

All businesses must be well organised to ensure all the jobs are carried out efficiently. Even if two people run a business, they need to decide what tasks need doing and by whom, but they can agree this informally, and even on a daily basis. If 20 or 200 people are employed, the situation is very different. Now each person needs a specific job role that 'fits' with all the others so everyone knows who is responsible for each area of work. Otherwise the result is likely to be chaos!

The way in which all these job roles link together is known as the **organisation structure**.

Describe it

Organisation structure refers to the way a business is organised internally to enable employees to carry out their job roles and communicate with each other.

Case study – **Dress sense?**

As a student, Magda worked part-time at a local fashion boutique. The owner relied on Magda to do many different jobs – from designing window displays to creating promotional flyers. Magda enjoyed the variety of work but did not like being on her own when it was quiet. She also lacked the courage to ask for a pay rise. She left when she got a better paid job with a large branch of a national fashion chain. There were six other sales assistants, two supervisors, a deputy store manager and the store manager, who reported to a regional manager. It was more formal, there were more rules to follow and Magda had less freedom to do different things. But she enjoyed the retail training she received, liked working with other people and was pleased she would have an annual pay review.

Types of organisation structure

There are various different types of organisation structure. The type chosen by a business is usually linked to its activities, its aims, its size and its scale.

Talk about it

There are many differences between working for a small and a large organisation. Identify those that Magda experienced and, as a class, add to these from your own experiences if you have (or have had) a part-time job.

Hierarchical structures

A hierarchical organisation has several levels. The fashion chain where Magda worked was hierarchical and can be illustrated as follows.

Regional Manager

Store Manager

Deputy Store Manager

Supervisor — Supervisor

Shop Assistant | Shop Assistant | Shop Assistant | Shop Assistant | Shop Assistant | Shop Assistant

A hierarchical business structure

The person at the top is the most senior and has the most power and authority. This is usually a manager who is responsible for the work of their **subordinates**, as well as for their own performance. They may have a deputy and/or supervisors to help them. The responsibilities of each group of people are different and their job title and salary usually reflect their 'place' in the hierarchy. Each employee normally receives instructions from the person immediately above them, to whom they are also accountable for their actions. This person is known as their **line manager**.

Pyramid structures

A pyramid structure represents an organisation that has progressively more people at each lower level. If it is also hierarchical the pyramid will be steep and there will be several levels. In a large hierarchical organisation it is important that managers are not responsible for more people than they can sensibly control. The number of people a person is responsible for is known as the **span of control**.

A pyramid business structure

Centralised structures

A centralised organisation has a head office that is separate from other parts of the business which may be situated in other areas of the country (or even the world).

In centralised structures, important decisions are usually taken by the head office and passed down to other parts of the business. National fashion chains, such as River Island and Next are structured like this, with a head office responsible for all main business functions, such as paying accounts and buying stock. Banks are another example of organisations with centralised structures.

A centralised business structure

The amount of freedom given to unit managers (like Magda's shop manager) varies. In some organisations, almost everything must be referred to head office for approval. In others, individual managers have more scope to use their own discretion.

Describe it

A **subordinate** is a person directly below you on the chart and for whom you are responsible.

Your **line manager** is the manager directly above you in the hierarchy (and connected to you by a line on an organisation chart).

Span of control means the number of subordinates a manager has to control.

Remember it

The opposite of **centralised** is **decentralised**. Most supermarkets are decentralised as the store manager can make most of the decisions about their own store.

Talk about it

In groups, decide the advantages and disadvantages of being a store manager in a centralised structure. Then suggest the advantages and disadvantages for the organisation in operating this way.

Just checking

What does the term 'organisation structure' mean?

Describe the main features of a hierarchical, a pyramid and a centralised type of business structure.

Remember it

The most senior person in an organisation may have the title **Managing Director** (MD) or **Chief Executive Officer** (CEO).

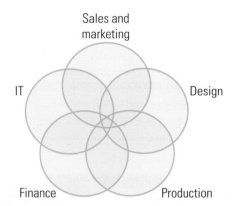

A collaborative business structure

Collaborative structures

A collaborative business is structured so that people can work together efficiently and effectively. This enables them to respond quickly to the challenges faced by the organisation. Teams are a common feature of collaborative organisations. The members may work together or communicate from a distance, using IT. These are known as virtual teams. Team membership will change so that the necessary expert skills are represented depending upon the type of task or problem. Usually expertise is more important than status or seniority in this type of organisation. The aim is to ensure those employees with the relevant knowledge and skills are involved in providing essential solutions needed by the business.

Circular structures

A circular organisation structure is the opposite of a hierarchical one. Another term for it is a flat structure. Here the most senior manager is in the middle looking out, rather than at the top and looking down.

This structure can be shown as a series of concentric circles. The people in the organisation have flexible job roles and can move in and out of different circles depending upon what they are doing or offering to the organisation at the time. The focus is on getting things done, rather than identifying who has the authority to do a particular task. People can be moved from a difficult task to an easier one (or vice versa) quite easily without it being seen as a promotion or a demotion. Again, this means there is more emphasis on team working and the organisation has more flexibility to respond to change.

Matrix structures

A matrix structure is often found in organisations that deal with specialised 'one-off' projects, such as civil engineering companies. These companies may be working on several projects at the same time such as a new motorway in the UK, a bridge in Europe and a high-rise office block in London. Each project (for example A, B and C) has an expert team responsible for seeing it through. These experts need the support of major functions of the organisation, such as finance, human resources and production. The project managers will be in constant contact with the managers of these functions about issues such as costs, staffing and design. The project teams work on the project until it is complete, then they are disbanded and a new team will be formed to work on a new project.

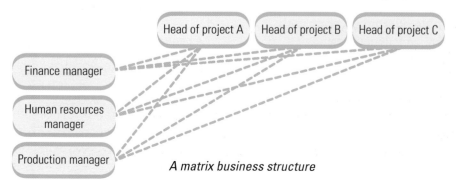

A matrix business structure

The impact of the organisation structure on business communications

Traditional business structures

Traditionally, most large organisations were hierarchical to give managers control over their subordinates. Business pioneers like Henry Ford believed that unless the workforce was closely monitored, very little work would be done! In this type of organisation, most communications are 'top down'. There are several dangers with this, particularly if there are several levels of authority.

- Employees may be frustrated that their voice is rarely heard, particularly if their manager 'tells' rather than discusses ideas.
- Information may become distorted as it is passed down from one level to another.
- If many people must be consulted about an issue, rapid decisions are less likely to be made.
- Crucial information may not be identified if senior managers only listen to their immediate subordinates, rather than to those with the best knowledge and skill for that issue.

These problems also apply to centralised organisations. Managers and staff, who must refer most issues to head office, cannot respond promptly to customers. They may also become demotivated as they may not feel their individual contributions are valued by their employer.

Modern business structures

Today's business world is very fast moving and many communications are instant. As a result, businesses need to respond quickly to a wide range of communications and issues, otherwise the consequences can be very serious.

To deal with these challenges most businesses need flexible ways of working, even when they employ a large number of staff. This also enables individual expertise to be harnessed and decisions are based on the most expert and up-to-date information possible.

In a collaborative or circular structure people can respond promptly to different types of communication. If they do not know the answer, they can refer a problem to someone who does. In a matrix structure, project leaders can obtain information promptly, and from the relevant person, on issues that relate to the project. Project teams can work together to solve complex problems.

Apply it

Identify the organisation structure of your school or college. Draw a diagram to represent it. Discuss with your tutor how the structure affects internal and external communications and how the organisation handles expert issues (such as complex IT problems) and urgent communications (such as an emergency on a student trip).

Hotlink

Find out more about complex projects and the people who work on them by visiting the Network Rail website and following the 'Our projects' link visit www.heinemann.co.uk/hotlinks.

Talk about it

Test your own management attitude. Your subordinate Hussein is working on an IT problem and says he will be able to concentrate better if he works from home tomorrow. Do you agree or do you think he just wants to skive off work for a day? What factors could influence your decision?

Modern business communication

Talk about it

In the 1980s, one chief executive insisted on reading all the mail, then wrote comments and instructions on each item before sending it to his managers. Discuss how feasible this would be today, as well as the likely outcomes!

Just checking

Describe the main features of a collaborative, a circular and a matrix type of business structure.

Explain the relationship between the organisation structure of a business and its communications?

Functional areas

Introduction to business functions

All businesses, whether big or small, have a number of functions they need to carry out to ensure the business runs smoothly. These also link to the aims and objectives of the business and what it wants to achieve. The aim of the fashion chain where Magda now works (see page 28) is to give all of its customers a wonderful experience. One objective is to increase sales by 5% from last year. The functions required to do this are shown in the diagram below.

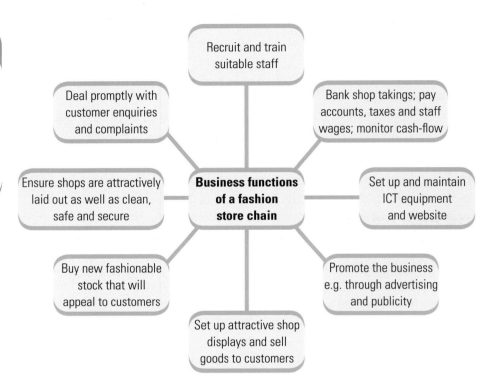

The business functions of a fashion store chain

Talk about it

In groups, identify exactly how each of these activities will contribute to achieving the aim of the business. Then discuss how the staff who work in each of these areas can help to achieve the objective of increasing sales.

Case study – Welcome to the Republic!

Republic is a high street fashion retailer with 93 stores in the UK (as of 2008). Its stated philosophy is given below.

'At Republic, we're all working towards the same goal: to help you find the products you're looking for and to ensure you receive the best customer service possible. So whether you're on our website or in a bricks and mortar store, your shopping experience with Republic will be the highlight of your day. Simple.'

As part of this philosophy, the company aims to provide customers with the most exciting brands at reasonable prices and to run promotions that offer fantastic value. Both the website and all the stores have been designed to make them relaxed and easy to shop in. In 2009 they successfully achieved their objectives of opening a total of seven mega-stores, including Westfield London, and in 2007 they launched their online store (visit www.heinemann.co.uk/hotlinks for a link to the site).

At the Republic Head Office in Leeds, you will find the following departments: buying, merchandising, marketing, ecommerce, retail operations, accounts, payroll, IT and personnel.

1 Working in small groups, link the titles of the departments at Republic's Head Office with the business functions in the chart on page 32. Compare your ideas as a class.

2 Suggest the type of functions a Republic store manager might be responsible for.

3 Republic says it wants to employ enthusiastic and passionate people who thrive in a results-driven environment. Its store managers and supervisors must be able to lead, inspire and motivate a team to get results. Explain why this is important if Republic is to achieve its aims and objectives.

Take it further

Do you think Republic is a centralised or a decentralised organisation? Give a reason for your answer.

The main functional areas

Many businesses, like Republic, are organised into functional areas that reflect the specialist tasks that have to be carried out. The most frequently found ones are shown below. In the next section you will find out in more detail what each functional area does.

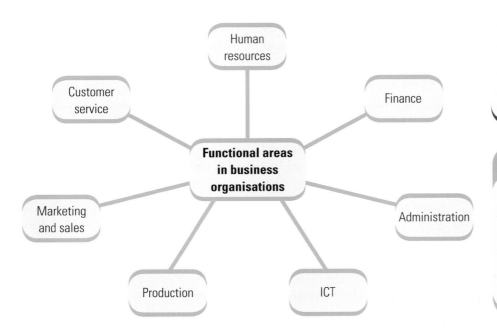

The main functional areas in business

Remember it

The titles of functional areas vary from one business to another. Republic, for example, has 'personnel' (not human resources) and 'ecommerce' (not ICT). You can expect these sorts of differences when you are investigating an organisation yourself (see page 38).

Just checking

What does the term 'business functions' mean?

Identify six functional areas (or departments) found in many businesses.

Explain the link between a business' functions and its aims and objectives.

The main aspects of functional areas

Administration

All businesses need administrators to carry out a variety of support activities to help the business operations run smoothly. Traditionally administration was centralised as one department on its own, but now it is more usual to find administrators employed throughout the organisation in other functional areas (see page 39). The main tasks administrators carry out are shown below.

(see page 39)

Research it

Arrange to interview an administrator at your school or college to find out about their job.

- **Organise, store and retrieve paper and electronic records.**
- **Distribute and dispatch mail.**
- **Organise meetings and prepare relevant paperwork.**
- **Respond to customer enquiries and deal with callers and visitors.**
- **Prepare and distribute documents by post and electronically.**
- **Order and store stationery items and office equipment.**
- **Keep records and files up to date (both paper and electronic).**
- **Make arrangements for travel or special events, e.g. sales conferences.**

Human resources

The term 'human resources' (HR) refers to all the people who work for the business. HR staff are responsible for all areas of staff employment and training. The recruitment process is expensive and time-consuming so it is important to attract and retain the right people. Training and development enables staff to reach their maximum potential and stay motivated. Another key role of HR staff is to ensure that the organisation complies with all laws relating to employment and health and safety. The main aspects of human resources are shown below.

Research it

Find out who is responsible for recruiting new staff at your school or college, who arranges staff training and who is responsible for health and safety. Arrange to talk to them about the jobs they do.

- **Advertising job vacancies, dealing with job applications and arranging interviews.**
- **Issuing a contract of employment to new staff and arranging induction.**
- **Notifying existing staff of promotion opportunities.**
- **Arranging staff training and development activities.**
- **Checking health and safety and keeping accident records.**
- **Monitoring and maintaining good working conditions.**
- **Maintaining staff records, including absences and pay rates.**
- **Liaising with any staff associations or trade unions.**
- **Ensuring compliance with current employment legislation.**

Arranging job interviews is one of the things carried out by human resources departments

Finance

If you owned a business you would probably consider this the most important function of all! As you will learn in Units 2 and 4, unless you pay your bills and forecast your cash flow you are unlikely to stay in business for long. The main aspects of the finance function are listed below.

- **Preparing and sending invoices.**
- **Receiving, recording and banking payments, and chasing up overdue payments.**
- **Checking and paying invoices received.**
- **Preparing the payroll and paying staff salaries and reimbursing expenses.**
- **Issuing departmental budgets and monitoring managers' spending.**
- **Producing cash flow forecasts and other financial reports.**
- **Producing business accounts and paying tax due.**
- **Advising managers about appropriate sources of finance.**

Research it

Who pays all the bills at your school or college and who monitors spending against the budget? What else do they do? Talk to them to find out.

ICT

Even small businesses today have a computer network and most also have a website or a webstore. Maintenance of the system, and its security, is the responsibility of the ICT function. ICT specialists will also help staff users who experience problems often via a 'help desk' facility. The main tasks carried out by the ICT function are summarised below.

- **Maintaining current computer systems and software.**
- **Advising on and installing new equipment/software.**
- **Training and assisting users.**
- **Obtaining/issuing computer supplies and consumables.**
- **Installing and monitoring security of the system to protect against hackers and viruses.**
- **Technical maintenance of the company website.**
- **Making sure staff computer use complies with company IT policy.**
- **Ensuring there is a back-up system for critical data so the system can be restored quickly in an emergency.**

Research it

Find out what the ICT staff do at your school or college. What is the IT policy and how does it affect what you can do as a user?

Production

This function is found only in manufacturing organisations, such as Heinz or Toyota for example, where a key activity is to produce goods. It may also encompass purchasing raw materials and stock control. Today many manufacturers operate a just-in-time (JIT) system where raw materials are delivered promptly when needed. This saves on storage space. There will also be many automated systems where the production process is done by machine or by robots. Production staff are responsible for the tasks listed in the table below.

- **Obtaining raw materials from approved suppliers.**
- **Checking and storing raw material stocks.**
- **Planning production schedules to maximise the use of available equipment.**
- **Producing or assembling the product and checking quality throughout.**
- **Resolving any delays or problems.**
- **Checking, packing and storing the end product and arranging distribution.**
- **Routinely inspecting and maintaining production machinery and arranging for any necessary repairs to be carried out.**

Research it

Ideally you should visit a production department to see how it operates. If this is not possible, you can see lots in operation on YouTube by searching for 'production lines', from the Nintendo Wii, to biscuits or Maclaren cars! A link to the website can be found at www.heinemann.co.uk/hotlinks.

Marketing and sales

Businesses earn money by selling their goods or services. This is the responsibility of the sales staff. Customers only find out about the business and what it offers through adverts, promotions, the website or by other types of publicity. Finding out customer needs and promoting the business is the responsibility of marketing. In some organisations marketing and sales are separate departments, in others they are a joint operation. The main aspects of this function are shown below.

- **Carrying out and analysing market research to obtain customer feedback on current and proposed products or service.**
- **Promoting the business and its products/services by advertising and public relations (PR).**
- **Obtaining a customer profile to target promotions accurately.**
- **Preparing and distributing promotional materials and linking these to sales promotions.**
- **Designing and updating the company website.**
- **Responding to sales enquiries and keeping customer records.**
- **Preparing quotations or estimates and selling the product or service.**
- **Negotiating discounts and providing technical advice.**

Customer service

Customer service is the way in which a business seeks to improve the level of customer satisfaction and the experience a customer has with that business. If that experience is positive, then it is more likely that the customer will come back and buy again from that business. This is where customer loyalty is developed. Customer loyalty is very important. It is no use advertising to attract new customers and then letting them down through poor service. For this reason many businesses have dedicated customer service staff or departments to give advice and information. This is particularly important for organisations that sell complex technical products or services, from engineering equipment to broadband. The main aspects of the customer service function are summarised below.

- **Providing specialist advice and information to assist customers.**
- **Investigating and responding to customer complaints.**
- **Solving customer problems.**
- **Providing after-sales service including supplying spare parts, arranging for repairs and replacing damaged goods.**
- **Keeping records of complaints and problems and analysing these to prevent repetition.**
- **Using customer feedback to improve service and satisfaction.**
- **Ensuring the business complies with consumer laws.**

Research it

Marketing is an important function in all organisations, both large and small. Talk to the owner of a small business to find out what marketing activities they do. Then arrange for someone from a large organisation to give a talk about their marketing function. As a class, identify the similarities and differences between marketing in a small and large business.

Talk about it

Many large organisations, such as BT and the Capital One bank, have outsourced their customer service facility to India because it is cheaper. Some organisations, such as the insurance company Arriva, also moved call centre operations to India but have now decided to relocate the service back in the UK. Do you think outsourcing customer service operations to other countries is a good idea or not? Discuss your views as a class.

Remember it

The term **aftermarket** is often used by automotive, engineering and industrial suppliers. This refers to customers who will need spare parts or other supplies after they have bought the product.

Just checking

Describe the main features of the following functional areas: administration, human resources, finance, ICT, production, marketing and sales, customer service.

Why do some businesses not have a production function?

Investigating functional areas

As part of your assessment for this unit, you will investigate and evaluate the functional areas of your larger, chosen business. This is likely to be a national or international organisation. You will then have to explain the importance to the business of one of the functional areas. This section helps you to understand what you may find when you are carrying out your investigation.

Assessment tip

Your tutor will guide you to find appropriate businesses to investigate, so don't worry about having to choose them on your own!

Differences in functional areas

There are several differences between the functional areas of different businesses. The names may be different (as we have seen with Republic), some activities may be spread across several departments (such as administration) and some may be outsourced (such as customer service). Other differences are summarised below.

Differences in structure

Businesses that provide specialist services or large global businesses may not name departments after standard business functions. Hospitals, for example, are structured into specialist areas such as outpatients, cardiology or paediatrics. A pharmaceutical company may be structured by products, for example drugs, toiletries and hospital supplies. An international business may be structured by geographical area, for example America, Europe and Asia.

Differences related to business size

The larger the business the more people will specialise in a particular job. In small businesses, employees often carry out different roles, such as administrators who record payments or organise repairs. In a medium sized business, these jobs may be done by different people. In a large business they may be carried out in different departments.

Specialist departments

Some functions are focused on one department because specialist equipment and expertise is required, for example production, sales and finance. Other functions may be carried out in several departments such as administration and purchasing. You might also find that purchasing is part of production or customer service is part of sales.

Assessment tip

Businesses can vary considerably in how they are structured and what they call their functional areas. Don't expect any two businesses to be identical or any business you investigate to fit with any textbook theory!

Remember it

Some businesses have an operations function, instead of a production department. Product design and development may be part of this, or there may be a separate R & D (research and development) department.

Talk about it

Which is best? To work in a small firm and be a 'jack of all trades' or in a large business and specialise? Discuss the pros and cons of each as a class.

Research it

Small businesses often outsource IT services. Larger businesses may outsource payroll, cleaning, security, distribution, customer service and public relations (PR). Find out which functions are outsourced at your school or college and why.

Apply it

A business wants to develop and launch a new product. Working in small groups, decide which functional areas would be involved, what each would do, and identify how they would have to work together for the launch to be successful. Present your ideas to the rest of the class.

Case study – The power of Cummins

Cummins Turbo Technologies is a large, global organisation which employs over 1,000 people in Huddersfield, West Yorkshire. It produces Holset turbochargers, which improve the efficiency of an engine, and sells these mainly to large truck makers. Departments at Cummins include Design and Development, Laboratory Operations (where turbochargers are tested), Production, Materials (i.e. Purchasing), Sales and Marketing, Accounts, IT and HR/Payroll.

The company prides itself on its industry-leading standards of customer care and has a separate Aftermarket Division to provide replacement turbochargers and spare parts.

Although Cummins could be described as a hierarchical organisation it also operates a system of team-based working. Staff at all levels liaise on cross-functional teams to contribute to project developments.

1 **What is meant by a 'hierarchical' organisation?**

2 **What benefits will Cummins gain by encouraging team-based working?**

3 **Identify the main role of each of the following functional areas: Design and Development; Production; Sales and Marketing; Accounts; HR/Payroll.**

4 **Explain the importance to the business of the Aftermarket Division.**

Working together – the interdependence of functional areas

Functional areas have to work *together* to achieve the stated aims and objectives of the business. Some examples are given below.

- Meeting sales targets does not just depend upon good sales staff. Production must also make quality goods and deliver them on time. Marketing must be able to identify consumer needs and help promote the products. The feedback sales staff give to marketing helps provide information to production on possible changes to design and specification of products.

- Quality targets mean purchasing staff must obtain the right raw materials, production staff must check quality throughout the manufacturing process and distribution must pack and transport the goods appropriately.

- Customer service targets involve all staff in the business. This is because customer service and sales staff rely on their colleagues in other departments for accurate and prompt information to answer queries efficiently.

Hotlink

Use the Cummins website to find out more about the company. A link to the site has been provided at www.heinemann.co.uk/hotlinks.

Just checking

Describe the differences you might find between functional areas in different organisations.

Explain why it is important that functional areas work together.

Communication between functional areas

You already know that functional areas have to work together to help to achieve the aims and objectives of a business. This obviously means they must communicate with each other. Functional areas also have to communicate with people outside the business as well as with each other. Their communications can therefore be divided into two types: internal and external.

- **Internal communications** are used between colleagues in the same or different departments or between branches of a company to request or provide information. Some written documents, such as reports, may be quite formal, particularly if they will be sent to senior managers. Others are informal, particularly if they are between colleagues of the same level. These include text messages, emails and even a quick chat over a coffee!
- **External communications** are sent to customers and suppliers and other business contacts outside the organisation. These are more formal and must be accurate, easy to understand and unambiguous.

Research it

An intranet contains information just for internal use. Investigate your school or college intranet and identify how it varies from the website, which is available to everyone.

Case study – You've got mail!

When staff first heard that HBOS could be taken over by Lloyds TSB in 2008, the chief executive, Andy Hornby, was deluged in emails from employees worried about their jobs if this happened. In response, he emailed all 70,000 staff to give them more information.

At one time the idea of staff contacting their CEO direct and getting a personal reply would be very strange. Email, though, has changed all that. Today anyone in an organisation can contact people by email, but this is not always good news. Emails full of spelling and grammatical mistakes to an important client will do more harm than good! Email in business tends to be very different to that which you may use between yourself and your friends. It is often more formal and there is an expectation that care will be taken over the presentation in most organisations.

Take it further

1 Discuss with your tutor why jobs were at risk when Lloyds TSB took over HBOS.
2 Find out the IT policy at your school or college and how it affects emails you send to other students or your tutor. Then find out how this compares with one other business organisation you know where computers are used.

Overview of communication methods

Communication methods can be divided into four types: oral, written, IT and visual. These are shown in the diagram below.

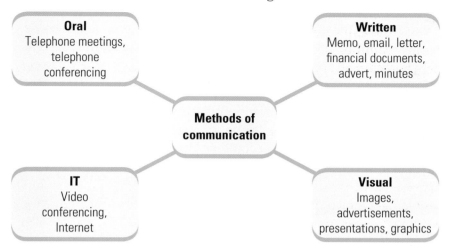

The type of communication that will be used in a situation will depend upon the following factors:

- **The recipient** – some types of communications (for example memos) are only suitable for internal communications. Similarly, business letters and advertisements are methods of communicating to external recipients.
- **The technology available** – you can only send emails to an external contact with an internet connection and if you know his or her email address. Even then you may be restricted on the type and size of attachments you can send.
- **The urgency** – electronic communications are quicker than traditional mail. Sending original documents quickly can be expensive, especially if a courier is used. Other methods of instant communication include the telephone, text messages, video conferences and Internet video/audio links.
- **The complexity** – complex information should be sent in writing. No one can understand a lot of information quickly if you communicate orally, especially over the phone. Complex information that needs to be compared is usually more understandable in a table or graph.
- **Feedback** – if you need immediate feedback to an idea or suggestion then you need to make personal contact by phone or by meeting that person.

Apply it

1 Draft an email to your boss asking if you can leave an hour early on Friday. Include a suitable reason. Ask your tutor to check your email for grammar, punctuation and tone.

2 Do you think you would be better to email your boss in this situation or go to see them in person? Suggest reasons when either could be best.

Research it

Owning a BlackBerry, a laptop and a mobile Internet dongle (used to obtain a broadband connection wherever you are) is becoming commonplace as many people in business need to communicate on the move. The Apple iPhone and Google phone are other options. In small groups, investigate each of these devices, identify how they contribute to business communications and share your ideas as a class.

Research it

Another method of communication is the podcast. Find out more about these and suggest how businesses could use them to their advantage. A useful outline of what they are can be found by visiting the link at www.heinemann.co.uk/hotlinks.

Remember it

The **tone** of a communication relates to its politeness and how appropriate it is for the recipient. When you are speaking, it involves using the correct tone of voice as well as the right words!

Just checking

What is the difference between internal and external business communications?

Describe four different communication methods used by businesses.

Explain the factors that affect which type of communication to choose in a specific situation.

Investigating and evaluating methods of communication

As you have seen, all businesses use different methods of communicating. Formal communications are normally used for important and serious matters, particularly when they are being sent externally. This is important if the issue is complex or if records must be kept for future reference, such as financial documents sent to accountants and shareholders, and information sent to employees about the terms of their employment.

On other occasions, informal communication methods will do the job perfectly, such as if you take a telephone message for a colleague and need to pass on the details. You could do this verbally, write a brief note, fill in a telephone message form or send an email.

Are you receiving me?

Many businesses use automated systems to send customers a text message reminding them about their appointment dates and times a few days before the appointment. The system was originally developed for hospitals, doctors and dentists but is now used by other businesses that lose money when appointments are forgotten or missed, such as hair and beauty salons, day spas and fitness studios.

Take it further

Many communication problems occur because people don't listen! How good a listener are you? Find out by working with a partner. Talk for five minutes about what you did last weekend. Your partner can take notes and check any details. Then reverse roles. Now see how clearly and easily you can tell your tutor what your partner said.

Oral communication methods

Oral communication methods are chosen because they are speedy, ideal for obtaining feedback and often resolve problems and queries rapidly.

Telephones

Telephones and mobiles are invaluable for discussing something with a person you cannot meet face-to-face. If someone is unavailable you can usually leave a message. Telephones are not suitable if the information is complex or if you need a written record, unless you confirm in writing later.

Meetings

These range from informal team briefings, in which staff contribute ideas and suggestions, to formal meetings to which external clients or shareholders are invited. In this case the audience mainly sits and listens to the speaker(s). The topics will vary depending upon the purpose of the meeting.

Telephone conferencing

In a telephone conference several people, often both internal and external, are connected simultaneously. This saves time and money as there is no need for people to travel to a set meeting place. It needs to be well organised or everyone may speak at once! For this reason, one person takes charge and 'chairs' the session to ensure everyone is involved and has the opportunity to contribute to the discussion.

Written communications

Written communications refers to text-based documents, such as letters, memos and emails which may be sent by post or electronically.

Memos

These are internal documents, used to send information between members of staff. Today email is often used instead. Memos are not signed and normally focus on just one topic.

Letters

Thousands of business letters are sent every day. Some are individually written and signed by their author. Others are mass produced to promote new products and services. There is a specific way to set out a business letter. The language is quite formal and slang or abbreviations are never used. The writer must also avoid using specialist jargon and technical terms the recipient would not understand.

Financial documents

These include quotations, purchase orders, invoices, statements, cash flow statements, profit and loss accounts, and balance sheets. You will see examples of these in Units 2 and 4.

Advertisements

There are two types of advertisements: promotional and informational. Informational advertisements may contain large amounts of text. They are used for technical or business-to-business (b2b) advertising and also when advertising for new staff. Descriptive information is also given in brochures and catalogues to promote products and services.

Minutes

'Minutes' is the name for the document that records what happened at a meeting. Some are in a brief, note format which records the decisions made and actions to be taken. Others are more detailed. The minutes are sent to everyone who attended as a formal record of what took place.

Email attachments/documents

Any type of electronic file can be attached to an email, such as a presentation, a video clip or a document. If a file is large it needs to be zipped (compressed) before it is sent. It is also sensible to notify the recipient in advance as some IT systems routinely block many types of email attachments, to protect against viruses.

Research it

Many specialist companies, such as 3+, exist to help businesses run conference calls, especially if they may involve hundreds or even thousands of people! Find out what exactly is involved by visiting the company's website (go to www.heinemann.co.uk/hotlinks).

Talk about it

Discuss with your tutor the type of meetings held at your school or college, who attends them and the range of topics discussed at each one. Find out which are formal and which are informal and the differences this makes.

Just checking

How would you find out which types of communication were used by a particular business?

Explain the importance of communications to people both inside and outside the business.

Visual communication methods

Text is not always the best way of conveying information. You would find it far easier to show what a house looked like, for example, by sending a photograph and a floor plan than by sending three pages of text!

Images and graphics

These include photographs, cartoons, graphs, charts, diagrams – the list is almost endless. If you want to see the range available quickly then go to the search engine Google and choose 'Images' from the options available.

Talk about it

In small groups, identify as many types of different images and graphics as you can and then suggest a business use for each one. Compare your ideas as a class.

Advertisements

Promotional advertisements use images, graphics, pictures and film clips to convey their message and ideas. 'Multimedia' means using more than one type of media to promote a product.

Research it

Find out all the ways in which BMW promotes its cars online by visiting their website and looking at the different models (go to www.heinemann.co.uk/hotlinks).

Presentations

Good visual communications can transform a presentation. The scope is far wider than a series of slides with bullet points! A sophisticated presentation can include film clips, animation and graphics.

Research it

Many large organisations pay specialists to prepare sophisticated presentations. Find out more by visiting the multimedia-presentation.com website via www.heinemann.co.uk/hotlinks.

Information technology

ICT is widely used for many different types of communications today.

Video conferencing

This enables two or more people in different locations to hold a meeting. They can just sit at their PC and be connected over the Internet. They simply need the appropriate hardware (speakers, webcam, microphone) and software. Alternatively, video conferencing

**Child Development:
An illustrated guide, DVD edition**
The popular guide to child development

Standard edition
- Lavishly illustrated in full-colour throughout, the popular *Illustrated Guide* provides a clear overview of child development from birth to 16 years.
- Additional sections covering developmental assessment, children with special needs and theories of child development help put development into context.

978 0 435420 48 2

DVD edition
- Includes a DVD providing video clips of children's developmental stages from birth to 8 years, giving you even greater insight into the development of this age group.
- Clear references to relevant video clips are provided alongside related information in the book, helping you to get the most out of the DVD.
- In addition to over 30 video clips, the DVD features an introductory video sequence that summarises the entire sequence of development from birth to 8 years.

Carolyn Meggitt
978 0 435899 87 5

Find out more at
www.heinemann.co.uk/childcare

Promotional advertisements can help to sell a product or service

Remember it

The name for a seminar or presentation streamed online is a **Webinar** or a **Webcast**.

equipment can be bought or hired, or a specialist firm can be hired to provide the facilities. The service does have to be paid for but is much cheaper than getting several people to travel large distances to meet up. An alternative is for a business to use specific communications software, such as that produced by WebEx, which enables it to hold its own web conferences with staff and customers.

Internet

The Internet has revolutionised communications for all types of businesses, and most customers. In 2008 there were over 100 million websites worldwide and by 2010 Internet sales are forecast to account for 20% of all retail purchases. Whether a business uses its website just for promotional and communication purposes or to sell over the Internet as well will depend upon its business activity and its aims and objectives.

Research it

Find out more about video conferencing by visiting the Miura Conference website. Investigate WebEx applications software by visiting their site. A link to both sites has been made available at www.heinemann.co.uk/hotlinks.

Research it

Check out other methods of communicating online by reading how Innocent Drinks communicates with its customers on page 50.

Case study – What a job!

Fatima works in the HR department of a large company. She liaises with a departmental manager who has a job vacancy. She prepares the advert and sends it to the manager as an email attachment for approval. She then places it on the website and in the local press. She sends applications to the manager to decide a short-list and interview date. She then writes to the candidates, books the interview room and ensures that everything runs smoothly on the day.

Individual managers often use different methods to communicate a new vacancy to her. The finance manager often sends her a detailed memo whereas the IT manager prefers email. The sales manager relies on his mobile or BlackBerry as he is often out of the office. The production manager prefers to have a short meeting with her.

1 **List all the different methods of communication Fatima uses.**
2 **Explain how each of the communications Fatima uses allows the HR department to work with the other functional areas.**
3 **Suggest the problems that could occur if Fatima did not communicate with the other functional areas effectively.**

Assessment tip

When you start to investigate the forms of communication used in a business, it is helpful to make a list of all the possibilities and tick those the company uses and cross out those it doesn't.

Just checking

Identify and describe the different types of oral, written, visual and IT communications commonly used by businesses.

1.3 Why are stakeholders so important?

What are stakeholders?

A stakeholder is anyone who has an interest or an involvement in a business. You are a stakeholder in your school or college. So too is your tutor, your parents and all the suppliers who provide items from books and chairs to bread and toilet rolls! You are also a stakeholder in all the businesses you regularly use, such as your local shops, cinemas and mobile phone providers, as well as anywhere you work.

Case study – The repercussions of being down and out

When XL Leisure, Britain's third largest travel firm, went bankrupt in 2008, 90,000 passengers were stranded abroad. Thousands more lost holidays they had booked and up to 1,700 staff found themselves out of a job. The chief executive was in tears as he blamed soaring oil prices for the problem. XL could no longer afford to pay its bills and owed large sums of money to Barclays and Straumur, an Icelandic bank.

Whilst rival airlines such as BMI and Ryanair were helping to fly home stranded passengers, at West Ham United the sales of replica shirts were suspended and plans put in place to redesign the roof of the East Stand. Why? Because XL was the team's sponsor. It had signed a deal worth up to £7.5 million only a few months before it collapsed and its XL logo was a feature of the East Stand roof.

Different types of stakeholders

There are several different types of stakeholders. These are shown in the diagram below.

The interests of stakeholders

All stakeholders have an interest in a business but these interests vary. As a student, you want to be taught in class, to cover the specification for your course and be given advice and help when you need it. Your tutor and other staff who work at your school or college will have different interests, such as wanting the opportunity to develop professionally, to have a secure job, to be respected as an employee and to be paid fairly according to the job they are doing.

A summary of the interests of different types of stakeholders is given in the table below.

Stakeholders	Main interests
Owners	To see the business grow, to make a profit, to be rewarded for the risks they are taking.
Customers	To buy products or services, to pay a fair price, to receive good customer service.
Employees	To develop their career, be paid fairly, treated with respect, have secure employment.
Financiers	To gain a return on their investment.
Suppliers	To be given orders to supply the business, to be paid promptly.
Local community	The employment of local people, which results in them having money to spend in local shops and so benefits the community as a whole; local businesses abiding by planning and environmental laws and taking account of local opinions.
Government	Receiving tax from successful businesses (the more profit a business makes, the more tax it pays); the employment of British citizens (which benefits the whole economy); all businesses abiding by laws and regulations relating to health and safety, employment, trading standards etc.

Apply it

Working in small groups, identify the groups of stakeholders involved in XL Leisure. Then identify the specific interest of each group and how each one was affected by its collapse. Compare your ideas as a class.

Take it further

Again in groups, identify all the stakeholders in the sporting team of your choice. Then decide upon the main interest of each group.

Just checking

What does the word 'stakeholder' mean?

Identify the different types of stakeholder in a business and explain the particular interests of each one.

Stakeholders and their influence

Some stakeholders are more important than others. This is directly related to the amount of power or influence they have. In a football club, star players like Wayne Rooney and managers like Alex Ferguson are important because their behaviour and performance directly affects the success of the club. Financiers, like Roman Abramovich, are also powerful because the club would struggle without their money. In businesses such as football clubs, especially with large clubs in the Premiership who are regularly supported by their fans, these two groups are more important than individual spectators.

This does not mean that individual customers or small suppliers do not have any influence on a business. Much depends upon the size of the business, its main activity and the ability of individual stakeholders to unite over a common cause.

Case study – Making the big boys back down

In 2007, HSBC bank was forced to reverse its decision to charge interest on student graduate overdrafts after the National Union of Students launched a campaign on Facebook. More than 5,000 joined the group and HSBC changed its stance, saying, 'Like any service-oriented business, we are not too big to listen to the needs of our customers.'

Social networking sites are being credited with helping consumers to organise their own campaign. An Internet campaign on Facebook, MySpace, Bebo and YouTube was launched to persuade Cadbury to start selling Wispa chocolate bars again. Cadbury agreed to give it a trial, saying that for the first time it would give the Internet a chance to prove itself!

Research it

Search the Internet to find out what other campaigns are currently in force. Then check out Grumbletext, an online consumer complaints website (go to www.heinemann.co.uk/hotlinks), and, as a class, discuss how effective you think such sites are in influencing business behaviour.

Tensions and conflict between stakeholders

The competing interests of stakeholders mean that it is often difficult to keep everyone happy, for example:

- A large business that wants to keep its selling prices competitive for its customers may drive a hard bargain with its suppliers. Small suppliers may not be in a position to turn down the order, but may make little profit from the deal.

- To please its financiers, a business may have to take decisions that do not please its employees, like foregoing a pay rise that year.

- To comply with Government regulations an organisation may have to take actions that do not suit all its customers, such as the new rules relating to healthy school dinners that have led many pupils to opt out.

- Different groups of customers may have different preferences. The suggestion to allow mobile phones to be used on airplanes has pleased some people and horrified others!

- To please customers the owner of a business may want to introduce changes that are not popular with the employees, such as extending opening hours.

- Employees may want profits spent on better working conditions or the latest equipment, whereas the owner or shareholders may want to keep the money in reserve.

How businesses meet the conflicting needs of stakeholders

The ways in which different businesses resolve these types of conflict varies. It will often depend upon the influence of the specific groups involved and the ability of the owner or managers to negotiate an agreement that keeps the most powerful stakeholders happy whilst, ideally, allowing some concessions for other interested parties. Sometimes this is easier than others! It will depend very much on the issue involved, whether the business could be adversely affected by bad publicity and the possible cost of the different solutions.

Usually the worst thing a business owner can do is to put off making a decision, as this is in no one's interest. It is better to focus on the best action for the business as a whole and explain the reasons clearly to anyone who is adversely affected as a result.

Just checking

Explain why some stakeholders have more influence than others.

Give examples of conflicting stakeholder interests and say what businesses might do in this situation.

Case study – Time to see red!

BT has a problem. In an age of mobile technology it still has a legal responsibility to provide and maintain public call boxes to ensure that everyone has access to a basic telephone service at a reasonable price. This means BT cannot use money as a reason to scrap phone boxes. For many people, the 66,000 kiosks still in existence are just a novelty. Most take less than £100 a year and are regular targets for vandalism. It costs BT an average of £1,409 per payphone to maintain them.

When BT said it was talking to Ofcom, the telecoms regulator, to see if it could scrap more boxes it received a large number of complaints. English Heritage, for example, argued the red kiosks were part of British history. BT has now come up with two schemes for local authorities. They can adopt a red kiosk, although the phone will be removed, and pay £1 for maintenance. Or they can sponsor a kiosk, complete with phone, and be charged £500 a year towards its running and maintenance. In the meantime, the police have joined the debate, arguing that the phones are still vital for use in emergencies and in many rural areas mobile phone coverage is still very poor.

1 **Identify all the stakeholders involved in the conflict above.**

2 **What action has BT taken to try to meet the needs of different stakeholders?**

3 **Do you think this action is appropriate? Could BT do more or should red phone boxes be scrapped? Debate the issue as a class and come to a conclusion.**

Why are customers important?

Businesses need customers in order to survive. This is because they must sell their products or services to get regular sales income. This income is essential to pay the costs involved in running the business, including staff wages. Unless the business earns enough sales income to cover its costs, it will go out of business.

For this reason, finding out what consumers' needs are, trying to anticipate how these needs will change and giving customers a positive experience and encouraging customer loyalty is vital. It is also sensible to listen to customers and find out their opinions. That way, the business knows what changes it can make to continue to attract customers and to stay competitive.

Case study – Not Innocent at customer relations!

Innocent Drinks is a multimillion pound fruit smoothie business. Its success has come from developing its ideas and making its customers part of the Innocent experience. In 1998 when the founders first tested their drinks at a music festival, people gave them the thumbs up. Today the business finds out what customers think through its website. It issues questionnaires and even held its own festival! It has its own blog, a twitter feed, a YouTube channel, Facebook page and Flickr group.

Take it further

Suggest how businesses like Innocent Drinks can benefit from the types of communication methods it uses. Compare your ideas as a group.

Note that you will learn more about the Innocent Drinks business if you also study Unit 3 (see page 158).

Talk about it

It costs five to ten times as much to attract a new customer as it does to keep an existing one, according to experts. In groups, decide why there is such a difference and what businesses should do as a result. Then compare your ideas.

Remember it

USP stands for unique selling point. This is an important feature of a business which makes it unique and differentiates it from its competitors.

The difficulties of capturing and retaining customers

New businesses have to work hard to attract their customers. They must tell customers that they exist, what they sell and the benefits of buying from them. Finding out what customers want is normally done through market research (see Unit 3 for more information on this).

Case study – Paws for thought

Irina and Matthew are vets. They have bought a small practice as the owner is retiring. They plan to build up a thriving centre focusing on small animal care.

Irina wants to attract and retain customers. She knows that Petplan, the pet insurance company, gives annual awards for outstanding care. In 2008, the Orwell Veterinary Group in Ipswich won the practice award; in 2007, it went to Feldon Veterinary Centre in Leamington Spa. Irina also knows their choice of receptionist will be very important.

Work in small groups to answer the following questions.

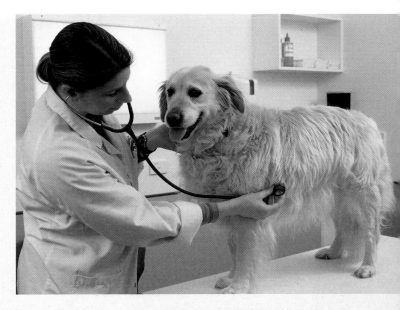

1 **Check out the websites of the Petplan award winners and identify the features of these practices that make them popular with their customers. Links to the sites have been made available at www.heinemann.co.uk/ hotlinks.**

2 **Suggest how Irina could communicate with customers to tell them about practice developments and new initiatives.**

3 **List the qualities and expertise you think the receptionist will need.**

4 **Suggest ways in which Irina and Matthew could encourage customer loyalty.**

Compare your ideas as a class.

Businesses then have to tempt customers away from their competitors. They can use several techniques. A small business may advertise in the local press and include a money off voucher against a first purchase. A larger business may offer discounted prices or a unique service. A new travel firm, for example, advertised free airport transport with every holiday sold.

The business must now meet the needs of its customers so that they will return again and again. There are many benefits of developing a loyal customer base. Loyal customers bring in additional income through repeat sales and also tell their friends and family about their experience, which is free advertising for the firm!

A common method of encouraging repeat business is a loyalty scheme. Even a small business can issue a card that is stamped on each return visit or purchase. After a set number of visits, the customer gets a bonus or reward. Large companies have more sophisticated schemes. Tesco's Clubcard doesn't just give benefits to customers as every time it is used it also helps Tesco build a profile of the customer. It records when they shopped, at which store, what they bought, whether the items bought were regular purchases or 'treats' and also how buying habits change during the year, for example, at Christmas and Easter, or on hot summer days. This enables Tesco to analyse the buying behaviour of its customers. It uses this information to target offers more precisely to its customers to encourage them to buy more.

Research it

The Tesco loyalty card data is managed by Dunnhumby, a British company that has since expanded into the US. Find out how it operates and read its case studies by visiting its website via www.heinemann.co.uk. (See also Unit 3, see page 127).

Just checking

Why do businesses need to attract customers and keep them happy?

Give examples of how businesses try to capture and retain their customers?

The power of customers

The ability of customers to make or break a business means that excellent customer service is crucial. So too is understanding and meeting the needs of customers, and recognising when these change.

Case study – Just the ticket

In 2008, Vue cinema chain announced it was screening some adult-only performances where no one under 18 was allowed in. The idea is to allow adults to watch a film in peace, without teenagers chatting and munching popcorn, or young people giggling in the dark.

This is only one of several Vue innovations. Others have involved installing new voice recognition technology to allow callers to request film information and screen times as well as letting them book and pay for tickets without waiting or queueing.

A development which has benefited most large cinema chains is the change from celluloid films to digital technology, with better quality digital pictures. The cost of the switchover could be too much for many small independent cinemas, which may be forced to close.

Describe it

Market share is the proportion of total sales for a product or service obtained by one brand or company.

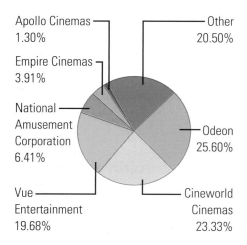

Apollo Cinemas 1.30%
Empire Cinemas 3.91%
National Amusement Corporation 6.41%
Vue Entertainment 19.68%
Other 20.50%
Odeon 25.60%
Cineworld Cinemas 23.33%

Market share of cinema chains (UK and Republic of Ireland) 2008 (Source: AC Nielsen Ltd)

What is market share?

The 'market' for a product or service is the total number of customers who buy it. Each business that offers that item then has a 'share' of that market. **Market share** is the amount of sales in relation to the total sales in the market accounted for by one firm.

Market share can increase rapidly in a new market. When Nintendo launched the Wii and Wii Sports at Christmas 2007 it gained market share against Sony and Microsoft, because the customer experience was so different from that obtained with the PS3 and Xbox 360. It boosted this success again when it brought out the Wii Fit in 2008.

In an established market, one way to increase market share is to take business away from competitors. The market for cinema goers is very competitive; not only do cinema chains have to compete with each other, they also have to compete with people deciding to buy or hire a DVD to watch at home instead. Vue wants to increase its market share. This is why it is focusing on new technology and other facilities and services to take customers away from the market leaders, Odeon and Cineworld.

The role of customer service

Customer service relates to the customer's total experience, from the moment they walk in to a business or view a website, to the after-sales service they expect, such as spare parts or repairs. Even though customers may demand value for money, they also want good service. Unless they have a positive experience they will look around for alternatives.

The benefits of providing excellent customer service include:

- It helps to retain customers so they return again and again and make repeat purchases.
- It improves the image and reputation of the business.
- Word gets around, which attracts more new customers.
- It improves customer satisfaction and loyalty.

However, superb customer service requires the commitment of every single person in the organisation. It is pointless sales staff being charming if the person who answers the phone the next day, to deal with a simple query, is rude or abrupt.

Apply it

What factors do customers take into account when they decide which cinema they prefer? In small groups, list your ideas with reasons. Remember to think about different customers, e.g. all age groups, families and those with disabilities.

Next identify the aspects of customer service that are important to cinema goers and suggest how a cinema chain can encourage customer loyalty.

Present your ideas to the rest of the class.

Meeting aims and objectives – the link to customer service

Excellent customer service can help a business to achieve its aims and objectives for very little cost. A business that wants to grow and expand, increase its profits and/or increase its market share must keep its existing customers happy and attract new ones. To do this it needs to meet – and preferably exceed – its customers' needs.

Talk about it

How wise do you think Vue has been to introduce adult-only screenings, given that nearly 50% of cinema goers are under the age of 25? What else could it do to attract more customers? Discuss your ideas as a class.

Assessment tip

If you need to evaluate customer service in one organisation, one way to do this is to survey a representative group of customers. You could practise this now by preparing a questionnaire about cinemas and deciding who you would ask to answer it.

Just checking

Explain the term 'market share' and describe the actions businesses may take to increase this.

Describe the role of customer service and the benefits of making sure this is as good as possible.

Case study – A driving force for customers

The Highways Agency is responsible for the country's roads. Its aim is 'safe roads, reliable journeys, informed travellers'. Its prime objective is to deliver a high quality service to all its customers. As part of this, it has developed a Customer Promise after talking to customers, stakeholders, staff and suppliers. You can read this on its website (go to www.heinemann.co.uk/hotlinks).

1 **Identify all the types of people who you think are stakeholders in the Highways Agency.**

2 **Suggest the main interest of each group you have identified and how much influence each one has. Give a reason for your decisions in each case.**

3 **In small groups, investigate how well the Highways Agency is meeting its customer service promises. Do this by looking on the website for evidence relating to its claims. For example, can you plan a journey or get**

traffic information easily and quickly? (Note: your tutor may give each group specific topics to research and report back on.)

4 **Assess how well you think the Highways Agency is fulfilling its promise and give reasons for your opinions.**

The needs of different customers

All customers have specific needs that they expect an organisation to meet. These vary depending upon the individual customer and the product or service they are buying.

Internal and external customers

Most people in the workplace have two types of customers.

- **External customers** are those outside the organisation who contact you for help or information.
- **Internal customers** are workplace colleagues who contact you for the same reason!

They are all your customers because they need your assistance to do something. An internal customer may need help to keep an external customer happy.

B2B and B2C customers

There are also two types of external customer.

- **B2B stands for 'business to business'** These are businesses who supply other industrial customers with goods for resale, raw materials or industrial products, such as Cummins (see page 39) and Innocent Drinks (see page 50).
- **B2C stands for 'business to consumer'** These are organisations that supply goods and services direct to consumers, such as retailers and travel agents.

Some businesses have both B2B and B2C customers. Examples include banks, computer firms and telecommunication companies like BT.

Case study – The wide, wide world of Siemens

You may spot the word 'Siemens' on your washing machine, computer or phone, or on traffic lights, security systems or hospital equipment! Siemens is a large global technology company which supplies both B2C and B2B customers. Its website and contact details are structured specifically to reflect this. Siemens was involved in helping the bid to bring the Olympic Games to London in 2012 and now supports the GB rowing team.

Identifying customer needs

The needs of customers vary, depending upon several factors.

- **Business customers** often buy complex, expensive products. They expect demonstrations and presentations, to negotiate discounts and payment terms, to talk about delivery, installation and contract terms and to have a guarantee of ongoing support and spare parts when needed.
- **Retail buyers** only stock goods they think their customers will buy and that fit with their reputation and image. Ideally they want products that sell quickly and on which there is a good margin of profit.

Remember it

Customer facing staff are those who deal directly with customers. Staff who do not are often called 'back office staff', such as finance or IT staff.

Take it further

Check out the difference between the products and services offered to B2B and B2C customers by visiting the Siemens website (go to www.heinemann.co.uk/hotlinks).

Talk about it

What are the main needs of students? List these as a class, then identify the facilities in your school or college that are specifically designed to meet them.

- **Private customers** have different needs depending upon their age, gender, culture, lifestyle, personal circumstances, individual preferences and income level. Their needs also vary depending upon the product or service they are buying (see below). Organisations can identify these needs by issuing surveys and questionnaires. Another method is customer relationship management (CRM). This involves using special software to capture and analyse customer data.

Take it further

Find out how CRM works by visiting the Business Link website and following the 'IT & ecommerce' link, followed by the 'Business applications' link (go to www. heinemann.co.uk/hotlinks).

Features of customer service and how these vary

Every business has to decide what customer services it will offer. These vary between different types of organisation and the needs of its customers. Your doctor or dentist, for example, will offer an appointment system, a personal consultation and a system for dealing with emergencies. These features are not appropriate for a fast food outlet or a clothes shop.

Take it further

Working in small groups, identify a local business that you know well and score it out of 5 (where 5 is excellent and 0 is awful) against each of the common customer concerns in the diagram below. Are there any other concerns that you have as a customer that are not listed in the diagram? Add these to the list. Then present your group's findings to the rest of the class.

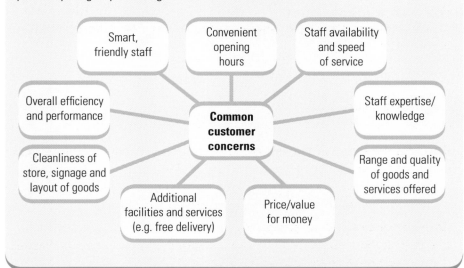

Apply it

The following are all customer service features – but not at the same business!

Free parking; gift-wrapping; home delivery; no quibble returns policy; order tracking; customer newsletters; help desk; email help facility; children's play area; spare parts; repairs; seating area with magazines; FAQs online; large print options; trial period; home visits; follow-up 'customer happy' phone calls.

1 Work in small groups to identify one type of organisation where each feature would be appropriate. Then add four more features of your own.

2 Identify how your own needs differ as a customer when you order a taxi, get on a plane, buy a pair of jeans, visit the bank and stay in a hotel.

3 Search for examples of good and bad customer service at YouTube. Then suggest four ways in which individual employees can make a fundamental difference to the customer's experience.

Just checking

Explain the differences between internal and external customers, and B2C and B2B customers.

How do the needs of each type of customer vary?

How do businesses identify the needs of their own customers?

Why do customer service features vary between different organisations?

Employees – their rights and responsibilities

Employees are a crucial group of stakeholders because they are essential to the success of the business. Employees who feel respected and valued by their employers are normally motivated to work harder than those who feel their contributions are ignored. Similarly, employers are normally keen to reward enthusiastic and productive staff rather than those who are lazy or uninterested.

In most workplaces, disputes between employer and employees are rare and most are solved quickly and informally. However, to protect both parties a number of laws have been passed. These give both parties certain legal rights and make it clear what they can and cannot do.

The expectations of employers and employees

Both employers and employees have the right to expect certain things from each other. When you start work you can expect to be paid the agreed salary. Equally, your employer will expect you to turn up in person and to do the job you are paid to do.

Case study – No way up?

Women today expect to have the same rights, pay and opportunities as men in the workplace. After all, it is more than 30 years since the Equal Pay and the Sex Discrimination Acts were passed. Yet two reports in 2008 found that there were still problems. The Office for National Statistics (ONS) reported that many women were paid less than men for doing the same job. Then the Equality and Human Rights Commission (EHRC) showed there are fewer women in senior roles in Britain than there were in 2003.

Talk about it

Reasons suggested for continuing differences between pay and opportunities for men and women include: fewer women having educational qualifications, women being less ambitious, continuing discrimination and prejudice, lack of jobs with flexible hours. Which of these do you think is the **most important** reason for the continued differences? Justify your answer and discuss your ideas as a group.

Employer expectations

These can be divided into four main areas.

Employees must meet the terms of their contracts

A contract of employment gives the terms and conditions of employment. You have the right to receive these in writing after you have worked for your employer for one month. They can be given in an offer letter and you may be told where to find other relevant information, such as your employer's disciplinary rules and procedures.

The contract contains essential information including your name and job title, the date your employment commenced, your hours and place of work, your pay, your holiday entitlement and the name of your employer. Once you and your employer have signed the document you are both bound by it. Breaking a term in your contract may give your employer the legal right to dismiss you.

Research it

Many people don't know their basic legal rights about sick pay, holidays and the minimum wage. Make sure you aren't one of them by using workSMART, the trade union site (go to www.heinemann.co.uk/hotlinks), to find out answers to the following questions.

1 **Will you get paid if you are off sick?**
2 **If you work a five-day week, how many annual paid holidays can you have and can you insist on taking Bank Holidays?**
3 **What is the current National Minimum Wage rate?**

Remember it

Statutory employment rights are those set down by Acts of Parliament. They apply to everyone. **Contractual rights** are personal. They are those stated in the contract of employment. They can never be worse than the legal minimum and may be better. You will learn more about contracts of employment if you study Unit 3 (see page 151).

Cooperate in meeting the objectives of the business

Your contract states the 'express terms' of your employment, such as hours and pay. Other terms are called 'implied terms'. These are considered so obvious they do not need to be written down, such as taking care of your employer's property and being honest. It is an implied term that you will work towards the objectives of the organisation. This is common sense. An organisation could not be successful if its employees were not focused on helping it to achieve its aims and objectives.

Follow health and safety regulations

This is another implied term. Your employer must comply with the Health and Safety at Work Act 1974 and other relevant regulations. Employees who are negligent and disregard health and safety laws can be dismissed and may face criminal prosecution for their actions.

Talk about it

Employees must comply with all laws relevant to their employment. Can you suggest three well-known laws that would apply to a van driver?

Treat other employees with respect

All employers have a legal responsibility to ensure staff do not suffer discrimination, prejudice, bullying, harassment or any other offensive type of behaviour. Most have policies and codes of practice on equal opportunities, diversity and other aspects of staff relations. All staff must comply with these policies and ensure they do not victimise anyone or treat them unfairly.

Research it

Find out the policies that exist in your college or school to ensure everyone is treated fairly.

Take it further

Working in small groups, identify six types of behaviour that demonstrate you are treating other people with respect. Compare your ideas as a class.

Just checking

Identify and explain the different expectations of employers.

Talk about it

If you are on a **salary scale** the **incremental rises** you will receive may be stated in your contract. Your contract may say when you will have a **performance review** but is unlikely to state any salary increase, or how much **bonus** or **commission** you will receive.

In small groups identify the meaning of each of term in bold. Then say why you think contracts rarely give specific information about payments and increases. Compare your ideas as a class.

Research it

Find out the difference between a trade union and a staff association.

Apply it

In small groups, decide upon the difference between harassment, victimisation, bullying and discrimination. Then give an example of each type of behaviour.

Take it further

Most organisations have policies to protect employees from this type of behaviour. Find those that exist in your school or college and identify how these are different for students and staff members.

The expectations of employees

These relate to the following areas.

Paid according to their contract

Your contract will state your salary, how often you will be paid and the method of payment. It will also include details of any bonus or commission schemes as well as information on sick pay. Your employer must honour all these commitments.

Provided with a safe working environment

This is a legal obligation of your employer, under the Health and Safety at Work Act 1974 and associated regulations. Employers who ignore health and safety requirements can be prosecuted. Your contract should state where you can read the company's health and safety policy.

Appropriately trained

Employers are responsible for ensuring that all employees receive appropriate health and safety training. Training is also essential when employees need specific qualifications to comply with the law (for example, staff who handle food) and if the job they are doing changes. Apprentices and young people under 18 have additional legal rights related to training.

Permitted to join trade unions or staff associations

The Human Rights Act gives all employees the freedom to choose whether to join a trade union or a staff association. They cannot be disciplined or dismissed for doing so.

Allowed access to confidential records kept on them

The Data Protection Act 1998 restricts the use of personal information stored on computer and in structured paper files. Employers must ensure that all personal data, such as that held on employees and customers, is processed fairly and lawfully, kept up to date and only kept as long as necessary. Employees can see what information is held on them although employers can make a small charge for supplying it.

Be treated equally with other employees

You have the right to be given the same opportunity as everyone else and treated fairly at work. Any differences irrelevant to someone's ability to do a job must be ignored at every stage of employment (such as sex, race, disability, religion, beliefs, sexual orientation or age). Employers must also ensure staff are not harassed, bullied or victimised by anyone else in the workplace.

The law and employment

The principle behind employment laws is to provide protection for all employers and employees. This protects you against unscrupulous, negligent or ignorant employers and also protects your employer too. The law gives employers the right to dismiss employees who breach their contract or fail to comply with company policies, either deliberately or accidentally. So, just as it is your employer's responsibility to know the law, you must also understand your legal rights and responsibilities.

The main principles behind current laws

The main principles behind most current employment laws are shown in the table below.

Aspect of employment	Principles behind the law
Equal pay	The Equal Pay Act 1970 states that men and women doing the same work or work of 'equal value' to the business must be paid at the same rate. The only exceptions are when there is an important difference not related to gender (e.g. the man is better qualified) or between the two jobs (e.g. the man works in a more dangerous environment).
Discrimination	Discrimination means treating someone differently and unfairly for some reason unrelated to their job. Laws relating to discrimination protect anyone from being discriminated against, victimised or harassed in the workplace on grounds of their gender (or gender reassignment), race, ethnic origin, sexual orientation, religion, belief, disability or age. This applies to all aspects of their employment, e.g. recruitment and selection, promotion opportunities, training, treatment at work, dismissal and redundancy.
Employment rights	Laws relating to employment rights have given employees the right to receive a written contract, the right to maternity and paternity leave, the right to parental and family leave, the ability to opt out of Sunday working, the right to a minimum notice period, the right to redundancy pay and the right to request flexible hours. Employers must consult employees about changes that will affect them and follow a specific procedure if there is a dispute.
Working hours	The Working Time Regulations restrict the number of hours employees can be asked to work per week and give all workers the legal right to a paid holiday each year.
Health and safety	The Health and Safety at Work Act, and the various regulations that followed, protect all employees and give them the right to work in a safe environment. They also protect visitors to the premises, such as customers or contractors.
Access to information and personal records	The Data Protection Act means that businesses are restricted in the type of information they can hold on individuals, how they can use it and how long they can keep it. Individuals have the right to check information held and can insist errors are corrected. The Freedom of Information Act gives members of the public access to information held by public authorities.

Case study – Who dares wins

Sharon Coleman went to the European Court of Justice to argue that she suffered 'discrimination by association' when she was forced to give up her job to look after her disabled son Oliver because she was refused flexible working.

The judges ruled that she had the right to take time off work to care for her disabled son. As a result other people who need time off to care for disabled or elderly relatives will have the same rights too.

1 Sharon Coleman was backed by the Equality and Human Rights Commission. Identify the main role of this organisation by visiting its website via www.heinemann.co.uk/hotlinks.

2 Many owners of small businesses are concerned that they cannot operate profitably if they have to offer flexible working to all their eligible employees. How justified do you think they are in this view? Give a reason for your answer.

Just checking

Identify and explain the different expectations of employees.

Describe the main principles behind current laws on equal pay and discrimination.

Solving disagreements and disputes

Many people work all their life without having a dispute with their employer. If they do, however, there is a specific procedure that must be followed to ensure people are treated fairly. This is laid down in the Employment Act 2002 (Dispute Resolution) Regulations. All firms must have specific procedures for dealing with dismissal, disciplinary action and grievances in the workplace. Employees are normally given this information as part of their contract of employment.

Reasons for disputes

Disputes can occur because of the alleged treatment of one individual employee or a group of employees. This can happen because

- people who work together have an argument
- employee(s) disagree with their line manager(s) or disobey a direct instruction given by their line manager(s)
- either the employee or employer breaches the contract of employment
- an employee, or group of employees, considers they are being treated unfairly, victimised, harassed or discriminated against.

Remember it

Fair dismissal is when an employee is sacked for a valid reason and the right procedures were followed. **Unfair dismissal** is when an employee is sacked for no good reason, e.g. being pregnant or joining a union and/or the right procedures were ignored.

Case study – United we stand?

In 2007, local authorities re-evaluated jobs and pay rates to implement a new single status pay deal for all workers. Some staff were winners, others were told they could lose £6,000 or £7,000 a year. UNISON and the GMB unions fought for more money to help solve the problem. As a result, the government agreed to release a further £500 million to local authorities to eliminate the pay gap.

The trade unions represented the employees in their dispute with their local authority employers. This type of dispute, which involves several people, is called a **collective dispute**. It was caused because the employer wanted to terminate current contracts and ask employees to sign new ones with different terms and conditions. If these will be worse, the trade unions will try to negotiate the best terms it can and all members will be bound by the majority decision.

People and organisations who help to resolve disputes

Many people and organisations can be involved in helping to resolve a workplace dispute.

- **The human resources department** will advise an employee about their rights.
- **Trades union representatives and staff association members** advise employees about their legal rights and whether they have a valid complaint. They may attend grievance or disciplinary meetings and if the problem goes to an employment tribunal they will provide support and advice. An employment tribunal is an independent body that judges the case. They also represent groups of staff with a common grievance.
- **The Equality and Human Rights Commission (EHRC)** monitors and supports all types of equality issues. Anyone can check its website or contact it for advice.
- **Several pressure groups and charitable organisations** will provide advice and support related to their own areas. For example, the Fawcett Society campaigns against gender discrimination.

Hotlink

Find out more about EHRC and ACAS by visiting their websites – go to www.heinemann.co.uk/hotlinks.

- **Employer forums** advise on good practice and assist employers who have a query or problem, such as the Employers' Forum on Belief (EFB) and the Employers' Forum on Age (EFA).
- **Acas, the Advisory, Conciliation and Arbitration Service** operates an arbitration and advisory service. Arbitration is where both parties to the dispute agree to an independent hearing of the case and agree to abide by the judgement made by Acas.

Steps in resolving a dispute

There are several steps in resolving a dispute, although few reach the highest level.

- Most disputes are resolved through informal discussions between staff and managers. This should quickly clear up any simple misunderstandings.
- If this does not work, the company's grievance and disciplinary procedures are invoked.
  - o **Grievance procedures** tell employees what to do if they have a serious complaint about a colleague or manager.
  - o **Disciplinary procedures** state what the employer will do if it has a serious complaint about the employee.
- The next step is arbitration (see Acas above). The arbitrator listens to both sides, asks questions and, after assessing the situation, suggests how the problem may be resolved.
- If this does not work, the issue is referred to an employment tribunal. Here, a special panel listens to the argument and questions any witnesses before coming to a decision.
- If there is an argument about the way the law was interpreted by the tribunal, an appeal may be lodged by either party. This will be heard by the Employment Appeal Tribunal.
- The final step is to refer the matter to the European Court of Justice. In rare cases, such as Sharon Coleman's case that you read about on page 59, this can result in a change to British law.

Step 6: Go to European Court of Justice

Step 5: Refer matter to the Employment Appeals Tribunal

Step 4: Take dispute to an Employment Tribunal

Step 3: Go to arbitration through ACAS

Step 2: Formal disciplinary or grievance procedures

Step 1: An informal discussion to solve the problem

Steps in resolving a dispute

Just checking

Identify common reasons for disputes in the workplace. Describe the people who can help to resolve one.

Explain the steps that should be taken if a dispute occurs and is not easily resolved.

Case study – It's not just what you say, it's where you say it!

Posting negative comments about your workplace online can have serious consequences. Thirteen Virgin Atlantic flight attendants were sacked when they described customers as 'chavs' on Facebook and made derogatory comments about the airline.

Joe Gordon was dismissed for gross misconduct by Waterstone's, the bookseller, after a disciplinary hearing over comments he posted on his blog. With help from his union rep he appealed. Although he was offered his job back he decided to take up employment elsewhere instead.

Answer the questions, then compare your ideas. A useful source of information is the Directgov website. Follow the 'Employment'

and 'Resolving workplace disputes' links. A link to the site can be found at www.heinemann.co.uk/hotlinks.

1 **The Virgin Atlantic staff were sacked for 'bringing the company into disrepute'. What do you think this phrase means?**

2 **What is a disciplinary hearing and why are union reps often involved?**

3 **If Joe Gordon had not been offered his job back, and wanted to take his case further, what could he have done?**

Unit 1 Make the Grade

Your assessment for Unit 1 involves carrying out an assessment task under **controlled** conditions, which has been set by Edexcel. The task involves answering questions about two businesses you have researched. One must be a local business and the other must be either a national or an international business. The questions cover aspects relating to every section of Unit 1.

Remember it

A **controlled assessment** means that your coursework is monitored by your tutor and you will do all your written work at school or college, not at home.

How does your assessment work?

- Your tutor will help you choose appropriate businesses. This will enable you to put the task into context and understand what you have to do.
- You may carry out the research on your own or in a group. This will probably depend upon whether anyone else has chosen the same business(es) to research.
- You will save your information in a research folder so that you can refer to it easily when you are writing your answers to the questions.
- Your tutor will record how long you spend researching, both in and away from your centre, and will also check your information to make sure it is all your own work.
- Your tutor will also supervise the writing up of your answers, which will be done in specific sessions allocated for this purpose. This is not the same as being in an examination but is to ensure that your written answers are entirely your own work.
- Your tutor will keep your work and your research folder safely between sessions.

Getting ready for your assessment

There are several things you can do to make the most of your assessment time. This is important because your time is limited.

- The maximum time you can spend on researching and investigating is 24 hours, over a period of eight weeks.
- The maximum time you have to write up your answers is 12 hours, spread over a period of four weeks.

At first glance this might seem like lots of time – far more than you think you will need. In reality, unless you are well prepared you could easily waste time, and then have problems because you have to do things in a rush.

Tips for planning ahead

- Think about businesses you would like to investigate. Are there any local firms you know well because someone you know works there? Are there any national or international businesses that really interest you because of the work they do or the products they make/sell?

Assessment tip

Remember that it's always easier to find out about a business if you or a family member or friend works there, and researching is always more fascinating if you are interested in what the business does.

- Test out your ideas with your tutor to see how realistic they are. Some businesses, like a small shop, may not be able to provide enough useful information. Others, such as large international organisations or public sector bodies, may be too complex to understand easily. Both are best avoided for your assessment.
- Remember that you can use many ways of finding out information. You can research the businesses online, visit the organisation, listen to visiting speakers and

obtain leaflets and other promotional materials. Write down all the methods that will be appropriate for each business you have chosen.

- If you are researching a business as a member of a group, agree first what aspects of the business you will each investigate. This way no one will waste time duplicating work other people have done.

- If you are going on a visit or listening to a visiting speaker, prepare in advance to ensure you get the most out of the event. Start by writing down the questions you need to ask. Take these with you if you are interviewing someone and write down their replies too (even better, find out if you can record the session). A visiting speaker can be given questions in advance. This helps everyone – you find out what you need to know and the speaker ensures the talk is relevant for everyone.

- Check that you can research online effectively. This means knowing how to explore all aspects of a website, what to do if you find information you don't understand and how to follow up positive leads through Google and other search engines.

Assessment tip

Remember that browsing aimlessly wastes time. So does getting distracted by other sites you like, such as Facebook!

- Only print out information that specifically relates to the task and bookmark other sites that may be useful later.

- Plan how you can use your time effectively. You cannot research properly in short bursts of ten or 15 minutes. Realistically you need to spend one or two hours focusing on the task. Planning ahead means you can choose times when you won't be interrupted. If you are researching at home, tell your family and friends what you are doing and enlist their cooperation to leave you in peace!

- Store the information you obtain safely in your research folder *the minute you obtain it*. You can sort through it and put it in order later. The main thing is not to lose anything important.

- Finally, read and re-read the task. Make sure you have information relating to every part of the task and store this in clearly labelled sections in your folder. When you are writing your answers, you won't have time to keep sorting through dozens of pages to find what you need!

Understanding the task

Your tutor will help you understand the task and what you have to do. An important aspect is the **command words** you will read. These tell you what you have to do. Some common command words, and what each means, are shown in the table below.

Command word	What you need to do
Analyse	Identify the main factors and say how these are linked. Then explain the importance of each.
Compare and contrast	Identify the main features of each item, then point out any similarities and differences.
Describe	Give an account that includes all the main points.
Evaluate	Use your information to make a reasoned judgement on the importance or success of something.
Explain or Justify	Give clear reasons to support your views.
Suggest or Recommend	Give your own ideas and views based on the information you have provided.
List	Write a list (don't put the items in sentences).
Outline	Identify the main points but don't go into too much detail.

Some command words are easier than others. It is simpler, for example, to write a list than it is to analyse a situation or evaluate it. However, you will need to be able to provide all these types of answers to gain high marks, so it is worth practising so that you know what to do (see below).

Assessment tip

You will meet command words in both your internal and external assessments, so the list on page 63 is useful for all the units. The table hasn't included words like 'calculate', 'check' and 'complete' (which you will meet in your external assessments). Make sure you know what these mean!

Skills focus

Although 90% of the assessment marks are awarded for the information you provide on your chosen businesses, you can also gain a further ten marks for demonstrating the following skills:

* Your time management, personal organisation and action planning.

Apply it

Jolanta, Seth and Ibrahim decided to research Asda. Ibrahim's father works there, mainly doing home deliveries, so Ibrahim promised to talk to him about the company. Seth promised to investigate the website. Jolanta said she would visit some stores, collect leaflets and talk to customer service staff.

Two weeks later the group met to review progress. Ibrahim had one page of notes which just focused on grocery deliveries. Jolanta had even less. She'd only seen one leaflet of any use and staff had been too busy to talk to her when she called. Seth, on the other hand, had pages of printouts from the website. He'd found lots on sustainability but nothing on how the business was organised. He had also printed the site map to help everyone decide what he should investigate next.

1 **Which member of the group has used their time the most effectively and why?**

2 **What is your view of the way the other members have used their time? Give reasons to support your opinions.**

3 **Suggest ways in which the group can solve the problems they face.**

* The way you use your data and solve problems you encounter.
* The role you and other people undertake when you carry out group work investigations and research.
* The suitability of your chosen presentation method(s).

As part of your assessment, you will be asked to think about these skills and explain what you think worked well and what did not. Bear in mind that you will do better if you provide evidence for your opinions.

Take it further

Working in small groups, suggest presentation methods for providing business information that work, and those that don't, with reasons for your choice. Think of written presentation techniques like headings, bullet points and tables, as well as oral presentations. Compare your ideas as a class. Then decide how important you think spelling, punctuation and grammar should be – and how you can improve these if you have a problem!

Sample materials

This section contains examples of assessment activities, student responses and comments on their answers, as well as some practice tasks to help you prepare for your assessment.

As you read each response, see if you agree with the comments. If you do not understand any of them, talk to your tutor.

Investigating what a business is and what businesses do

Student Activity: For your first task, choose your two businesses and give the reasons behind your choices.

Shahida's answer:

The two businesses I have chosen are ABT law, a local firm, and Warburtons Ltd, which produces bread and bakery products. It has bakeries in Scotland, Wales and all over England. I have chosen them because I am interested in what they do. Also, they carry out different activities and one is large and the other small, so it will be easier to compare them. I can find out about ABT law because my aunt works there. It also has a good website because it specialises in online conveyancing. I am interested in Warburtons because we visited our local bakery last year and staff were very helpful. They also have a good website and I'm sure we could arrange for someone to talk to us or perhaps visit them again. They are keen on community work and education so I'm sure they would help. The business is very successful and it will be interesting to find out how it continues to meet different challenges.

Comments on Shahida's answer:

This is a very good start to the activity. Shahida has thought hard about her businesses and has chosen two which should be very interesting to compare and contrast. She has also considered how she can find out information and how responsive the businesses will be. Her explanation is clear and thorough and she will achieve good marks if she continues this standard of work.

Zoran's answer:

My businesses are Jack's Motors, a garage near my home, and the football team I support, Arsenal. Jack's Motors does repairs and MOTs and hires cars too. It's run by two brothers and their sister who are family friends. I want to write about them because I like cars. I go to all Arsenal home matches as I've got a season ticket. I can find out about it from its website. It also has an annual report for fans and there's lots of useful information in this year's I can use.

Comments on Zoran's answer:

Zoran has chosen two contrasting businesses in which he is interested, which is good. He should be able to find out information about Jack's Motors but needs to think of additional ways to research Arsenal. This is important because some aspects he needs to investigate, such as functional areas and communications, are unlikely to be on the website. He should also guard against copying out large chunks of information from a particular document, no matter how useful it is!

Assessment tip

Never copy out huge chunks of information from a leaflet or website, and always acknowledge your sources. If you don't know how to do this, your tutor will tell you.

Apply it

Agree your two businesses with your tutor and then write a statement which clearly gives appropriate reasons for your choice.

Investigating the businesses

Shahida and Zoran must now find out about the aims, objectives, purpose and activities of their businesses, and their main competitors. They also need to know the form of ownership and how at least one business responds to ethical and sustainability issues.

Note that many small local businesses don't have written aims and objectives. You can find out what these are though by talking to the business owner(s) about what they aim to achieve and how they plan to do it.

Student Activity: Compare and contrast the aims, objectives, purpose, activities and main competitors of your two businesses.

Shahida's answer:

ABT Law was formed in 2007 by three partners who now employ two staff. Their main purpose is to provide an online legal conveyancing service. They specialise in property and conveyancing work, which is the business activity, and clients who are buying or selling a house can do everything online. This is ideal if people are working all day and haven't time to go to long meetings. It also means the business can have clients all over the country. Its main competitors are not local solicitors but online e-conveyancing companies.

Warburtons is completely different. It is the largest independent bakery in the UK with over 4,000 employees. There are 13 bakeries and 11 depots in England, Wales and Scotland. Its main activity is to produce bread and bakery products. It is a family business and was founded in 1876. Its main competitor is Hovis.

Comments on Shahida's answer:

Shahida has identified the business activity of both her businesses. She needs to provide more information about the purpose of Warburton's and also include the name of several competitors for both businesses. She could also find out about Warburtons' current market share. Shahida has said that Warburtons is completely different from ABT Law. This is not really true because, despite its size, ABT Law operates on a national basis, so there is at least one similarity she should mention. Shahida should also include appropriate business terminology in her answer to get a good mark.

Apply it

When Shahida investigates the ownership of ABT Law, she is told it is an 'LLP'. Find out what this is and the implications of this if the business becomes insolvent.

Analysing how businesses are organised

You are only likely to have to investigate how your *larger* chosen business is organised because a smaller business is unlikely to have a formal structure or be divided into functional areas. You will also have to research the forms of communication used and whether they allow the functional areas to work together.

Assessment tip

Remember that for some tasks you might only have to find out information about ONE business, not both. If you don't realise this, you could easily do more work than is necessary!

Analysing means identifying the main factors relating to the way the business is organised and its functional areas, as well as the links and communications between the functional areas. You then need to use this information to explain how each functional area contributes to the business. Then use your information on communications to assess if these allow the functional areas to work together.

Apply it

Shahida has found that Warburtons has job roles in the following areas: Manufacturing, Engineering, Business Development, Distribution, Site Support and Site Food Specialists. The website also lists head office functions as Marketing, National Accounts, Category Management, IT, Finance, Technical Support and Food Safety, Purchasing and Packaging, Centre Engineering and Centre HR. By checking job roles and job vacancies on the recruitment part of the website she discovers Business Development is similar to Sales.

1 **Investigate the website yourself and identify the main work carried out by each functional area. A link to the site can be found at www.heinemann. co.uk/hotlinks.**

2 **Use the titles of the job roles and information about head office functions to suggest the type of organisation structure the company has.**

3 **As a class, discuss the benefits and limitations of obtaining an organisation chart from a business.**

4 **In small groups, investigate one functional area each and prepare a statement which explains its importance to the business. Present this to the rest of the class.**

5 **Suggest some questions Shahida could ask a visiting speaker from Warburtons about their communications.**

Evaluate why stakeholders are so important

The last section relates to the stakeholders of ONE of your chosen businesses, in particular its customers and employees. First decide which business would be best to choose. Start by identifying all the stakeholders and then decide their interest in the business and how they contribute to its success.

Next, think about the needs of the customer and how they can influence the business. What is their view of the customer service – how can you find this out? Finally, you need to investigate the rights and responsibilities of the employer and employees, and issues such as the problems legislation and regulations have imposed on the business.

Assessment tip

Don't automatically think you should always investigate your largest business when given the option. If you have to investigate problems caused by legislation and regulations then you may find better examples in a small business (with limited resources).

Student Activity: Identify the stakeholders of one chosen business and evaluate why one group of stakeholders is particularly important.

Zoran's answer:

Arsenal FC has many stakeholders. First there are the employees, especially the manager and the players, who are all crucial to the team's success. Then there are the supporters who are vital for team morale. The money they pay to see matches is income for the club. Some are shareholders. Arsenal also does lots for the local community, including schools and charities. The main shareholders are the owners/directors, led by Daniel Fiszman, and they have over 45% of the shares. Two rich financiers also have shares. Alisher Usmanov, a Russian, owns over 24% and Stan Kroenke, an American billionaire, owns 12%. The directors prefer Kroenke and don't want Usmanov to own more shares. The club also gets money from sponsors (especially Emirates) and TV companies. All Premiership clubs try to get into Europe to get more money. They can use this to buy more good players, so it becomes self-perpetuating really. So, I think the most important group is good players, because otherwise results would be poor, income would fall and supporters would lose interest. This is why fantastic footballers are paid so much.

Comments on Zoran's answer:

There are some very good aspects to Zoran's answer. He has identified most of the stakeholders, assessed their contribution and then used this information to evaluate which group he thinks is particularly important. His answer would be better if he included other stakeholder groups, such as local suppliers, and if he differentiated between casual supporters, season ticket holders and businesses which hold corporate events at the Emirates stadium. Lack of detail and use of business terminology also let Zoran down. There are no details of the Emirates deal or other sponsors. Neither does he say what could happen if Usmanov bought more shares. Zoran also needs to stick to answering the question, which doesn't involve justifying footballers' wages!

Talk about it

In groups, identify the stakeholders at Zoran's other choice of business: the garage. Debate whether Zoran's task would have been easier or harder had he chosen this business instead.

Unit 2 Financial Records

Describe it

Financial records show transactions that take place on a day to day basis.

Profit and loss accounts show the revenues and costs of a business for a given amount of time, usually a year.

Balance sheets show a business' financial position – it is a snapshot of the business at a particular point in time.

Businesses use many different documents to keep **financial records**. These documents are extremely important as they keep records of money received by the business, payments made and statements that show all the money that is flowing in and out of the business. In this unit you will learn about the different types of documents that are important to businesses and why the format of these documents is crucial. You may have heard of some of these documents before, for example invoices, cheques, receipts and delivery notes. There will be some new ones to learn about too and by the end of this unit you should understand the part that each document plays in a business.

Profit and loss accounts and **balance sheets** are two financial statements used in business. You will learn what each type of statement is for and the meaning of terms used. Some words you may be familiar with such as 'profit' or 'assets' but other words will be new. You will also investigate how ICT is used to produce these statements.

This unit contains all the information that you need to know about financial records, with lots of exercises and information to help you with your studies. You will have many opportunities to think about all aspects of financial recording and complete practical activities that will help you to apply the techniques that you are learning for the examination of this unit.

In the final part of the unit you will find out how you can make judgements about how well a business is doing based on its **liquidity** (how well it can make payments and keep trading) and **profitability** (how much money it makes after costs have been taken away). You will learn how to measure liquidity and profitability using **ratios**. You will be able to comment on these ratios and learn how ratios are used by different groups of people. These groups include the owners of the business, lenders of money and the Government.

Would you choose this person to look after your financial records?

Describe it

Liquidity measures how much cash a business has available to pay what it owes.

Profitability measures how much profit a business makes over a given amount of time.

Ratios are calculations used to work out measurements of liquidity or profitability.

Apply it

Receipts are one of the most common financial records that you probably come across in your everyday life. Although businesses may include different information on their receipts (which you will learn about later in this unit) there is lots of common information. In small groups, look at the receipt on the right.

1 Now write a list of all the information that you can find out from this receipt.

2 Is there any information on a receipt that you don't understand or know what it is for?

3 Now find another receipt and compare the information that appears on both. What do you notice about the two receipts? Is the information the same or different?

This unit covers the following topics:

2.1 Investigating the flow of financial documents used in business trading
2.2 Investigating business payment methods and costs
2.3 Investigating the nature of financial statements in business
2.4 Investigating the importance of financial statements to business

The Corner Shop	
2 Brampton Road	
Swansea SA2 4GG	
Tel: 01792333222	
Choccy-nut bar	0.60
Blue pen 2 @ 0.30p	0.60
Newspaper	0.80
Milk semi-skimmed 1 pint	0.50
Mints	0.45
Total	£2.95
Cash	£5.00
Cash change	£2.05

Today you were served by KATY.
Thanks for shopping at The Corner Shop –
please call again!

VAT number:123 456 789

Date: 08/04/09   Time: 12:53

A receipt

How you will be assessed

This unit is one of two compulsory units that you will need to study for the Single Award in Applied Business and one of four compulsory units that you will need to study for the Double Award in Applied Business. Your learning for this unit will be assessed in an external examination. The examination lasts for one hour and you will be given different types of questions including multiple choice, short and extended answers to work on. In this unit you will learn about different formulae that you might be asked to use in the examination, but you do not need to memorise these as you will be given them in the examination. You will, however, need to remember how to use them!

2.1 Investigating the flow of financial documents used in business trading

Types of financial documents

In business, there are lots of different types of financial documents that are used. Of these, there are nine main ones that you are going to learn about and then be expected to use. You will need to understand why and how they are used. You will also need to think carefully about how important they are to a business and be able to make judgements about them.

The nine documents that you are going to study are shown in the diagram below.

Think about it!

You have probably heard of some of the documents listed opposite. In small groups, write down everything you know about each document (for some this might be nothing and that is OK at this stage!). What do you know about the documents? When have you seen them used? Who was using them? Why? How? Think about the names of the documents – what does this tell you about them? Are there clues? You may be surprised by how much you already know about business!

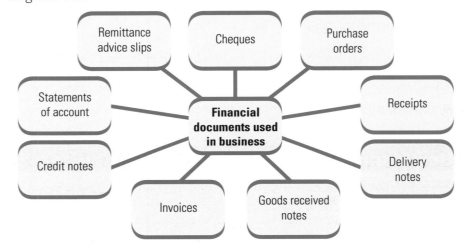

Purchase orders

A purchase order is the document that is used in business to place an order. It is very important because it gives details about:

• what the customer wants to order

• when it was ordered

• who ordered it and the quantities involved.

It is very important that a purchase order has all the information the business needs so that it can satisfy its customers. From a legal point of view, a purchase order is the contract between the business and the customer. This means if the customer orders goods or services and then does not pay for them, the business can take the customer to court to try to get their money.

You can see in the purchase order shown opposite that a lot of information is needed. Using a purchase order means that a business should be able to try and reduce mistakes that could be made and be very clear about what customers actually want.

Recycled Paper Products Ltd
West Quay Road
Southampton
SO14 7AB

Purchase Order

Customer Name and address:
Pencils and Everything Supplies
15 Rathbone Road
Southampton
SO22 6PU

Item	Description	Qty	Unit cost	Total
1	Best white paper 100gsm	5 reams	5.00	25.00
2	A4 Lever arch files (boxed x 10)	6	9.50	57.00
			Sub total	82.00
			VAT at 17.5%	14.35
			Total order value	96.35

To be delivered to: 15 Rathbourne Street, Southampton
Delivery date: 2 May
Requisitioned by: A. Buyer
Authorised by: A. Budgetholder
Signature: *A. Budgetholder*
Date: 20 April

	Item	Cost centre	Amount
	1	801	29.38
	2	801	66.97

A purchase order

Remember it

The **VAT** amount on the purchase order is shown as 17.5%. Remember that on December 1 2008, VAT was reduced to 15%. This is a temporary measure and, at the time of writing, is set to last until 31 December 2009.

Research it

Purchase orders can be done online as well on paper. Find out how this can be done and the advantages there may be of completing and receiving purchase orders in this way.

Apply it

Briana and Holly have been running a business selling gardening products and tools made from 100% recycled materials for approximately three months. They receive orders over the telephone, by email and in person in their shop. They have been having some difficulties with the orders. When orders arrive, it can be sometimes hard to understand what is wanted as they sell a lot of different types of some items, for example five different types of spade. Tags to put on plants are sold in packs of ten and sometimes there is confusion when a customer wants ten tags – they might receive 100 (ten packs of ten) when they actually only want one pack of ten. The business' prices appear on the website and in the paper catalogue, but sometimes the prices do not match up and customers get confused about which is correct. Briana and Holly add a £5 delivery charge regardless of the size of the package, which sometimes means they lose money on orders. One of their customers even took delivery of an order for £250 and then refused to pay. Holly had taken the order over the phone but then lost her record of the conversation.

1 **Explain to Briana and Holly how they would benefit from using purchase orders.**

2 **Using paper or IT software design a suitable purchase order for their business.**

3 **Identify each of the problems the business has had over the past three months and then suggest how each one could be overcome.**

Take it further

Do you think there are any limitations to a purchase order? Explain what these limitations might be. In the light of your answer and the work you have covered so far, give a judgement about how useful they are to businesses.

Just checking

What information is found on a purchase order?

From a legal standpoint, what is a purchase order?

How can using purchase orders benefit a business?

Delivery notes

A delivery note is a business document that provides information when a product is delivered to a customer. Remember that the customer could be another business (B2B) or the final customer (B2C). When an item is delivered, the delivery note gives all the details and the customer is asked to sign to say that they have received the order.

Assessment tip

You will need to think of ways to help you remember why different documents are important in business. You may find a helpful way to do this is to remember a sentence or phrase to remind you. For example, delivery notes are **PRACCT**ical in business because they provide Proof, Recording, Auditors, Confirmation, Checking and Tracking. Now try and make up your own rhyme or sentence to help you remember why these documents are so important.

The name of the business

Customer address

The invoice is the way the customer is charged

Date order sent from Happy Chocolate

By signing for the goods as being received in good condition it is harder to return them

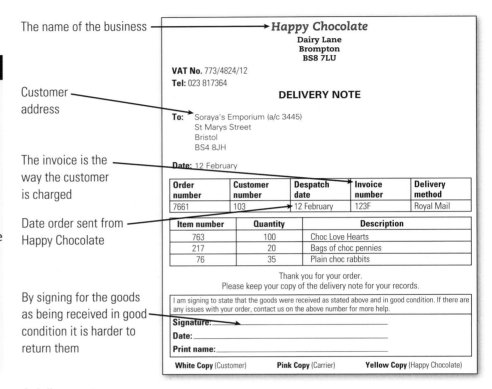

A delivery note

Research it

Look at different types of delivery notes that are available online or in paper form (just type 'delivery note' into a search engine on the Internet to find some examples). What do you notice about the different layouts that are available? Make sure you understand all the different types of delivery note that are available in preparation for the exam.

Delivery notes are really important for lots of reasons. They help businesses track goods that have been sent out, check that they were received by the right customer and that they were of appropriate quality. The benefits of using delivery notes include:

- They provide proof that the goods have been delivered.
- They give a record of what has been delivered for both the customer and the business.
- They are useful for auditors so they can check the movement of goods.
- They are used for checking what has been delivered against the invoice to be sent.
- They confirm that the goods have been received in good condition or record any problems that were found.
- They can be used to track where goods have gone and therefore avoid them being stolen or used by someone else.

Goods received notes (GRN)

Small businesses may only use delivery notes to check that the stock they have ordered has been received or that appropriate amounts have been sent. In larger organisations, there may not be time to go through the order in detail when it arrives so the delivery note will be signed and the stock moved to the storeroom to be unpacked. When it is unpacked, staff at the business will go through the order and check it on a goods received note (GRN), making a note of anything that is missing or damaged. The goods received note will then be sent to the accounts department so that when payment is requested on an invoice, the payment can be adjusted or new goods sent through.

Apply it

Complete the GRN below using the following information:

Soraya received the chocolate from Happy Chocolate on Order 7661. She unpacked the order but found two of the bags of chocolate pennies had holes in (each bag cost £1.99 plus VAT) and 98 chocolate hearts (costing £1.25 each plus VAT) had been delivered instead of 100. Soraya also placed an order (number 7662) on 16 February for 35 chocolate chicks, which were all received, and 45 chocolate crisp parcels, although she only received 40. The chocolate crisp parcels were priced at £2.35 each plus VAT.

Soraya's Emporium
Goods Received Note

Goods received from:

Supplier a/c no.   GRN no.
                           Delivery note no.
                           Delivery note date:
                           Checked by:

Order number	Quantity ordered	Quantity delivered	Item description	Enter details here to state received, damaged or other

Research it

Produce a poster showing the advantages to businesses of using GRNs and the impact to businesses if they are not used. Add a judgement about how important they are to any business.

Take it further

Using the Internet, books and journals, find as many different examples of companies using goods received notes as you can. You may wish to print some of them out to look at them. Explain why they are used, including the advantages and disadvantages. How do businesses make use of technology when using goods received notes?

Just checking

Give four benefits of using delivery notes.
What is the difference between a delivery note and a goods received note?

Talk about it

Before we look at an invoice, in a small group, talk about the information you think would need to be on it. Think back to the information that was contained in each of the documents you have already studied. What information do you think is most important and why?

Invoices

Purchase orders, delivery notes and goods received notes all relate to goods being ordered and delivered. The invoice is the next important step as it is the way requests for payment are made. An example of an invoice is given below to show you what they look like. It is important to make sure you learn each part of an invoice and why it is important. Invoices need to be accurate and sent out in a timely way to make sure the money is received for goods as quickly as possible. This is important because it is only if businesses receive money from sales that they have the cash to buy the resources they need for production and maintain their liquidity.

Happy Chocolate
Dairy Lane
Brompton
BS8 7LU
VAT No. 773/4824/12

INVOICE

Invoice no. 123F
Order no. 7661
Date: 19 February
Due date: 5 March

To: Soraya's Emporium (a/c 3445)
St Marys Street
Bristol
BS4 8JH

Item no.	Quantity	Description	Unit price (£)	Value (£)
763	100	Choc Love Hearts	1.25	125.00
217	20	Bags of choc pennies	1.99	39.80
76	35	Plain choc rabbits	0.75	26.25
			Sub total	191.05
			VAT 17.5%	33.43
			Total	224.48

Payment terms
Payment within 14 days please by cheque or to the following account:
Anybank plc, Sort code: 20 79 25 Account no: 123456

An invoice

Invoices must show all the necessary information that is needed by a business to make sure that goods or services are paid for. This includes:

- the date
- who the customer is
- details of the goods or services
- other reference information, including the amount owed, the length of time to pay and how to pay.

Invoices also need to be accurate and complete. Unless they are filled out correctly, a customer may not understand how to pay or what they are paying for.

Research it

Carry out research in your school or college with someone from your administration department. Interview them and ask them about the most common mistakes that they come across when checking invoices. Write a list of the ones that they have come across. Ask your teacher to check through your list and help you identify any other common errors that are made. You will need to remember common invoice errors to help you avoid them in your exam for this unit.

Take it further

Think about the different lengths of time that are shown on invoices for payment. They may be anything from seven days to six weeks or more. Judge the importance of invoices to a business when thinking about money coming into and out of the business by answering the following questions:

1 **How important do you think it is for businesses to have short payment dates on invoices?**

2 **What happens if a customer does not pay an invoice on time and what would the business need to do in this situation?**

3 **Why might businesses choose to give a longer payment time?**

4 **Make a judgement about how important invoices are to any business or not-for-profit organisation.**

Case study – DHL

DHL is an international delivery company that operates in 220 countries and has more than 300,000 employees. As it is so large, invoicing is a major job and over the past few years, DHL has decided to make use of online invoicing for larger clients.

There are lots of advantages to using online invoicing and these include the following:

- Saving on costs as invoices go via email rather than post.
- Automatic tracking of invoices.
- Ease of dealing with customer issues.
- Better tracking of payment.
- Online statements of account are updated immediately, as well as online payments.

1 **What are the advantages of online invoicing for customers?**

2 **Are there any disadvantages of online invoicing, for both DHL and its customers?**

Assessment tip

You will need to know the difference between purchase orders, delivery notes, goods received notes and invoices. It might help you to draw a diagram showing the ordering and delivery process for a business and one of its customers. Refer to each of the documents we have looked at so far and explain what each document is for and at what stage in the process they are used. You could use the following example: Stanhope Electrical Goods has ordered 24 boxes of blank CDs from Holywell Audio Supplies.

Are there any gaps in your knowledge? Do you understand each type of document, what they are for and can you make a judgement about their usefulness? If not, go back over the relevant section and do some more research to help you.

Just checking

What is an invoice?

What are the advantages of using online invoicing compared to paper based?

Remember it

A **credit payment** is when a business pays money into a customer's account rather than takes it out. This means that the amount the customer owes is reduced.

Credit notes

You have already learned that sometimes when businesses send out goods they get damaged or not enough are delivered. Rather than give the customer their money back each time this happens, some businesses give credit notes instead. A credit note gives a customer the right to purchase replacement goods from the business. It is effectively a credit on the customer's account. An example of a credit note is shown below.

Happy Chocolate
Dairy Lane
Brompton
BS8 7LU
VAT No. 773/4824/12

CREDIT NOTE

Credit note no. 12345
Due date: 26 February

To: Soraya's Emporium (a/c 3445)
St Marys Street
Bristol
BS4 8JH

Item no.	Quantity	Description	Unit price (£)	Value (£)
763	2	Choc Love Hearts	1.25	2.50
217	2	Bags of choc pennies	1.99	3.98
			Sub total	6.48
			VAT 17.5%	1.13
			Refunded amount	7.61

Reasons for returns
Chocolate Love Hearts missing
Chocolate Pennies damaged

A credit note

Credit notes mean that a business is able to retain a customer rather than possibly losing them to a rival business as it encourages customers to stay with the business. They are also a good way of judging if there are problems in certain areas of the business or with certain products. If businesses track credit notes very carefully they should be able to ensure that in future they do not keep having goods returned and so keep their customers happy.

Statements of account

You have already learned the importance of different financial documents in business and hopefully appreciate that these documents help businesses track deliveries and the flow of money in and out of their accounts. A statement of account brings all of these documents together as it provides a summary for the business and for the customer of what has happened in a set period of time. This might be a month, a few months or even a year depending on the size of the business and the customers they work with.

Apply it

Look at the statement of account for Soraya from Happy Chocolate. Notice that the invoice amount is a **debit** (money that needs to be paid) and that there is a **credit** amount (for credit note 12345). You will remember that Soraya received another delivery from Happy Chocolate that had some items missing (see page 73). Add the second credit note to the statement of account. The credit note number is 12348. Soraya also ordered 300 bags of New Year sweets (invoice number 733K) but they arrived too late and were returned. The bags cost 75p each plus VAT. Add this information to the statement of account and then complete Amount now due section.

Happy Chocolate
Dairy Lane
Brompton
BS8 7LU
VAT No. 773/4824/12

STATEMENT OF ACCOUNT

To: Soraya's Emporium
St Marys Street
Bristol
BS4 8JH

Date: 28 February

Date	Details	Debit	Credit	Balance
	Balance brought forward			123.27
	Invoice 123F	219.71		
	Credit note 12345		7.45	
	Credit note			
	Invoice			
			Amount now due	

- -

Remittance Advice Slip

From: Soraya's Emporium   **Customer a/c no.** 3445
St Marys Street
Bristol
BS4 8JH

Amount enclosed ....   **Date of statement** 28 February

Your ref ....   **Date of payment** ....

Method of Payment ☐ Cheque ☐ Credit card ☐ Debit card

Please add details here including the card holder's name, card number, expiry date of the card and security code (written on the back of the card). Please make cheques payable to Happy Chocolate.

....
....
....

Describe it

A **debit** on a statement of account is money that needs to be paid by the customer – money owed. **Credit** is the money that has been put back into the account as credit for goods returned or damaged.

Remember it

Statements of account are very important as they help businesses track customer payments and items returned.

Remittance advice slips

When you looked at the statement of account on page 77 and worked out the final total due, you probably noticed the remittance advice slip at the bottom of the statement. Remittance advice slips are used by customers to send in payment by post. They are provided so that they do not have to send a letter explaining which account they are sending payment for as the remittance advice slip shows all the details. Some remittance advice slips also include the banking details of the business the customer needs to pay so that they can be taken to a bank. Remittance slips may also be attached to an invoice as well as a statement so that individual invoices can be paid.

Apply it

Use the remittance advice slip below for the following payment: Happy Chocolate is owed £75.21 by Juice Bars Ltd for their statement dated 31 March. Juice Bars Ltd is based at 22 Pentridge Way, Eastbourne, EA2 8MU. They have decided to pay by credit card – the name on the card is Juice Bars Ltd and the card number is 5278 3982 1123 2222; the expiry date is 11/11 and the security code is 123.

Remittance Advice Slip

From: Customer a/c no.

Amount enclosed ....   Date of statement ....
Your ref ....   Date of payment ....
Method of Payment ☐ Cheque ☐ Credit card ☐ Debit card

Please add details here including the card holder's name, card number, expiry date of the card and security code (written on the back of the card). Please make cheques payable to Happy Chocolate.
....
....
....

Remember it

When you are completing a remittance advice slip, it is important that you check and then double-check your calculations. You must also make sure you have included all the relevant information such as the account number, the date and who has paid the money in.

Research it

Visit the Money Matters to Me website and look at the pages on 'What money is' in the 'Money Matters' section (go to www. heinemann.co.uk/hotlinks). There is lots of information provided on issues relating to money and an interactive video showing how to write out a cheque properly.

Cheques

The remittance advice slip shows that there are different ways that money can be paid to businesses by customers. Cheques are one way that this can be done. Cheques used to be the most common method of payment but this is starting to change now. You will learn more about how cheques work on page 84.

Paying by cheque is a good way of keeping a record of payments made as the stub of the cheque book can be filled in with the details. This can be referred to later.

Receipts

Receipts provide a record for the customer and the business. The customer keeps their receipt so they can prove that they have paid for goods or services and so that they can return goods if they are faulty. The business keeps receipts as proof that money was paid in and that a customer received goods or services. Receipts may be produced by a cash register (till), a receipt book or, as is becoming more common now, may be emailed to the customer after they have paid.

From: **Mad About Books!**<customerservices@madaboutbooks.co.uk>
To: **A Customer**<a.customer@hotmail.co.uk>

Dear A. Customer

We thought you would like to know that your order **MAB234156** at www.madaboutbooks.co.uk has been dispatched.

Order contents: **1 x Edexcel GCSE Applied Business Student Book**

Sub Total:(GBP)**18.99**
Delivery: FREE
Grand Total:(GBP)**18.99**

Delivery address: A. Customer, 19 The Street, My Town AA13 2GB

If you provided card details for payment, your card has now been charged and "**Mad About Books**" will appear on your statement.

If you wish to contact us, please send a message to: info@madaboutbooks.co.uk

Kind regards,

Mad About Books.

An email receipt

Apply it

You have now learned about the nine most important business financial documents and you should be able to answer the following questions for each of them.

1 **When is it used?**
2 **Why is it used?**
3 **How is it used?**
4 **What information does it contain?**
5 **How important is the document to a business?**
6 **What would happen if the document was missing or incomplete in some way?**
7 **What does it look like – can you produce one yourself and complete it?**

If you find there are any gaps in your knowledge, go back over the appropriate sections.

Remember it

When writing a **cheque** yourself or taking a cheque as payment, make sure you check the following:

- the correct date (cheques are only valid for six months after they have been written)
- the amount in words matches the amount written as numbers
- any changes or alterations are signed by the person writing the cheque or it may be rejected
- the cheque must be signed – without a signature it is not valid
- there must be enough money in the account or the cheque will 'bounce'. Taking a cheque guarantee card number will reduce the risk of a cheque bouncing although the payment is only guaranteed to £50 or £100 maximum.

Assessment tip

Produce a set of revision notes or posters for the business financial documents we have looked at to help you revise for the exam.

Just checking

Name nine different types of financial document used in business.

What is the difference between a remittance advice slip and a statement of account?

Why are cheques being used less in business today?

Give three reasons why large businesses would benefit from using goods received notes.

What is a purchase order?

Paper-based accounting systems can be slow-going!

Computerised accounting systems

You have learned so far in this unit that many organisations are moving away from paper-based systems for all their financial documents and are using computers more and more. Years ago all accounting systems worked using paper documents.

Nowadays, most businesses make use of a personal computer and many use systems that are linked through the Internet. Many of the documents you have learned about are automated so, for example, it is possible to enter the details of a purchase order online immediately. Delivery notes may be emailed and invoices and credit notes can be accessed by logging into a computerised system. Statements of account may not even be sent in the mail but viewed by customers online when they want rather than waiting until the end of the month.

Using computerised accounting systems means that orders can go directly from the customer into a business' system. This means when a purchase order is raised, rather than needing to be sent and then the order processed, it can be done automatically.

Case study – Amazon

Amazon conducts virtually all of its business online and makes very good use of computerised accounting systems. This is because all of Amazon's orders and receipts are completed using email and it is possible to check on the progress of an order at any time. The Amazon website even recognises existing customers so they don't have to log in and can make personalised recommendations based on what they have bought before. When an order is received, a receipt is automatically sent to the customer and then when the item leaves the warehouse another email is sent to the customer letting them know their order is on its way.

Advantages of computerised systems compared to manual systems	Disadvantages of computerised systems compared to manual systems
Fewer errors should be likely as calculations are automatic.	Money needs to be invested into systems and therefore may create an additional cost for the business.
Paperwork cannot become lost as it is recorded automatically on the system and is usually emailed rather than sent through the post.	It takes time to set up a system and staff will need to be trained. Both of these issues take time and resources.
Computerised documents are quicker to produce as many of the parts of the document can be completed automatically, for example the date.	It may not be worth investing in a system if the payments received by the business are very small (the **cost-benefit** must be assessed).
Money is saved as postage costs do not have to be paid in order to send the document.	Sometimes computers have problems such as viruses or they breakdown – information could then be lost.
Customers can log in to their accounts and check payments or receipts if the business has a self-service facility.	Someone may gain access to a computerised system in order to find out information about the business. This is possible with paper but not as easy to do.
Extra passwords and codes can be added to a computerised system to stop unwanted people viewing the information.	

Describe it

Cost-benefit means what the cost of something is to a business and what the benefit to the business is. For example, if the cost of a computerised accounting system is more than the benefit, it is not worth putting the system into place.

Research it

Find out by searching the Internet what types of computerised accounting system there are. Produce a table showing the features of each. Which one would you recommend to someone starting up a new small business trading online?

Take it further

Make a judgement about whether or not you think all small businesses should use computerised accounting systems. Think of reasons for and against and then make your judgement. Make sure you give a reason (support) for your judgement.

Just checking

What are the advantages of using computerised accounting systems?

2.2 Investigating business payment methods and costs

In your everyday life, you will have come across two types of payment: cash and non-cash. Cash is when you physically hand over notes or coins. Non-cash means any other methods that you might use including cards, cheques and transfers. To understand how businesses work you will need to investigate why businesses use different types of payment methods and the costs, time, advantages and disadvantages of each method.

Types of cash and non-cash payment methods

We will now look at the following types of cash and non-cash payments:

- cash (notes and coins)
- cheques
- credit cards
- debit cards
- credit transfer
- direct debit
- e-cheques and other online payments.

Cash

Cash is the payment method that you will probably be most familiar with. You are likely to have bought items at shops or paid for lunches in your school or college canteen with cash. Cash comes in two forms: notes (£5 and over) and coins (from 1p to £2). Cash is still one of the most popular methods of payment in the UK today.

When businesses use cash they receive the money immediately. This means there is no wait for the money to flow into the business. Businesses may take money using a till or via handover of cash on delivery. Having cash means it should be easier and quicker to pay for business expenses. Although there are no direct charges to a business for accepting cash, equipment is needed to store it, for example a safe. People or machines are also needed to collect and count the cash. Any cash received by a business will need to be taken to the bank to help keep it safe.

Cash is a fast and simple payment method for everyday use

Talk about it

When businesses use cash, they need to consider the security aspects of using this payment method and the type of cash they may be willing to take, in terms of currencies and denomination (for example, some companies won't accept coins below 10p in order to avoid processing small change). Answer each of the questions below in small groups and discuss some of the issues related to using cash on a daily basis.

1 **How might using cash affect the physical security arrangements of a business?**
2 **What effect might using cash have on the insurance that a business has?**
3 **What additional training might staff need to handle cash?**
4 **What equipment might a business need when using cash?**

Research it

Make a list of ten businesses that operate in your local area. Find out how many of them take cash ONLY. How many of them accept other payment methods and which methods are they? Display your results in a graph.

Apply it

Djoulde is setting up his own mobile car tyre replacement business. He has decided to only take cash for payment in his first year of trading. Car tyres are priced at between £20 and £100. He plans to go to the workplaces and homes of customers to change the tyres. He expects, on average, to change between 4 and 6 tyres per day and will charge £10 to change and rebalance the tyres. Djoulde wonders how being a cash only business might affect his customers.

1 **What would you tell Djoulde are the advantages and disadvantages of trading in this way?**
2 **Would you recommend any changes to Djoulde's plan and, if so, what would they be?**

Research it

In late 2008, there were difficult times for many people with the advancing 'credit crunch'. As a result, many businesses and customers decided to use more old fashioned methods of payment instead of cash. 'Bartering' works when people exchange goods or services for other goods or services, for example exchanging a book you have read with a book you haven't read, or giving away food surpluses and then changing them for other foods. Many websites have taken advantage of this new interest in bartering, which can be seen as a form of recycling. Links to some of these sites can be found by visiting www.heinemann.co.uk/hotlinks.

Produce a presentation on the advantages and disadvantages of using barter instead of cash.

Just checking

Identify two advantages and two disadvantages of being a cash-only business.

Cheques

Cheques are very detailed and give clear information about the amount of money that is to be paid and who it is being paid to. When a cheque is given to a business, it must be paid into a business account at a bank or building society for the money to be transferred. It has to be 'cleared' by the bank before the business receives the money.

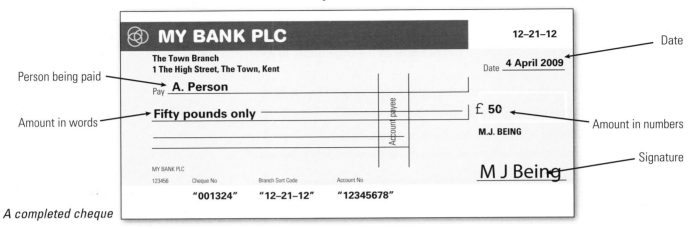

A completed cheque

Advantages of cheques	Disadvantages of cheques
An immediate record of the payment is created giving full details.	Many businesses face a charge by their bank for processing cheques, which can make it not worthwhile to accept them, especially for small amounts.
No cash needs to be carried so may be a little safer.	Funds need to be **cleared**. The time between a cheque being paid in to the bank and funds being received can often be up to three days.
Money spent can be tracked by completing the cheque book stub.	Cheques can 'bounce' if there is no money available in the person's account.
Useful for paying for large amounts of money (no need to withdraw and carry around large amounts of cash).	A cheque book needs to be carried around, which can be inconvenient and it may get lost.
	Cheques must be paid in to a bank within six months of the date or it will become invalid.
	As cheques are handwritten, they can be completed incorrectly or they may be altered in order to commit **fraud**.

Describe it

Clearing of a cheque means the time taken between the cheque being presented to the bank and the money being received into the account.
Fraud means crimes that are committed involving money.

Take it further

Marks and Spencer, Argos, Asda, Boots, Currys, Morrisons, Next, PC World, Sainsbury's, Shell garages and WH Smith are just some of the businesses that do not allow customers to pay by cheque. Think of as many reasons as you can why these businesses have chosen not to accept cheques. To what extent do you think not accepting cheques might affect trade for these businesses?

You can find out more about businesses and cheque payments by following the links provided at www.heinemann.co.uk/hotlinks.

Credit cards

A **credit** card is a type of payment card that allows you to borrow money and then pay it back later or in instalments. There are two ways that a business might use a credit card. The first way is to use a credit card themselves to pay for goods and services. The second is to offer their customers the opportunity to pay using a credit card. A credit card works in the same way as a loan except it is normally for a shorter period of time. A statement is sent every month showing what transactions have been made, what payments have been received, what the balance is and any interest that has been charged. The statement may be sent in paper form or provided online. Other information on the statement will include how much can be borrowed, the rate of interest that is charged on any outstanding balance and payment options.

There are lots of different types of credit card available for businesses and customers to use. Different cards will offer different rates of interest and may also have other incentives attached to them such as points or **cashback**.

THE PLATINUM CARD

Account Number	1234 5678 9876 5432	25 July
Credit Limit	£5600	
Available Credit	£4021.80	
Previous Balance		£1165.13

Transaction Date	Description	Amount
24 Jun	B & Q	£51.96
25 Jun	W M Morrisons	£43.17
28 Jun	Marks & Spencer	£98.50
Spending on your account		**£193.63**
Minimum payment – due by 19 August		**£39.45**

Please note: If you pay by direct debit your next payment will be **£1578.20**. This will debit your nominated account on **19 August**. Your estimated forecasted interest amounts to **£46.50**. Estimated interest is based on an amount which would be payable by you if you paid the minimum amount for this statement period and it reached us on the last day of payment.

A credit card statement

Describe it

Credit comes from the word *credere* (Latin) meaning 'trust'. Credit is where a person buys something and agrees to pay for it later.

Advantages of credit cards	Disadvantages of credit cards
Enables businesses to accept lots of different currencies, which is very important if they trade in other countries.	Interest rates can be high, especially when using credit cards to borrow cash.
The risk of fraud is reduced, especially when a PIN is used.	The business may be fined if payments are late.
Can offer insurance protection to the business if something goes wrong with the purchase.	
A credit card receipt into the business is guaranteed.	
Payments can be made online.	
Cash can be borrowed.	
The business' employees can pay for expenses when they are working rather than having to use their own money and claim it back.	

Giving customers the option to pay by credit card

When a customer uses a credit card, the credit card company pays for the goods or services and the customer pays the credit card company back over a period of time. If the customer does not pay the credit card company back within the agreed timeframe, the credit card company will seek payment from the customer, not the business. Customers benefit from purchase protection, which means that if the business goes into **receivership**, the customer should get their money back.

Businesses often allow credit cards for payment as they enable customers to pay over a longer period of time and so increase sales. Small businesses will often decide on a minimum customer payment when a credit card is used so that the charge is worth paying (which was 70p in August 2008). Some stores, such as Ikea, ask their customers to pay for the privilege of using a credit card.

Describe it

Receivership means when a company has been taken over by a receiver. A receiver takes control of companies that are about to go bankrupt and sorts out their financial arrangements.

Describe it

Chip and PIN is where a credit or debit card has a digital chip within it which holds information about the business or customer.

PIN means personal identification number, which is a four digit number only the card holder should know.

Debit cards

Debit cards work in a similar way to credit cards but instead of the money being borrowed, it is taken out of the customer's or business' account. When payment is made with a debit card, the business is guaranteed payment although not immediately (often up to three days later). Debit cards also allow payments to be made in different currencies and online. **Chip and PIN** facilities used with both types of card help to reduce fraud as the **PIN** must match the details held on the system of the organisation issuing the card. Like credit cards, charges are made for using debit cards so businesses need to make sure that they can cover these costs.

Apply it

Andrew's Party Gifts has received the following receipts this month: ten cheques, 23 direct debits, 64 debit card payments and 43 credit card payments. Referring to the bank charges in the table above, how much will these receipts cost the business (also assuming that the business is charged 70p per credit card transaction by the credit card company). How much money would the business save if the credit card company decided to reduce its charges to 50p per transaction?

A debit card

Case study – Lloyds TSB bank charges

In July 2008, Lloyds TSB made the following standard charges for all business customers. They are very typical of the charges all banks and building societies make their business customers, although sometimes a business can negotiate special deals for their particular needs.

1 **Find out what is meant by 'direct debit', 'standing order' and 'ATM'.**

2 **Which type of payment method might a small business prefer its customers to use?**

Lloyds TSB Bank Charges for Business Customers	
Cheque	65p
Direct debit	40p
Standing order	40p
Transfer (transfer to another account in your name with the sort code starting 30-xx-xx)	Free
Debit card transaction (excluding ATM)	40p
ATM withdrawals (free from a Lloyds TSB Cashpoint® machine)	45p

Credit transfer

Credit transfer allows businesses to move monies from one account to another. Credit transfer can be a one-off movement of money between accounts or regular payments. The transfer may be from one business to another, from a customer to the business or even movements of money between the business' own accounts. Regular transfer payments are known as standing orders.

There are many reasons why businesses might prefer to use credit transfer rather than other methods:

- They are able to move funds between accounts and gain interest on the money while waiting to pay their bills.
- Transfers can be done online at the press of a button.
- International payments in other currencies can be accepted, e.g. euro, and these can be exchanged into pound sterling automatically.
- Repeat payments may be easier as payment information does not need to be set up again.
- Real time processing can detect fraud or payments where there are problems (businesses would need to pay a higher charge for this service).

Credit transfers usually take time to clear unless extra payment is made for real time processing (this means processing straight away). The business may have to wait a few days for the money to be paid into their account and will need to plan for this.

The final way that a credit transfer may be used is if a customer needs a refund for goods and services. Rather than offering money back, the business may transfer credit to the customer's account so that the next time they want to purchase something they know they have this money available.

Some businesses may ask their customers to pay them by standing order. This means that the same amount of money will be taken from the customer's bank account each week or month and will then be paid across to the business. Using standing orders means that there is no need to physically count or check the money as the bank will do it automatically. The customer or other business puts the standing order into place so the business has no direct control over them. The customer may cancel their payment without notice and so the business will need to have procedures in place to collect payment if this happens. Banks will charge businesses for processing standing orders, like other forms of payment.

Research it

Choose six organisations that you know well and find out how many of them accept standing orders as a method of payment. How commonly are they used? Which methods of payment are less commonly used by these businesses? Explain why.

Take it further

International payments can be accepted by credit transfer and then be automatically transferred into pounds. How might changes in currencies affect these transfers and how can businesses plan for such changes?

Just checking

What is the difference between a debit and credit card?

Apply it

Organic Food Deliveries has decided to expand into your area. They sell home-delivered organic food, including fruit, vegetables and dairy products. Produce a factsheet for them about direct debits. Include information on how direct debits may help them with payments and also include information on at least three of the possible disadvantages that they might face.

Research it

Find out what 'Direct Debit Guarantee' means.

Explain **one** way it can help a business. Explain **one** way it can help a customer.

Direct debit

Direct debit, like standing orders and credit transfers, is a way of transferring money automatically. Unlike a standing order, a direct debit payment is set up by the business that is receiving the money and not by the customer. This means that the amount of money taken can be increased or decreased depending on the number of goods bought or the cost of the services provided.

Many businesses make payments using direct debit for goods or services they use regularly, good examples being electricity, gas or water. Often discounts will be offered for paying in this way and it can be extremely convenient for both the customer and business. Direct debit payments help businesses to plan more effectively as:

- they are guaranteed payments
- customers do not have to remember to pay them because they are automatic
- they cannot get lost in the post
- the amount of money and the date when it is taken can be changed automatically.

Setting up a direct debit is relatively simple. The customer simply needs to complete a direct debit instruction form.

Direct debit payments are convenient and can save time, but sometimes paying this way may actually cost a business more money than if it accepted payments in other ways. This is because when receiving direct debits, the business will need to pay a charge for each one. When making payments by direct debit there are also sometimes other charges. For example, paying insurance or car payments monthly may result in interest being added to payments. Sometimes this can be as high as 20% extra. This would not be a cheaper way for the business to pay. Of course, this does mean that a business could charge its customers for offering this facility and may even be able to cover additional costs in this way. The business may also be charged if they miss a payment or are unable to pay. This may be as much as £35, so they need to ensure they have funds available. Some customers also worry about direct debit payments, especially if they are on a low income or are elderly.

- - ✂ -

Instruction to your Bank or Building Society to pay Direct Debits
PLEASE FILL IN THE WHOLE FORM AND SEND IT TO:
A BUSINESS

DIRECT Debit

1 Name and full postal address of your Bank or Building Society branch

To the Manager _____ Bank/Building Society

Address _____

_____ Post Code _____

2 Name(s) of Account Holder(s)

3 Bank or Building Society Account Number

Originator's Identification Number

4 Branch Sort Code

□□ – □□ – □□

A Business Reference Number **6**

5 Instruction to your Bank or Building Society

Please pay A Business Direct Debits from the account detailed in this Instruction subject to the safeguards assured by the Direct Debit Guarantee. I understand that this instruction may remain with A Business and, if so, details will be passed electronically to my Bank or Building Society

Signature(s) _____ Date _____

Banks and Building Societies may not accept Direct Debit instructions for some types of account.

Please indicate your preferred payment frequency | Monthly ☐ | Quarterly ☐ | Half Yearly ☐ | Yearly ☐

A direct debit instruction form

E-cheques

E-cheques are payments that are made over the Internet from one account to another. Unlike a credit or debit card, an e-cheque payment comes straight from a customer's bank account to the business' online account. An e-cheque takes between seven and ten days to clear, so it is important that the business waits for the money to clear before it sends out the goods. If a customer does not have enough money in their account, the e-cheque will 'bounce' (not be paid) in the same way as a normal paper cheque. E-cheques are not yet common in the UK but are used more in the United States with digital signatures.

Because businesses have to wait up to ten days for an e-cheque to clear, customers paying in this way may have to wait longer to receive their order than other customers paying with different methods. If the item is being sent via the post, their order may take as long as 14 days to be completed. Some customers may not be willing to wait this long.

PayPal

E-cheques are just one method of online payment. New methods are being introduced all the time, and one of the most commonly used is PayPal, which you may have used yourself. PayPal works by allowing customers to pay money into a PayPal account, often via a debit or credit card. When the customer wants to buy something they arrange for a transfer to be made from their PayPal account to the seller's account. This means that they do not have to send their credit or debit card details to the seller. This makes PayPal a relatively secure method of payment.

Mobile phone payments

payforituk.com is just one of a new type of payment service that is offered in the UK – payments by mobile phone. The cost of low value items are added to the phone bills of mobile phone users instead of payment being required by credit or debit card. Users of mobile phones are able to buy credit for their phone in £10 packages and these can then be transferred into a UK cash voucher that can be used online.

Have you ever paid for something using your mobile phone?

Take it further

Like all methods of payment, there is the possibility that criminals may use e-cheques to commit fraud. Produce a poster giving hints and tips to businesses on ways to avoid fraud (information can be found on the Internet by entering 'e-cheque fraud' into a search engine).

Assessment tip

You may find it useful to copy and complete the table below as part of your revision for the exam. Try to identify at least two advantages and two disadvantages for each payment method.

Payment method	Advantages	Disadvantages

Research it

Go online and investigate ten of the businesses you like to buy goods and services from. How many of them allow you to pay with PayPal? Copy and complete the table below and then draw a graph based on your results. What do you notice and why?

Name of business	Type of goods/services	Accepts PayPal – Yes or No?

Just checking

How do payments made by direct debit benefit businesses?

How can a mobile phone be used for payment?

Sources of revenue and costs

Describe it

Revenue means income coming into the business from sales, through a grant, the leasing of premises or interest on money in the bank.

Costs mean any payments that are made from a business, for example telephone bills or the manufacture of products to sell.

There are two very important words you will need to learn and understand for your exam: **revenue** and **costs**.

Every business has to have revenue because without money coming in it cannot survive and pay for everything it needs. The type of revenue will depend on the type of business.

Apply it

For each of the businesses or business people below, identify the possible sources of revenue they may have. Think of as many different sources as you can.

- Local hairdressing salon
- Garage advertising online
- Commercial radio station
- Monthly magazine
- Self-employed artist
- Market trader selling fruit and vegetables
- Football club
- Accountant

As well as money coming into the business, money also needs to be paid out to cover the costs of producing products or services. All businesses have to pay for costs to start up in the first place and then to run. As you would expect, these costs are called **start-up costs** and **running costs**.

Spending money on start-up costs is important for the good running of a business as it can lead to cost savings at a later stage. For example, money spent on market research in order to work out how many customers the business is likely to have, where it should advertise and the type of promotions that it should offer (for example, discounts or buy one get one free) can help the business plan effectively and not spend money unnecessarily.

Describe it

Start-up costs are costs that a business has to cover when it is first set up. Those costs that are only paid at the start of a business might include buying a lease for a shop or a computer for an online business.

Running costs are those costs that the business must pay regularly, for example business rates or electricity bills.

Take it further

Market research allows businesses to collect data about lots of different aspects of the market that they are in. Find out what is meant by market research and the different types that may be possible: primary and secondary.

Case study – The nail bar

Matthew is setting up a nail bar business in the high street. He is trying to work out which costs are running and which are start-up costs. In pairs or small groups, tick next to each cost whether it is a start-up cost or a running cost. Think of three other types of cost that are not listed here, add them to the table and decide whether they are start-up or running costs.

Cost	Start-up cost	Running cost
Nail polish		
Fast nail dryer		
Sinks		
Chairs		
Tables		
Electric nail-polishing brush		
Soap		
Towels		
Cleaning liquid		

Case study – **Jared's burger van**

Jared has always wanted to run his own burger van and is currently thinking about his costs. Using your best estimating skills and research from the Internet, work out his running costs per month and the start-up costs he needs to pay out before he can start his business. He expects to sell, on average, 50 burgers per day and he is going to work six days per week. He is going to pay himself £200 per week in wages.

Cost	Running costs per month £	Start-up costs £
Burgers and buns		
Cleaning materials		
Cutlery, napkins and plates etc.		
Gas for the cookers		
Insurance for the van		
Ketchup, mustard etc.		
Licence from the council		
Mobile phone		
Painting of advertising logo on van		
Petrol		
Purchase of two cookers		
Purchase of fridge freezer		
Purchase of cash register		
Purchase of van		
Regular advertising		
Staff wages		
Totals		

Just checking

Define the following words and phrases: revenue; costs; start-up costs; running costs.

Apply it

You may already be thinking of different ways you might want to run your own business in the future. One way that is becoming increasingly popular is to run a business through eBay or Amazon selling second-hand items. There are a number of different businesses already trading through eBay, such as miss-bargain.com, which trades in designer clothes.

Make a list of all the start-up and running costs you think you might need to pay if you ran a business through either eBay or Amazon. What are the advantages and disadvantages of running an online business compared to an offline business?

Costs between businesses can vary for many reasons. They can even vary between businesses that offer similar goods or services. Some of these reasons are shown below.

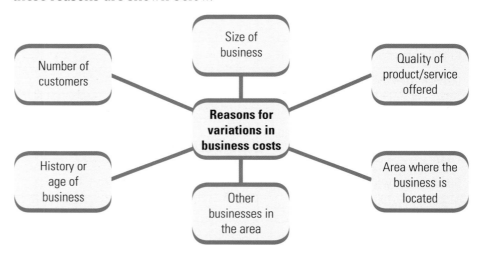

Take it further

Can you think of any other reasons why businesses have different costs and revenues even though they are offering the same service or product? Think about the difference in costs between jeans made by Levi and those made by Primark. What makes the difference in costs and revenues? Why?

Talk about it

What do you think is meant by the term 'primary sector'? What do you think is meant by the term 'secondary sector'? Use the clues in the terms to help you and have a discussion as a small group to see if you can work it out together.

So far we have looked at the costs and revenue that relate to two service sector businesses (or tertiary businesses). These are the most common businesses in the UK. They offer something to their customers such as manicuring their nails or selling them food, as with our two examples on pages 90–91, but these businesses do not actually extract or make products themselves.

There are two other business sectors you might have heard of: primary and secondary. You will need to be able to compare costs between businesses in the same sector and between those in a different sector.

The term 'primary sector' means the first industry, so businesses that operate in this sector are involved in the extraction of raw materials from the ground (mining and quarrying, for example), agriculture, fishing and forestry. The costs which relate to this type of business can be quite different to that of a business providing services. Think of the costs associated with farming, for example.

Apply it

Copy and complete the table below to work out the costs businesses from the primary sector may have to pay when they are trading. You may need to conduct research to find out the answers.

Primary sector business	Costs	Revenues
Fisherman		
Coal mining company		
Farmer		

How are these costs different to costs in service sector businesses? How are revenues different? In your exam you will need to be able to compare and contrast.

The secondary sector relates to businesses that take raw materials such as milk from cows (primary) and then make them into products that can be sold. Examples of businesses like these include dairies, furniture makers, cake producers such as Mr Kipling, and so on.

Research it

Using your research skills now do the same exercise for secondary sector businesses as you did for the primary sector by choosing from one of the examples below or thinking of one of your own.

- Cadbury
- Clark's Shoes
- Dairy Crest
- Weetabix
- Ford
- Heinz

Think about the costs and revenues that these businesses have. How do they compare to the primary sector and how do they compare to the tertiary sector? In your exam, you may be asked to compare costs from different sectors so it is important you understand the meaning of each.

Remember it

Primary sector means businesses that extract raw materials from the ground or land so they can be made (by the secondary sector) into something new.

Secondary sector means businesses that take raw materials and make them into products, for example cheese making from milk.

Tertiary sector means businesses that provide services, such as restaurants and taxi firms.

The role of ICT

The role of ICT is very important when thinking about costs. You have already learned about different ways that money can be saved by using online purchase orders and statements (see page 80). Using ICT can make a big difference to the way businesses operate.

Many businesses are now run online. You have seen how Amazon makes use of automated systems to send out delivery notes and provide statements to customers (see page 80). Ordering in this way means it is much quicker and easier than operating in a manual way. Using ICT to take payments means that businesses and customers are paying for goods and services in advance more often, they can automatically receive a receipt via email and deliveries can be tracked online at the touch of a button.

Case study – Vodafone

If Vodafone has a problem with a handset, most of the delivery tracking and receipt is done using ICT. When the handset is received at its depot for repair, a text message (SMS) is sent to the customer letting them know it has arrived, and when it has been repaired another text message is sent saying it is on its way back. Having automated ICT systems like this means that the customer knows what is happening at all times and feels more in control.

Can you think of other businesses that make use of ICT to keep their customers happy and interested? How does this have a positive effect on customers?

One of the main reasons businesses choose to use ICT is so they can become very responsive to customer needs. For example, it has become common for businesses to hold less stock and be able to be more responsive to customer needs – when ordering a new car it is possible to choose the make, model and extra features that you want and then the car will be delivered to order.

Case study – Make it your own

Nike has launched on its website the option for customers to personalise their own trainers and clothes. By allowing customisation of their products, Nike is not only able to satisfy the needs of its customers but is also only producing what is needed to fulfil orders. This reduces stock costs as shoes and clothes only need to be made when orders are received. Visit the Nike website to find out more (go to www.heinemann.co.uk/hotlinks).

The business spreadshirt.net works in much the same way, enabling customers to design their own T-shirt. Cashflow is improved as customers pay online when they order, meaning that the business receives payment before the product is made.

Apply it

You have been asked to carry out research into the advantages and disadvantages for customers of businesses using ICT for payments and ordering. To carry out the research you need to produce a questionnaire that you can use in your class and with friends and family.

You will need to think about the different types of question you might want to ask. You may wish to include some questions about personal information, such as their age range or their gender, to see if this has an impact on how often people buy online. Some examples of different types of question are given below to get you started.

- Do you shop online?   Yes   No
- How many times per month do you shop online?
  1   2   3   4   5+
- I prefer to buy online. (Choose one of the following.)
- Strongly agree   Agree   Have no opinion   Disagree   Strongly disagree
- Why do you shop online? _____

Don't forget to test your questionnaire before you give it out to check that everyone understands your questions. You will also need to think about what information you want to get from your questionnaire and how you will handle the data when you have collected it. How easy will it be to interpret? Will you be able to produce useful graphs, charts etc. that tell you what you want to know? Are there questions included that do not help to tell you what you want to know? If so, do not ask them and waste your time as well as your audience's.

When you have collected your completed questionnaires, write up a report of your results. It is important to remember that your results must tell you something – what have you learnt in relation to the task you have been set?

ICT is also used in and around retail stores to help businesses run more effectively. You probably see barcodes on a daily basis. They are there to help stores understand how much has been sold and how much they need to order.

Apply it

Think of as many ways as you can that ICT is used in businesses. It might be in the ordering process, in the way that information is transmitted to customers or even the way that customers pay. There are lots of cost savings to be made using ICT, for example using e-newsletters to advertise products to existing customers or by using a website rather than having a shop. See how many you can think of. You can learn a great deal by keeping your eyes open and observing carefully when you go out shopping!

Just checking

Describe how ICT can help businesses become more efficient when ordering stock.

2.3 Investigating the nature of financial statements in business

Describe it

A **profit and loss account** shows a business' financial performance measured by its costs and revenues over a period of time, usually a year.

A **balance sheet** shows a business' financial performance at a point in time.

So far in this unit, we have looked at some of the key business documents and how they are used in business. We have also learned about methods of payment and the costs that are associated with running online and offline businesses. One of the key reasons businesses trade is to make a profit and provide a return on the investment made in the business by their owners. In this section we look at two key documents that really help the owners of a business understand how it is doing financially: the **profit and loss account** and the **balance sheet**.

Before we look at profit and loss accounts and balance sheets in more detail, you will need to understand the meaning of some key terms that are found within them. Each of these terms is explained with examples over the next few pages.

Terminology in financial statements

Sales turnover

Sales turnover means the sales that the business has made in a specific time period. This is worked out by multiplying the number of goods sold by the price. The net sales is the amount of sales less any returns for products that are damaged or lost. The terms 'sales revenue' and 'total sales' are sometimes used instead of sales turnover, but they mean the same thing.

Let's take an organic fruit and vegetable business as an example: if the business sells apples online by the kilo for £2.69 and during a given period of time they sell 258 kilos of apples and nothing else, they would have a sales turnover of £2.69 x 258 = £694.02. If they had two kilos of apples returned or lost, their net sales would be £694.02 – £5.38 (2 x 2.69) = £688.64. In reality, the business sells lots of different fruits and vegetables so their sales would be made up of the sales of all the fruits and vegetables, each of which will have different prices.

Cost of sales

It is important here not to get confused by the term 'cost'. Remember, 'price' is the amount of money the customer has to hand over to acquire a product or service. 'Cost' refers to the spending by the business on the resources needed for production of the goods or service. Cost of sales, therefore, means the actual cost of producing goods or making services available that were sold. For example, if you sell 100 sweets that were bought in for 10p each, the goods would cost £10.00 to produce. If the sweets were sold at a price of 30p each, the sales turnover would be 100 x 30p = £30.00 but the cost of sales would be 100 x 10p = £10.00.

Apply it

Happy Chocolate had the following sales figures and costs for the six months to April 2009. Work out the total turnover and cost of goods sold for Happy Chocolate.

Month	Sales £	Returns £	Cost of goods £
April	3400	200	2000
March	2300		1500
February	1500		900
January	1300	100	850
December	1400		875
November	1800		

Apply it

Now work out the cost of sales for the organic fruit and vegetable business if it costs them £1.50 to produce a kilo of apples and they sell 308 kilos.

Gross profit

Gross profit is the amount of money left from the goods or services sold less the cost to buy them (cost of goods sold). For example, if a business sells £15,000 of sales and the resources used to make those sales cost £2,000, the gross profit would be £13,000.

Apply it

Amel runs her own dressmaking business. She made £4,000 in sales and the dresses cost her £3,458 to make. What is her gross profit?

Luke has a motorcycle business. He made £5,000 gross profit in May. The cost of buying in the bikes he sold was £10,000. What was his sales turnover?

Expenses

Expenses are the costs that the business must pay in order for it to trade. Examples might include gas, electricity, rent or any other costs that need to be paid by the business. It is important that you understand which items represent expenses and which represent income.

Apply it

Draw two boxes on a sheet of paper or in a document using IT. Label the boxes 'Expenses' and 'Income'. Now put each of the following items into one of the boxes. Compare your answers with those of a classmate.

Sales; electricity; advertising; insurance; interest paid to the company; legal fees; administration; petrol; lighting.

Just checking

What do sales turnover and cost of sales show?

Net profit

Net profit is gross profit less any expenses the company has paid out. Net profit therefore shows the amount of money made by a business after it has paid all of its bills.

Apply it

Mohammed has set up his own business selling flowers for events and parties. His gross profit for the first six months is £15,000 (based on sales of £25,000 and cost of sales of £10,000). He runs the business from home and his sales are all done over the Internet or phone. In small groups, work out what you think his expenses might have been and then calculate his net profit. Compare your answers with another group – what was the same, what was different and why?

Assessment tip

You will need to be able to explain the difference between gross and net profit – check your understanding now by writing down a definition of each and checking it.

Take it further

You may have already thought about a business you would like to run when you leave education. Using that business idea as an example, think of all the possible expenses you might incur. Add them up and see how much money you will need to cover to set up and run the business for a year. How many sales will you need to make in that year to generate a profit of 10%?

Fixed assets and current assets

Assets are very important to a business. This is because they are things which are owned by the business that they are going to be keeping for some time. Fixed assets are those things which are for continuous use by the business, such as buildings, machinery, equipment, vehicles etc. Current assets, like fixed assets, are also owned by the business but unlike fixed assets they could be more easily turned into cash (and include cash) such as stock. Stock represents future sales and so can be turned into cash relatively quickly. Current assets also include people who owe the business money for goods or services; these businesses or individuals are known as debtors.

Current assets are things like stock

Fixed assets are things like buildings and land

Apply it

Archie has been running his own cheese shop for more than ten years. He owns the shop (he bought the shop and lease in 1998). He has £200 in the bank and has approximately £2,600 worth of cheese in the shop. Last year he had three new fridges put into the shop at a cost of £500 each. To serve the cheese, he has a range of knives and cutting equipment which he bought for £350 from the previous owner – they are now estimated to be worth £200. The fixtures and fittings of the shop were updated in April of this year and included things like a counter, blinds etc. They cost approximately £5,000 but, if re-sold, would be worth £2,000.

1 Identify the fixed assets and their value. Identify the current assets and their value.

Research it

Choose three different businesses in your area or online. Think about the possible fixed and current assets they own. Which types of fixed asset do they own? Which types of current asset do they own? Why might online businesses have fewer fixed assets than offline businesses?

Just checking

What is the difference between gross profit and net profit?

What is the difference between fixed assets and current assets, giving examples of each?

Remember it

A good way to remember the difference between current liabilities and long-term liabilities is to think of current liabilities as being like current affairs or current issues, i.e. happening now (or within a year for current liabilities). Long-term liabilities are as they sound and payable over a longer term.

Remember it

Debtors are businesses or people who owe a business money. **Creditors** are businesses or people a business owes money to.

Current liabilities and long-term liabilities

Liabilities in its most simple form means money that the business has to pay out. It is the money the business is liable or responsible for paying to others – debts that they owe. Current liabilities are those debts that need to be paid within a year. Long-term liabilities are debts that need to be paid over a number of years. They may be from a few years to 25 or 50 years, for example a long-term loan or a mortgage.

Apply it

Look at the table below listing different types of liabilities and decide which are current and which are long term. Put a tick or cross in the right box.

Type of liability	Current	Long-term
Mortgage over 25 years on a property		
Payment owed to a supplier for stock		
Electricity and heating costs to be paid		
Loan over ten years		

Take it further

Businesses have liabilities over different periods of time. These liabilities represent funds that are used for different reasons. You will need to conduct research into the different types of loan a business might use and why they might be used.

Explain the advantages and disadvantages to a business of taking out a business loan over 25 years compared to one over a year.

Working capital

Working capital is the difference between current assets and current liabilities. You can think of it as being like your own wallet or purse. Assets that you have that can be easily used might be cash (current assets), less the money that you owe to your friend for buying you a meal last week (current liabilities). This leaves you with the money you have to work with, which is working capital. Continuing with our example, if you have current assets (cash) of £10 available, and you owe your friend £5 (current liabilities), your working capital is £5.

Apply it

Andrew has set up his own business making freshly-made sandwiches and cakes. It is going to be called 'Buttery Buns'. His assets and liabilities to the end of June are shown below.

Asset or liability	Amount £
Cash in the till	55.23
Orders waiting payment	250.25
Delivery van	5,000.00
Money in the bank	6,000.00
Bank loan to be paid off within a year	5,000.00
Oven and equipment	10,000.00
Flour, eggs, sugar and sandwich fillings in the stock room	500.00
Money owed to suppliers	1,000.00

Use the information above to calculate Andrew's:

- Current assets
- Current liabilities
- Working capital

Apply it

Using the information below, calculate the following for each business:

- Current assets
- Current liabilities
- Working capital

Chocco Desserts Ltd	£	Ice Snax Ltd	£
Bank	200.00	Bank	500.00
Creditors	400.00	Creditors	200.00
Loan from bank	2,000.00	Loan from bank	750.00
Debtors	750.00	Debtors	300.00
Stock	600.00	Stock	1,000.00
Cash	300.00	Cash	250.00

Capital

Although 'capital' sounds similar to 'working capital' it is quite different, so make sure you understand the difference. Capital still relates to money, but rather than being the difference between what you have and do not have, it is the amount of money that is used to set up the business in the first place.

Sometimes small business owners may borrow capital from a bank to get their business up and running. They may do this by securing a loan against their own property or assets so that the bank can get its money back if the business fails to pay back the loan. Another way a business may raise capital is by asking individuals or other businesses to invest in return for shares. This means that the investors own a share of the business and is known as 'share capital'.

Just checking

What is the difference between capital and working capital?

Profit and loss account

Now you have become more familiar with all the terms that you are going to find in the profit and loss account, you need to understand how all these terms are put together to form the profit and loss account. A profit and loss account is a very important document for a business because it shows the income, expenses and level of profit (or loss) the business has made over a given period of time (often a year).

Erin is running her own business called 'Sweet Thoughts'. It sells lots of different types of sweets and cakes. Her profit and loss account for the year ended is shown below. The top part of the profit and loss account shows the movement of stock and the gross profit. It is known as the trading section and is shown in blue.

	£	£
Sales turnover		150,000
Less cost of sales		
Opening stock	5,000	
Purchases	51,000	
Less closing stock	6,000	50,000
Gross profit		100,000
Less expenses		
Rent and business rates	15,600	
Advertising	2,000	
Wages and salaries	28,000	
Administration	1,000	
Insurance	2,000	
Interest on loans	2,100	
Telephone	600	
Accountancy fees	900	
Legal fees	1,000	
Bank charges	400	
Repairs and maintenance	300	
Heat and light	600	
Miscellaneous	300	
		54,800
Net profit before tax		45,200

Erin's 'Sweet Thoughts' profit and loss account for the year ended 31 March

Apply it

Answer the following questions about Erin's business by referring to her profit and loss account:

1 How much is the gross profit?

2 What is the total amount of expenses that Erin paid out?

Compare your answers with those of a classmate.

Assessment tip

You will need to learn the layout of a profit and loss account so that you can produce one if necessary. Remember, businesses can make both profits and losses. If a business has made a loss over the period of time being considered, it is either shown as a negative figure, for example -£25,345, or is shown in brackets, for example, (£25,345).

Case study – L&C T-shirts

Li and Charlotte have been selling T-shirts all over the world through their website. Their turnover and expenses for the past six months are shown below. Produce a profit and loss statement for them based on this information.

- They sold £50,000 worth of T-shirts.
- They started the six month period with £3,500 of stock and bought £7,500 worth of stock.
- At the end of the six months, they had £1,000 left over.
- Their expenses included £20,000 for wages, £2,000 for advertising, £2,000 for insurance, £400 for the telephone, £1,000 for web hosting, £600 for heat and light, and £300 for miscellaneous costs.

Make sure you include the gross and net profit sections of your statement.

Balance sheet

A profit and loss account shows the money that has gone in and out of a business over a given period of time, but does not show any of the items that the business owns (assets) or any of the money that it owes (liabilities). Assets and liabilities are shown in a balance sheet, which is used to work out how much a business is actually worth. A balance sheet is called a *balance* sheet because it must balance! This is because the total assets less the current liabilities (those that need to paid in less than a year) must equal the amount of money that has been used to finance the business. It shows where money has been invested and who is owed money.

Remember it

A **profit and loss account** represents money flowing in and out of a business over a period of time.

A **balance sheet** is a picture of what the business owns and what it owes at a particular point in time – it is a snapshot of the business at one point in time.

Apply it

We have already looked at the difference between assets and liabilities in this unit. Try to put the following items from a balance sheet into two categories: assets and liabilities.

Cash in the bank; overdraft to be paid; cash in the till; advertising bill to be paid within 20 days; bank loan to be paid over five years; stock in the store room; a business van; shelving for the shop; mortgage to buy the shop; business rates to be paid within one month; tools used by the business; office furniture; tax to be paid; customers who owe the business money.

On the opposite page you can see an example of a balance sheet. You will notice that the total assets less the liabilities and the capital employed are both shown in blue. These are the two areas of the balance sheet that must balance. When you are working out your own balance sheet calculation, you must make sure you do not make the same mistake that has been made in this example. The balance sheet must balance; if it does not then you have made an error in your calculations.

Many businesses now use ICT to help them organise their profit and loss accounts and balance sheets. You have learned about the some of the advantages and disadvantages of using computerised accounting systems on page 80.

Rapid Cycles Ltd
Balance Sheet 1 April

	£	£
Fixed assets		
Shop premises		75,000
Fixtures and fittings		5,000
		80,000
Current assets		
Stock		15,000
Debtors		1,000
Bank		3,000
Cash		1,000
		20,000
Less current liabilities		
Creditors	7,000	
Overdraft	4,000	
	11,000	
Working capital	9,000	
	89,000	
Total assets less current liabilities		
Financed by:		
Long-term liabilities	10,000	
Bank loan	60,000	
Mortgage	70,000	
Capital and reserves	19,000	
Capital	89,000	
Capital employed		

A balance sheet

Just checking

What is the difference between a profit and loss account and a balance sheet?

2.4 Investigating the importance of financial statements to business

You have hopefully been making progress with your understanding of the terms used in financial statements and how such statements are used by businesses to show the:

- profit or loss they have made (profit and loss account)
- real value of the business by showing assets and liabilities (balance sheet).

These statements are most useful when you can use calculations to investigate what is happening in the business in more detail. In this section you will learn about the different calculations (known as **ratios**) that are used to work out how profitable a business is (known as profitability ratios) and how easily a business is able to pay its bills (liquidity ratios). The final part of this section looks at why financial statements are so important to people who have an interest in a business or are affected by it (i.e. stakeholders), as well as the way ICT might help us interpret financial statements.

Before we start looking at ratios, there are some very important key terms you will need to know. These are shown in the table below.

Describe it

A **ratio** is simply one number divided by another.

Cash	Cash means the amount of physical money you are able to get to quickly. This might be money in the till or cash in the bank. It is money you have in your hand. If a business does not have enough cash available to pay the bills, it will not be able to continue to trade.
Profit	Profit is the amount of money you expect to get when all of your costs and expenses have been taken away from your income. This is the amount left over. It is possible for a business to think it is going to make a profit at the end of the year but not have enough cash in its accounts to continue trading. Profit is only a 'real' amount of money when the business has reached the end of the financial period in which it was trading.
Liquidity	Liquidity means how easily a business can pay its bills and turn any assets into cash if it needs to.
Profitability	Profitability means how much profit is being made by a business in relation to how much has been invested in it. For example, if a business makes a profit of £1,000 but has invested £100,000, its profitability is low. Investors may choose to invest elsewhere in future. However, if the profit is £50,000 in relation to an investment of £100,000, it would be considered far more profitable.

You will learn more about these terms and how they are used to work out how profitable or liquid a business actually is as you work through this section.

Case study – **Troubled Times Ltd**

Look at the profit and loss account below and answer the questions that follow.

Profit and Loss Account for the six months ended 30 September

	£	£
Sales turnover		10,000
Less cost of sales		
Opening stock	5,000	
Purchases	1,000	
Less closing stock	2,000	4,000
Gross profit		6,000
Less expenses		
Rent and business rates	10,000	
Advertising	2,000	12,000
Net profit before tax		(6,000)

1 What profit/loss has the business made?

2 What could Troubled Times do to help it become more successful? Think about how profit is generated – the difference between revenue and costs. You might need to think about how the business could change its costs, expenses, purchases of stock and so on.

3 What could Troubled Times do to change its sales turnover figure?

4 What do you think Troubled Times should do in the short term and longer term?

Apply it

Now look back at the balance sheet for Rapid Cycles Ltd on page 105 and consider its assets and liabilities.

1 In light of what you have learned in this section, what do you think of its situation?

2 Which type of assets does it mostly own? How does having lots of this type of assets help it pay its bills if necessary?

3 What is its level of current liabilities? How does this affect the business?

Research it

Many businesses make use of IT to help them manage their accounts. Conduct some research into the different accounting software packages such as Sage that are available to help produce financial statements in business.

Remember it

Profitability ratios work out the level of profit compared to the amount of sales that have been made.

Profitability ratios

As well as looking at the profit and loss account and balance sheet, it is possible to apply ratios to the figures shown in each statement. The three main ratios you need to know about for profitability are:

- gross profit margin
- net profit margin
- return on capital employed (ROCE).

Each ratio gives information about the profit being made. Comparing different ratios helps the business and investors to see what is happening to the business over time and how well (or badly) the business is performing compared to other similar businesses. It helps to give an indication of the financial health of the business.

Gross profit margin

The gross profit margin is a way of working out how much profit a business has made compared to the sales it has made. The ratio is worked out by calculating the gross profit as a percentage of the turnover. It shows how much gross profit is made for every £1 in sales. The higher the percentage, the better. A business would rather generate a gross profit of 60p for every £1 it earns in sales than 20p!

$$\text{Gross profit margin} = \frac{\text{Gross profit x 100}}{\text{Turnover}}$$

Net profit margin

Gross profit margin takes into account the sales revenue and the cost of sales. To get net profit we need to subtract the expenses the business has had to make. The net profit margin works out the amount of profit after expenses and calculates how much has been made compared to turnover. The ratio is worked out by calculating net profit as a percentage of turnover. The higher the percentage, the better for the business. Net profit will almost always be lower than the gross profit for obvious reasons!

$$\text{Net profit margin} = \frac{\text{Net profit x 100}}{\text{Turnover}}$$

Return on capital employed (ROCE)

The return on capital employed works out the amount of net profit that has been made as a percentage of the amount of money used by the business. This shows the return on the amount of capital invested. To better understand this it is useful to think of two businesses operating in the same market which are exactly the same size in terms of the money they use (the capital employed). If Business A used £100,000 worth of capital to generate profits of £20,000, it would clearly be more effective at using this money (its capital) than Business B which also had £100,000 of capital but only generated £3,000 in profits.

The problem is that not every business is the same size, so ROCE can be used to compare profitability. ROCE is worked out by calculating net profit as a percentage of capital employed. The higher the percentage, the better. It is useful to think about the age of a business when working this calculation out – new businesses may find it harder to have a good return on capital employed when they first start up as they need to establish themselves first. ROCE should ideally work out between 20 and 30%. This figure should also be compared to competitors and regularly monitored.

$$ROCE = \frac{Net\ profit \times 100}{Capital\ employed}$$

Apply it

You have been asked to comment on the profitability of the following three businesses for the past year. Work out the gross profit margin, the net profit margin and the ROCE for each.

Name of business	Gross profit £	Net profit £	Turnover £	Capital employed £
Alex's Designer Online Shoes	7,500	1,000	20,000	15,000
TJ's Bike Shop	25,000	5,000	50,000	80,000
George's Organic Sauces	4,500	3,000	18,500	25,000

1 Which of these businesses has the highest gross profit margin?

2 Which has the highest net profit margin?

3 Which has the highest return on capital employed?

4 Which one would you invest your money in and why? Discuss this question in small groups or with your teacher.

Research it

Businesses always like to have the highest gross and net profit margins as possible. This is because it shows they are being profitable. Based on your understanding of how profit is made, research ways that businesses can improve their profitability. Try to produce a list of the top ten ways in which you think profitability can be improved or increased.

When thinking about the return on capital employed, businesses often compare the amount they could have earned in interest on their capital in a bank to the amount of money they have made through the business. Look up the current Bank of England Base Rate of interest and, using the three businesses that we have already looked at, compare the amounts of interest that could have potentially been made if the money was invested in a bank using the base rate. Where would you invest your money?

Assessment tip

You will need to be able to understand how to use profitability ratios and be able to calculate and comment on examples like these. Make sure you understand each one.

Just checking

How do you work out the gross profit margin of a business?

What is the calculation for ROCE and what does it show?

Liquidity ratios

Liquidity ratios are very important in helping businesses plan how easily they are able to pay their bills. It is important that businesses have money to pay their bills in a timely way but do not have so much money in their accounts that it could be making more if it was in a bank account or reinvested in improvements to the business. There are two ratios you need to learn and be able to apply. These are:

- current ratio
- acid test ratio.

Current ratio

This ratio gives an indication of the liquidity of a business, i.e. how easily the business can pay its debts. The ratio should be at least 1, and ideally somewhere between 1.5:1 and 2:1. If a business has a ratio of 1, it means that its debts equal its income and there is nothing left over. Even if a business has a ratio lower than 1.5:1 it may still mean it has trouble paying its debts. This is because it will not have much money left over to cope with unexpected costs, such as a machine breaking down. If the ratio is greater than 2:1, it means the business is probably holding too much stock or other assets that could be used more effectively within the business. Not investing money back into the business or inefficient use of resources is just as bad as not having enough money. This is because there is an opportunity cost to the business – this is the cost of losing out on an opportunity to make even more money by not investing.

$$\text{Current ratio} = \frac{\text{Current assets}}{\text{Current liabilities}}$$

Acid test ratio

Some analysts also use the acid test ratio as this measures liquidity but doesn't take account of stock. This is because stock can be difficult to sell off quickly or may become out of date and therefore cannot be sold at all. Like the current ratio, the acid test ratio should be at least 1 (this means that the current assets minus stock are equal to the current liabilities) but ideally should be between 1.5:1 and 2.1:1.

$$\text{Acid test ratio} = \frac{\text{Current assets less stock}}{\text{Current liabilities}}$$

Liquidity ratios are extremely useful to businesses, but it is important to remember that they do have some limitations. Like balance sheets, they are only a snapshot in time, so if stock is sold the next day or additional cash is received into the business, the ratio may significantly change almost overnight. Ratios also only show what has happened rather than what is going to happen. It is also important to remember that businesses that have seasonal trade, such as holiday parks and ice cream makers, are likely to have points in the year when they have better liquidity than others. As long as they are prepared and have reserves to cope with these periods, they should be able to avoid having problems paying their debts.

Remember it

Liquidity ratios work out how easily a business is able to pay its expenses.

Apply it

Name of business	Current assets (including stock) £	Stock £	Current liabilities £
Alex's Designer Online Shoes	25,000	10,000	15,000
TJ's Bike Shop	50,000	40,000	35,000
George's Organic Sauces	20,000	15,000	5,000

You have already looked at the profitability of these three businesses, now you need to consider their liquidity.

1 **Work out the current ratio and the acid test ratio for each and consider which business is most able to pay its debts and which is most likely to struggle.**

2 **What do you notice about the amount of stock each business is holding? What impact is this likely to have on their ability to pay bills?**

3 **Where would you invest your money and why?**

Just checking

How is profitability different to liquidity?

How would you calculate current ratio?

What is the difference between current ratio and acid test ratio?

Importance of financial statements to stakeholders

You have already learned about the different stakeholders a business has (see page 46). We are now going to look at these stakeholders and the different financial information they use and analyse in order to find out how a business is doing. Each of the different groups will want to use the financial information available differently and it is important you understand how and why they do this.

(see page 46)

Owner(s)

Financial statements are very important to owners of businesses as they show how much profit (or loss) is being made by the business and the assets and liabilities that give the true worth of that business. Many owners have invested in their businesses and want to make a return on their investment (profit) and therefore the greater the return, the better!

Businesses may be owned by individuals, partners or have external investment by shareholders. All of these different types of owner will want to see a measure of business performance in order to make decisions on what to do in the future. Using ratios helps businesses to prepare to pay their bills or to invest more/less in stocks.

Talk about it

Think about the different groups of stakeholders you learned about on page 46. They all have different needs. In small groups, talk about each group of stakeholders and what they want/expect from a business. Make some lists and compare yours with those of other groups.

Case study – L K Bennett

Linda Bennett opened her first designer fashion store in Wimbledon in 1990. She continued to expand the business until July 2008 when she sold part of her stake to two large investment companies, Phoenix Equity Partners and Sirius Equity. She now retains a 30% ownership in the company, which has 101 stores in the UK, Jersey, Dublin and Paris. Linda Bennett no longer runs the business herself because she has now become a **non-executive director**. A new chief executive will manage the business and Linda will continue as a non-executive director. It is expected that there will be the potential for another 19 stores to open in the UK and plans are in place to expand the business further in the future.

1 **How important will financial statements be to Linda Bennett now and in the future? Why?**
2 **Which ratios might she be interested in and why?**

Managers and employees

Managers and employees are both groups of stakeholders who will be interested in how a business is doing. This is because they depend on the business to earn money. Managers and employees will be interested in the finances of a business because:

- they give them an idea of how safe their jobs are
- they are likely to show if the business is going to expand or reduce in size

Remember it

A **non-executive director** is someone who does not run a business on a day to day basis, but monitors how it is doing.

- they may be used to award increases in pay per year based on how well the company is doing
- they may be used by unions and other staff groups to negotiate increases in pay for all employees
- they may be used to award bonuses to individuals or groups of employees or managers.

Lenders

Lenders are the banks and other financial organisations who have lent money to a business. They will be interested in the finances of a business as they want to make sure they will receive money back on their investment. If the liquidity of a business is poor, it may mean that it cannot pay its bills and therefore will not be able to continue trading. Lenders will also want to see financial statements in order to consider whether or not to lend a business more money, for example to expand or update facilities. Lenders will work out the risk they think they are facing when loaning money. The higher the level of risk, the higher the possible interest rate and the lower the chances of receiving a loan.

Research it

Choose a business that you know well – you might have a part-time job there or you might have completed work experience there. Or, if this is not possible, you can find some company profiles on the Biz/ed website; just click the Company Info tab (go to www.heinemann.co.uk/hotlinks).

Find out as much as you can about a business' financial statements.

1 **How easy is it to get hold of this information?**

2 **How easy is it to understand the information?**

3 **What impact might these statements have on managers and employees?**

Apply it

You are working for an organisation that lends money to small businesses and have been approached by two small businesses, each asking for a loan of £5,000. Financial information taken from the profit and loss accounts and balance sheets for both businesses is shown below.

In small groups, using the information and ratios you have learned so far in this unit, give a presentation to the rest of the class on which business you would lend money to and why. In your presentation, explain what other information you would like to know to help you in your judgement, for example experience of the business managers, past sales or competitors. What do the ratios tell you about the two businesses?

Name	Number of years trading	Gross profit margin	Net profit margin	ROCE	Current ratio	Acid test ratio
Juice Bar	2	50%	20%	15%	2	1
AMR Pets	10	40%	30%	10%	2	1.5

Just checking

Why might a business' employees be interested in seeing its financial documents?

Why might a lender be interested in a business' financial statements?

The Government wants businesses to do well

Government

The Government will also want to know how businesses are doing financially for many different reasons.

- To ensure they pay the right amount of business tax.
- So they continue to be secure and employ people (who pay taxes and do not need to claim unemployment benefits).
- So they export goods abroad (where appropriate) and help keep the UK economy strong.

Talk about it

Businesses pay taxes to the Government. In small groups, make a list of all the different ways this money is used. Pool your results as a class and see how many you come up with.

Case study – The Swift Group

The Swift Group is the largest producer of caravans in the UK. They are based in Cottingham, East Yorkshire. They make about 80% of all caravans manufactured in the UK. Following a slowdown in sales, the company made approximately 250 people redundant in 2008, but they are hopeful that in the future sales will go up and more people may need to be employed again.

1 **Identify and describe why each of the groups below would be interested in the financial statements of the Swift Group:**

- **its employees**
- **local people**
- **Government**
- **competitors.**

Take it further

In 2008, the UK Government became involved with the finances of several large banks, including Northern Rock and Halifax Bank of Scotland (HBOS). They loaned the banks money so they could keep lending money to other institutions including small businesses.

1 **Outline one advantage to the Government of lending this money to the banks.**

2 **Describe one disadvantage that there might be for the Government.**

Customers

Customers are keen to know how a business is doing so they can be sure that money they have paid to a business will result in them getting the goods or services they order. If a business has trouble paying its bills, it might close down and then the customer may never receive their goods or money back.

Suppliers

Like customers, suppliers want to know that a business is financially strong so they can be sure they will be paid for the goods or services they have supplied. If a business goes into liquidation, not only is the business and its customers affected but its suppliers may also lose money too as the business cannot afford to pay them back.

Case study – Arvella Bridal

In June 2008, the Arvella Bridal boutique went into receivership leaving 170 brides without wedding dresses. Lisa Clarkson, the owner of the business based in Lyndhurst Hampshire, owed over £400,000 in debts. The brides all lost hundreds of pounds worth of dresses. Some of them had only two or three days to find new dresses.

The brides wanted refunds but were unable to claim them as they could only attend a creditors' meeting together with other organisations wanting their money too, for example banks and suppliers. It was found when the company went into liquidation that no accounts had been filed for the boutique and they were long overdue.

1 **How might seeing the financial statements of Arvella Bridal Ltd before using the business have influenced customers?**

2 **Conduct research into businesses in your local area that have closed leaving their customers without products or services. Explain why customers usually do not bother to look at the financial statements of a business before they decide to buy. Think about whether you consider the finances of a business before you spend your money.**

The role of ICT

As you have already learned, ICT is helping suppliers and customers access more information about businesses they are using or working with as company information is now available online. ICT is very important to all businesses as it helps them produce financial statements, and software packages such as those you investigated on page 107 can help a business highlight problem areas.

ICT packages can help businesses interpret financial information precisely and carefully and are able to highlight issues to managers and employees. This is because a computer is able to analyse large amounts of data more quickly than the human eye. It can turn financial information into colour coded formats, graphs and charts so that it is more easily understood. A computer, however, cannot actually know what to do as a result of the financial information it has analysed. Humans are needed at this stage to make decisions about what to do next. But who knows what will happen in the future!

Take it further

It is possible for you to look at the financial status of companies by doing research at Companies House – you can access its website via www.heinemann.co.uk/hotlinks.

Apply it

Thinking about ICT and its use in business finances, answer the following questions:

1 **How can ICT be used to produce financial statements?**

2 **How can it be used to monitor what is going well and not so well in a company finances?**

3 **How can ICT be used to monitor suppliers and customers?**

4 **Which types of charts and graphs could be produced using ICT to analyse the finances of a business?**

5 **How can ICT be used to calculate ratios?**

Just checking

Why might the Government be interested in the finances of a business?

Where can suppliers and customers find out information about companies they use/work with?

Outline two advantages to a business of using ICT to keep financial records.

Unit 2 Make the Grade

This unit is assessed by a one hour exam, which you will need to prepare for. It is important that you learn about the different types of financial documents and statements that are needed for the exam. You will need to think of ways to remember the key terms and be familiar with how the key financial documents are created and what they are used for.

This section is designed to help you prepare for the Unit 2 exam. It comprises six main sections:

- Revision tips
- Common mistakes
- Revision checklist
- Examiner's guide to the exam
- Sample questions with student answers
- Practice questions

Revision tips

There are seven key points for revision listed here to help you. Look through each one and think about how you can try to ensure that your revision is really effective.

Remember it

You may have heard the saying, 'Failing to plan is planning to fail!' Make sure you use the tips that follow to get the best grade possible and always have a revision plan.

Resources

When planning your revision, make sure that you think about the place, how much time you have and the materials you will need. It is really important for this exam that you practise creating and completing the key financial documents and ensure you are confident in being able to do the calculations that are required.

Learning styles

You have probably heard about different learning styles. This means that individuals tend to prefer to learn in different ways. Some people find images, mindmaps and other visual ways of presenting information easier to digest and understand, whilst others prefer to learn through written material that is clearly laid out. It is helpful to revise in a way that suits your preferences, but you should also try to use different ways to revise and not rely on just one method – remember, the exam will be a written paper-based assessment.

Using IT

You may find it useful when you are revising to make notes and this may be on a computer or by hand. If you use a spreadsheet package like Microsoft Excel, you may be able to set up some of the financial documents as a template and then keep practising on them using different figures. It is also useful to make use of online websites such as Biz/ed as they have lots of learning materials you can use. The website has a particularly useful accounting section with lots of information to help you with the content in this unit. You can find a link to the site at www.heinemann.co.uk/hotlinks – just enter the express code 4011P.

Planning

You should make a plan of your revision. This unit requires a lot of learning and you need to apply it very carefully in the exam. Break down your revision into small chunks so you can learn it effectively. You will need to start your revision much earlier than you think – remember that Business Studies will be one of six to eight subjects you will have to revise for.

Looking after yourself

Make sure you drink plenty of water and take regular breaks to keep yourself focused and concentrating. Your revision should be little and often. Good planning will mean that you can keep on top of your revision, feel good about your progress and also have a life as well! Looking after yourself mentally as well as physically is vitally important.

Timing

Make sure you plan your time well during the exam. There is nothing worse than not finishing an exam in the time allowed. It is very important that you attempt all the questions as there are marks to be gained at every stage of the marking process, even if your answer is not perfectly correct! The questions will have different marks attached to them: six, eight and ten marks, for example. Remember that you have about one minute for each mark so think about your timing and spend around ten minutes on a question worth ten marks, six minutes on a question worth six marks, and so on. Don't spend ten minutes struggling with a question worth only two marks – you can use the time better to tackle other questions that you are more comfortable with and which will gain you more marks. It does not matter how long you spend on a two-mark question, the maximum amount of marks you can get is two!

Presentation

Remember that the examiner will need to be able to read your writing and understand your workings in the calculations. Make sure you write as clearly and neatly as possible.

Common mistakes

- Confusing 'statements of account' with 'profit and loss accounts'.
- Not understanding the difference between how a debit and a credit card work.
- Getting confused when looking at APR (interest rate) and thinking that the higher the APR on a credit card, the better! This is not true – the lower the APR the better as the customer pays less interest.
- Thinking that a credit card and a credit transfer are the same – check you know the difference.
- Not understanding that 'revenue' and 'income' mean money coming in, and 'expenditure' or 'costs' mean money going out.
- Not understanding the difference between the terms 'price and 'cost', which we use interchangeably in everyday life. This can cause confusion in business studies. Price is the amount of money that has to be given up to acquire a good or service. Cost refers to the expenditure by a business on resources (rent, wages, raw materials, machinery etc.) to produce goods and services.
- Confusing 'balance sheets' and 'profit and loss accounts'. A balance sheet is a picture of what the business owns at a given point in time whereas a profit and loss account represents money flowing in or out of a business over a period of time. Think of a balance sheet like a picture as it captures a view at a moment in time. Take the picture at a different time and it will be different.

Revision checklist

1. Financial documents

You will need to know the purpose of the following *nine* financial documents, as well as how to create and complete them:

- purchase order
- delivery note
- goods received note
- invoice
- credit note
- statement of account
- remittance advice slip
- cheque
- receipt.

2. Computerised accounting systems

You will need to know how computerised accounting systems are changing the way that businesses look after their records, including their advantages and disadvantages.

3. Balance sheets and profit and loss accounts

You will need to be able to use a balance sheet and a profit and loss account, knowing what information they give and what the relevance of the information is.

4. Payment methods

You will need to know the difference between cash and non-cash payments and the importance/ difficulties associated with each of the following:

- cash
- cheques
- credit cards

- debit cards
- credit transfer
- direct debit
- e-cheques and other online payments.

5. *Revenue and costs*

You will need to be able to identify the sources of revenues and the costs for different small businesses and put them into one of these two categories.

6. *Key terms*

You will need to be able to define and understand the following key terms:

- sales turnover
- cost of sales
- gross profit
- expenses
- fixed assets
- current liabilities
- long-term liabilities
- net profit
- current assets and net current assets
- working capital
- capital
- profit and loss account
- balance sheet.

7. *Ratios*

You will need to know how to calculate the following accounting ratios:

- gross profit margin
- net profit margin
- current ratio
- acid test ratio
- return on capital employed.

8. *Stakeholders*

You will also need to name the different stakeholders who would be interested in a business and why, including:

- owners
- managers and employees

- lenders
- Government
- customers
- suppliers.

Examiner's guide to the exam

In this section you can read some advice from an examiner, which may help you to do even better in the exam.

- Unit 2 represents 40% of the whole marks for your Single Award GCSE in Applied Business or 20% for the Double Award so, clearly, it is important. There are 60 marks available and the exam lasts for one hour.

- In the exam, your learning will be assessed in lots of different ways, which will include:
  o multiple choice questions
  o short answer questions
  o extended answer questions.

- You will be given a scenario/context to read and then some structured questions to answer. You should write all of your answers in *black* ink. When you see an asterisk (*) next to the question number, it means that the examiner will be judging your use of written communication (including spelling and grammar) as well as the content of your answer, so take extra care.

- It is absolutely vital that you understand the different assessment objectives on which you will be judged. There are three of these:
  o A01: Recall, select and communicate knowledge and understanding of concepts, issues and terminology.
  o A02: Apply skills, knowledge and understanding in a variety of contexts and in planning and carrying out investigations and tasks.
  o A03: Analyse and evaluate evidence, make reasoned judgements and present appropriate conclusions.

You must remember that 70% of the total marks awarded for the qualification are for A02 and A03. You must, therefore, remember that knowing lots of content is only a part of the learning for this qualification. The examiner is more interested in how you use your knowledge and the skills that you demonstrate. Make sure you understand these assessment objectives, get to know the way in which they will be assessed, how questions are framed to assess these skills and what the examiner is looking for. If you ignore the importance of the assessment objectives then you risk not doing as well as you can in the exam.

- Attempt all the questions on the paper and do the best that you possibly can!

Sample questions with student answers

Student Activity: Natural Sweetness

Baljeet and Luke have been running a juice bar business called Natural Sweetness in their local town centre for the last few months. They produce fruit smoothies and soups made from fresh organic ingredients. All of the ingredients are bought from wholesalers in bulk so that they can benefit from discounts. They are given 20 days to pay for those goods.

Baljeet and Luke have really good levels of customer service and are passionate about their business. They are not very confident in the financial recording side of the business so have asked you to help them.

Q1 When the orders arrive at Natural Sweetness from the wholesaler, the delivery driver asks Baljeet and Luke to sign for them. The document they sign is an example of:

- A delivery note
- An invoice
- A purchase order
- A credit note

(1 mark)

Max answers:

- An invoice

Comments on Max's answer:

There is one mark available for this question, which is shown in brackets after the question (1). Unfortunately, Max has not answered correctly. It is a delivery note that arrives with goods and is checked and signed. An invoice is the document used to request payment. Max achieves no marks for this question.

Q2 Some of the oranges received with the delivery are bruised and damaged. Luke phones the wholesaler to say that he is not happy. Luke is a very good customer so they immediately agree to make an adjustment to his account. They do this using:

- A credit note
- An invoice
- A purchase order
- A statement of account

(1 mark)

Max answers:

- A credit note

Comments on Max's answer:

This is the correct answer – one mark awarded.

Q3 The following orders arrived the next day from the wholesaler (account 7765):

Order 12: 50 boxes of oranges, but 20 boxes contained bruised and damaged oranges; 20 boxes of strawberries, but only 10 boxes were delivered.

Order 13: three boxes of bananas, which were received in perfect condition.

Complete the details missing from the Goods Received Note below using today's date and signing as the checker. Include details of any goods that need to be sent back.

(7 marks)

Max's answer (shown in blue):

Natural Sweetness
Goods Received Note

Goods received from:

Supplier A/c No.

GRN No. 7834
Delivery Note No. 2
Delivery Note Date:
Checked by:

Order No.	Quantity	Quantity delivered	Description	Enter details here (stating received, damaged or other).
12	50	50	Boxes of oranges	
12	20	10	Boxes of strawberries	Only 10 delivered
13	3		Boxes of bananas	

Comments on Max's answer:

There are a possible seven marks to gain for this question but Max has not completed the information at the top of the Goods Received Note and so has not gained any marks here. Given that this is worth over half the total marks for this question (four marks out of seven) it is an expensive mistake. Max needs to make sure he answers every part of the question. Max has also forgotten to make the adjustments for the bruised and damaged boxes of oranges so, in total, has only managed to get two marks out of a possible seven.

Q4 Luke and Baljeet only allow customers to pay by cash as there is an ATM (cash machine) in the high street outside their business. Give one advantage for Luke and Baljeet in only allowing customers to pay by cash.

(2 marks)

Max's answer:

When customers can only pay by cash, Luke and Baljeet get their money immediately so they can use it in other ways in the business.

Comments on Max's answer:

The answer is good as it makes two clear points: Luke and Baljeet get their money immediately (1 mark) and they can use this money in the business (1 mark).

Q5 Give one disadvantage of Luke and Baljeet allowing customers to only pay by cash.

(2 marks)

Max's answer:

Customers might not have any cash on them.

Comments on Max's answer:

This is a very basic answer. Although it makes a valid point, it is not developed and so Max only achieves one mark here.

Q6 Luke and Baljeet are considering allowing their customers to pay in other ways in the future. Examine the different methods of payment they could allow and how this decision is likely to benefit them.

(6 marks)

Max's answer:

They would benefit from allowing customers to pay by debit card or credit card as this would mean they would get more customers. It would also mean that customers might spend more money in the business by maybe having a smoothie and a soup rather than one or the other. Baljeet and Luke could also accept other methods of payment, such as payment by mobile phone. This could get them some younger customers who may not have a credit or debit card but who are likely to have a mobile phone with credit.

Comments on Max's answer:

Max has first identified an alternative payment method (credit and debit cards), which gains him one mark. A reason behind this choice of payment has also been provided, which would gain a second mark. Max also gains a mark for then giving an advantage to Luke and Baljeet of accepting this type of payment. The last part of Max's answer could have benefited from some explanation of what 'payment by mobile phone' is. Although he gives a reason why this would be an advantage to Luke and Baljeet, the examiner would not be sure what Max means by 'payment by mobile phone'. He would only gain one mark here.

Assessment tip

The command word in Q6 is 'examine'. This means that you must consider both the advantages and disadvantages of an issue and question some of the assumptions that underlie it.

Max's answer to Q6 could have been improved if he had considered some of the drawbacks of accepting payment by credit/debit card and mobile phone.

Practice questions

Apply it

Have a go at answering the following questions about the Natural Sweetness business.

1 Explain why Luke and Baljeet might prefer their customers to pay with a credit card rather than a debit card.

(3 marks)

2 The acid test ratio is given by the formula:

$$\text{Acid test ratio} = \frac{\text{Current assets less stock}}{\text{Current liabilities}}$$

Baljeet and Luke have current assets of £2,500, stock to the value of £500 and current liabilities of £5,000. Calculate the acid test ratio.

(2 marks)

Comment on the acid test ratio for Baljeet and Luke that you have calculated.

(4 marks)

3 Many large suppliers do not accept cheques for payment anymore. How might this affect the way Natural Sweetness makes payments to its suppliers?

(4 marks)

4 Identify **one** possible start-up cost and **one** likely running cost for a business like Natural Sweetness.

(2 marks)

5 Explain the difference between a start-up cost and a running cost for a business like Natural Sweetness.

(3 marks)

Unit 3 Investigating People, Business and Change

Describe it

Customers are individuals or organisations who buy goods and services.

Employees are individuals who carry out work for an employer.

Changes in the **external environment** include things like a change in the law, a change in technology, or a change in the wider economy. A business has little or no control over these types of change.

This unit develops some of the themes from Unit 1. It looks at factors that allow businesses to develop over time. As businesses change, issues arise which affect people involved in the business. This unit first looks at **customers** and **employees**. Customers have expectations about the goods and services they want business to provide for them. Employees provide the workforce for a business. They are recruited and trained by the business. They need to be flexible so that they can help the business to change over time.

Changes also take place outside of a business, such as the way in which businesses have to face higher costs when there are increases in the prices of raw materials they buy. To change successfully businesses need to respond to customers, recruit and develop their people and respond to the external environment.

Case study – Reggae Reggae Sauce!

A good example of a business that has grown quickly is Reggae Reggae Sauce. Reggae Reggae sauce is used to make food like chicken more spicy and interesting. In 2006, the entrepreneur and reggae musician Levi Roots was able to persuade Peter Jones of Dragons' Den fame to invest £50,000 for a 40% stake in his business. Three weeks later the sauce was on Sainsbury's shelves. Roots learned the recipe from his mother and in 1991 set up a stall at the Notting Hill Carnival. Customers told him that they really enjoyed his sauce and in 2004 he sold 4,000 bottles at the Notting Hill Carnival. Working with his children as his only employees, they used a big cooking pot at home from which they were able to fill 36 bottles at a time.

Today the sauce is advertised nationally and sold through many supermarket chains. Each factory batch makes 150,000 bottles and many people are employed in the process. The ongoing success of Reggae Reggae sauce depends on it continuing to be popular with customers, as well as making sure that the business responds to changes in the **external environment**.

Apply it

Some of the most rapidly growing businesses in Britain in recent years have been coffee shops. Costa Coffee is a good example. It was set up in London in 1971 by the Costa brothers, Sergio and Bruno. Today Costa shops are on most major high streets, as well as airport lounges and many motorway service stations. They offer a warm and welcoming atmosphere and a great range of coffee drinks, cakes and pastries. Today Costa is owned by the large and well known business Whitbread, which also own pubs, hotels and restaurants.

At a Costa coffee shop, you can buy a range of different types of coffee. For example, a Café Espresso, which is a concentrated coffee drink. In contrast, a Café Mocha is made up of one-third espresso and two-thirds steamed milk.

Working in pairs carry out some research to find out the range of coffees sold in a Costa shop or other local coffee shop. What are the different varieties, sizes and prices? Why do customers want this variety?

Why have coffee shops become so popular? What is likely to be the effect of large numbers of people losing their jobs in the City of London on spending in these coffee shops?

Remember it

Large established businesses often take over successful existing businesses in order to grow. This was the case when Whitbread acquired Costa Coffee. Whitbread owns pubs and restaurants and has expertise in supplying coffee and ready to eat foods. So Costa provides a good example of business growth.

This unit is divided into three sections:

3.1 Why are people so important?
3.2 How do businesses develop?
3.3 What are external factors?

How you will be assessed

This unit is one of four compulsory units you will need to study for the Double Award in Applied Business. Your learning for this unit will be assessed through controlled assessment tasks (internal assessment). The task is set by Edexcel and requires you to select two businesses to research: one local and one national or international. You will answer a number of set questions based on the content of this unit about your selected businesses. You will be able to use the materials you have researched to answer questions given a set time frame.

Your tutor will give you guidance about suitable businesses to investigate and you will find lots of useful hints and tips in the Make the Grade section at the end of this unit (see pages 178–81).

3.1 Why are people so important?

Customer needs, expectations and satisfaction

Talk about it

Why do you think the **retail outlets** described here have chosen to set up and sell their goods and services at Heathrow's Terminal 5? Talk about each of the examples given. What retail outlets are there at another airport or a railway station you have visited recently? Did you use any of them? What were you expecting to find or buy there?

The departures lounge at the Terminal 5 building at Heathrow Airport, which opened in March 2008, is for British Airways flights. It boasts a range of fashionable shops, cafés, restaurants and pubs. Typical examples include the fast food outlets Wagamama and Pret a Manger, shops selling expensive women's shoes and handbags, like Kurt Geiger, and even a specialist sunglasses shop, Sunglass Hut. The famous department store Harrods has a prominent outlet. There is a Travelex where you can exchange pounds for euro, as well as other currencies. WH Smith sells books, magazines and sweets.

Without customers, businesses like retailers could not exist. The retailers operating from Heathrow Terminal 5 will most likely have carried out detailed market research before they decided to set up. They wanted to find out whether they would have enough customers to enable them to make a profit. They had to find out exactly what sorts of products they would need to sell to tempt air travellers to make purchases from their shops.

Remember it

Retail outlets sell to the end customer. Retailers usually hire the space for their shops from a landlord. They therefore have to make a lot of sales just to cover the cost of the space they hire.

Retailers need to anticipate and identify (find out) what customers' needs are and try to satisfy these needs. They also need to know what customers are likely to buy. This is not easy, especially trying to predict how consumer behaviour will change in the future. To help them, businesses carry out **market research**. For example, clothing retailers at Heathrow Airport Terminal 5 need to find out what customers flying to various destinations are likely to purchase. They need to bear in mind that in winter some of their customers are flying to the southern hemisphere where it will be summer. The clothes they sell will need to be different from those stocked in their other outlets.

The fashion company Reiss has a store at Heathrow Terminal 5. They provide stylish clothes for fashion conscious men and women round the globe. The store acts as a shop window to global travellers. Armed with information about what customers are likely to purchase, Reiss fashion buyers purchase supplies of clothes they hope will meet consumer needs and will sell. The fashion buyers purchase two main types of item:

Describe it

Market research uses different methods (including interviews and questionnaires) to try and find out what consumer needs are and what response consumers give to the products and services retailers sell.

- Statement items – these are not necessarily the bestselling items, but they draw customers into the shop. They are usually displayed in the shop window, for example a dress designed by a leading designer.
- Stock items – these are items that are expected to sell in large numbers. They need to meet most customers' expectations, for example this season's must-have top or pair of shoes.

Case study – Europe's BIGGEST new shopping centre

At the end of October 2008, the new £1 billion Westfield Shopping Centre opened at Shepherd's Bush in London. The centre was built and is owned by the Westfield Group, a company that owns shopping centres in Australia, New Zealand, the US and the UK. Westfield rents out shops in the centre to retailers such as Top Shop. Westfield contains 265 shops and 50 restaurants, and has parking spaces for 4,500 cars. The shopping centre is designed to cater for a variety of different types of consumers. For example, there is a Burger King, a Nandos and a 14 screen cinema. The upmarket zone is called 'The Village' and houses retailers such as Prada and Dior, as well as Mulberry, Gucci and Versace. At the centre of the complex are five major established retail 'superstars': House of Fraser, Waitrose, Marks and Spencer, Next and Debenhams.

1 **Why do you think customers are prepared to travel to huge retail complexes like Westfield?**

2 **What market research would you expect the owners of Westfield to have carried out before deciding to go ahead with the project? Note: the Westfield Group is an Australian multinational group which owns retail centres across the globe.**

3 **Westfield is now going to set up another centre in Stratford, East London, ready for the Olympic Games in 2012. What factors would the owners take into consideration before deciding on the size and facilities that will be offered in this new centre?**

Check out the Westfield website and find out more about the Australian-owned Westfield organisation and their other super-sized retail outlets. A link to the site is available at www.heinemann. co.uk/hotlinks – just enter the express code 4011P.

Case study – Internal and external customers

Read Eva's account below about working in a coffee shop at a busy airport.

On a busy day, eight to ten employees work in the coffee shop. Most of them deal directly with customer orders. But there were others, like me, who simply made the drinks. I have learned that there are two types of customers: internal customers, who are the other employees taking customer orders (the front of counter servers), and external customers, who are the people buying sandwiches, cakes and drinks.

When I moved onto serving customers directly, I learned that customers expect to be provided with good value for money. For example, well-made sandwiches and drinks served at the right temperature. They also expect the tables to be clean, and to be served with a smile. It is also important to be helpful, for example answering questions about which sandwiches were vegetarian or contained Halal meat. It is important to provide additional services, such as directing customers to toilets and baby changing facilities.

1 **Working in groups, draw up a list of things a business needs to do to meet customer needs and expectations.**

The most important person in any business is the customer. If you anticipate and identify their wants and needs, your business is already off to a good start. Provide them with good value products. A good value product is one for which the customer feels that they have had a good deal. The price may be low or it may be high – the important thing is that the customer thinks the price was worth paying.

Customers want information about the products they buy. For example, are they healthy? Are they compatible with other products? Customers also want important details such as delivery dates and what to do if things go wrong. After-sales service is another important customer need. Will the customer be cared for after they have made their purchase?

Just checking

Explain the difference between an 'internal' and 'external' customer.

Outline the main types of expectations that customers have when buying a particular good or service.

Remember it

A **churn rate** is a measurement of the customers lost by a business over a period of time. The term is used when customers are subscribers to something, e.g. clubs, magazines or even credit cards. It is calculated by dividing the number of subscribers to a business by the number giving up their subscriptions during a given time period, expressed as a percentage. For example, if a fitness club has a thousand members and one hundred give up their membership each month, then the churn rate is 10% per month.

Measuring and monitoring

Satisfied customers return to a business time after time. Repeat business saves a lot of time winning new business. For example, gyms and fitness clubs are well known for having a high **churn rate**. They want to lower this figure by keeping customers satisfied, maybe by offering things like personal training or tailored fitness programmes.

It is important for businesses to use measures such as churn rate and to monitor them over a period of time. These figures enable businesses to check how effective they are at keeping customers satisfied.

Case study – Measuring customer satisfaction at British Airways

British Airways measures its customer satisfaction through GPM (Global Performance Monitor). This measures customer satisfaction with all aspects of a BA plane journey. The survey was widely tested before it was first used. It is used on all major air routes. In 2007, 48,000 customers filled in the survey every month.

British Airways uses such a wide survey because it wants to get a representative view from all customers. The survey includes questions about how happy customers were when booking tickets, the service in the airport, the quality of the meals, the friendliness of staff, and whether customers would recommend the airline to a friend.

The results of the surveys are shared with employees at every level in the organisation, and can be used to identify better meal options, organisation of seating arrangements on flights, seat types, legroom and many other details.

1 **What is the main purpose of carrying out the survey?**

2 **What other information might BA want from passengers to help identify customer needs?**

3 **Do you think the results of the surveys are likely to be representative of the views of all British Airways customers? Justify your answer.**

4 **How else could British Airways go about measuring customer satisfaction?**

Hotlink

Check out the Enterprise-Rent-A-Car website to find out more about the services offered and the customer satisfaction philosophy (follow the 'About Us' link) (go to www.heinemann.co.uk/hotlinks).

Enterprise Rent-A-Car provides car rental from key locations such as railway stations and airports. The company believes that customers are their top priority. Enterprise uses a measure known as ESQi (Enterprise Service Quality index) to measure customer satisfaction. Customers are surveyed by telephone and asked if they were completely satisfied with the service they received. Each Enterprise branch around the country earns a rank depending on the percentage of customers who said they were completely satisfied.

The simplest way of measuring sales performance is to keep a record of sales. The value of sales made can be described in a number of ways. Sometimes sales figures are referred to as 'sales revenue' or simply 'sales' but they are also known as 'turnover'. The following table shows Arsenal Football Club's sales revenue from football activities between 2005 and 2007.

Year	2005 (£m)	2006 (£m)	2007 (£m)
Turnover (£m)	115.0	132.1	200.8

(Source: Arsenal PLC Annual Report 2007)

If you look at these figures, you can see a rapid rise in income in 2007, which was a result of Arsenal moving from its old ground Highbury to the much larger Emirates Stadium. This improvement in sales performance helped Arsenal to become more competitive in terms of raising revenue with other top European football clubs.

Ongoing sales growth helps business to establish a strong position in the market. This is illustrated by Pink Ladies, a women-only cab service set up by Andrea Winders and Tina Dutton in Warrington in 2005. By 2008, Pink Ladies had a fleet of 14 bright pink Renault Kangoos and employed 45 staff. The workforce includes female drivers who are trained in self-defence, first aid and customer care. Sales revenues increased from £0.5 million in 2007 to £1.5 million in 2008. Pink Ladies now operates on a licence basis in a number of British cities and has plans to expand abroad.

Loyalty card records are another way of checking on customer satisfaction, as well as spending patterns. In the UK, Tesco has been a leader in using loyalty cards to keep its customers happy. Interestingly, Tesco owns 83% of a company called Dunnhumby, which analyses all the data that Tesco gets through its loyalty cards. Dunnhumby can then build up a detailed picture of who spends what, when, how often, on what and how much at Tesco. Tesco is then able to offer promotions and special offers targeted at particular customers based on this information. Customers benefit from loyalty cards by getting discounts, however, every time they use their loyalty cards they are providing Dunnhumby, and hence Tesco, with lots of details about their buying patterns and preferences.

Other ways in which businesses can measure and monitor customer satisfaction is through numbers of customer complaints or returned goods.

The Pink Ladies women-only cab service

Hotlink

Check out the Pink Ladies website to find out more about the company and how it operates (go to www. heinemann.co.uk/hotlinks).

Research it

Working in small groups of three or four, choose a business you could carry out a customer satisfaction survey for, e.g. your local cinema or a coffee shop. Write a list of no more than ten questions that could be used in a survey to measure customer satisfaction. Try out the survey on some of your friends.

Assessment tip

The assessment for this unit will require you to show how a particular business maintains, monitors and improves its customer service. Your teacher may arrange for a local customer service manager to talk to your class about how this is done. Alternatively, you may want to carry out some Internet research using the search words 'customer service' or 'improving customer service' and the name of a chosen organisation.

Just checking

Identify and describe at least three ways of measuring customer satisfaction.

Research

Perhaps the most important aspect of business is that of meeting customer needs. Market research can help businesses identify customer needs. For any type and size of business, four of the most important marketing questions are:

- Who are we selling to?
- What do they want?
- When and where do they want it?
- What price are they prepared to pay?

Market research is expensive and has to be well planned. To be effective it must:

- be systematic, which means being clear and organised and planning research step by step
- gather information, so a business must know what it is looking for and collect only useful information
- record information and keep clear records of what is found out
- analyse information, which means ordering and making sense of the information gathered in order to show trends and conclusions.

Market research information is either primary or secondary. Primary information is information you gather yourself; secondary information is information that someone else has already gathered and published.

Case study – The Trunki

Designer Rob Law came up with the idea of a ride-on suitcase for children, which had wheels and was brightly covered. He initially pitched his idea on BBC's Dragons' Den, but it was rejected. However, John Lewis saw the product's potential after the show was broadcast and its interest led to its launch.

A key aspect of the market research for the Trunki involved approaching large stores to find out how much they would be prepared to sell the product for. By 2008, Rob Law had sold his 100,000th Trunki and won his 11th award.

1 **If you were going to carry out some market research for the Trunki, how would you go about finding answers to the following questions?**

- **Who are we selling to?**
- **What do they want?**
- **When and where do they want it?**
- **What price are they prepared to pay?**

Apply it

The three founders of juice company Innocent, Richard Reed, Adam Balon and Jon Wright, knew that their families liked their product when they come up with the idea. But would the market like it? They decided to test the drink out at a music festival in London in 1998. They spent £500 on buying fresh fruit to make 1,000 bottles of an orange, banana, and pineapple drink – a smoothie. They set up a stall with a sign reading, 'Do you think we should give up our jobs to make these smoothies?' Two bins were set up for empty bottles: one labelled 'yes' and the other 'no'. At the end of the festival the 'yes bin' was overflowing and Innocent was born. In 2008,

Innocent launched an orange drink blended with at least 12 types of pure orange. They will have a lot of competition from existing juice sellers, such as Tropicana.

1 Do you think setting up the two bins at the festival can be regarded as market research? Explain your answer.
2 What market research questions do you think Innocent needed to ask before launching its new orange drink?
3 How could Innocent collect information which would help it find out about its customers, e.g. popular flavours, satisfaction with products?

Primary information is usually obtained by interviewing a **sample** of the target market. The questions asked should be clear and simple, and wherever possible tested in a pilot survey which is tried out on only a few people. It is often easier to analyse the results of a questionnaire if you give interviewees alternative answers to questions which requires them to choose one option. These are called 'closed questions'. For example:

How often do you shop here?

A Every day   B Once a week   C Once a fortnight   D Hardly ever

Questions can be asked in person (often the best way), through the post (can be slow and produce a poor response), by telephone (quick and easy, but perhaps not very reliable) or via a website. Another approach is to use email marketing, but this is likely to have a very low response rate. To increase response rates, it can be helpful to offer a reward in return for completing a questionnaire, e.g. a £20 gift voucher for an 'on the spot' street interview, or a discount on online purchases. Many businesses gather useful information on guarantee forms which have to be returned to register the product.

Observation involves looking at how customers behave when shopping. An example of this is watching how supermarket customers typically walk around a store in order to plan its layout. Observation has revealed that shoppers usually like to start in the fresh produce department. Having bright and attractive fruits and vegetables at the front of the store also gives an appealing and inviting entrance.

A customer panel involves bringing together a group of customers to talk about a product and the choices they make. The panel might also be given a list of topics to discuss or asked to test products and give their reactions. Researchers watch and listen to the customers to pick up ideas about what products will and will not be successful. A customer panel is sometimes called 'a focus group'.

Describe it

A **sample** is a selection of 'units' (for example, people or businesses) from a population of interest. The sample might be random, which in effect means anyone who is available, or it might be structured, which would mean selecting people from the target market. A sample should be chosen in such a way that it reveals something worthwhile about the population from which it is chosen.

Research it

Find out how a local business in your area carries out its market research. What other methods could it use?

Just checking

What are the four most important market research questions?

How can market research be carried out to ensure it provides useful results?

Employees – recruitment

People are at the heart of business success. Most modern jobs involve employees dealing directly with customers, either face to face, by phone, by letter or online. Employees have other key responsibilities, including:

- operating in a safe way so as not to endanger other employees or the public
- looking after company resources – this involves having a good understanding of ways of minimising waste and respecting the environment
- meeting deadlines and working in an efficient way
- meeting the needs of internal customers as well as external customers
- acting as a visible representative of the business and the brand
- being enterprising and taking the initiative where appropriate.

It is essential then for modern businesses to attract, motivate and retain the best possible people. **Recruitment** involves attracting the right standard of applicants to apply for vacancies.

Describe it

Recruitment is the process of identifying the need for a new employee, defining the job, attracting candidates and selecting those best suited for the job.

Case study – Fit for the job?

David Lloyd Leisure is the leading racquets, health and fitness club group in the UK, with over 70 clubs across the country, over 350,000 members and over 5,000 team members. The company attributes its success to employing the best talent in the market and there is a comprehensive development programme for ambitious and successful team members from junior to senior management.

The Careers section of the David Lloyd website states:

'Everyone in the David Lloyd team shares a real passion for working in this rewarding industry. And if you share our love for fitness and you'd like to develop your career with the market leader, it would be great to have you on board.

'At David Lloyd we don't have ordinary jobs – we have fulfilling careers. We're on the lookout for amazing new people who want to help us create and deliver the best experience for our members and guests.'

1 **What do you think would encourage a person to seek a job working for David Lloyd?**

2 **Why do you think David Lloyd makes a distinction between 'ordinary jobs' and 'fulfilling careers'?**

3 **When you leave school or college, will you be looking for an ordinary job or a fulfilling career? Why is this important to you?**

4 **Why might teamwork skills be important when applying for a job with David Lloyd?**

Hotlink

Visit the David Lloyds website to find out more about the company and their recruitment (go to www.heinemann.co.uk/hotlinks).

Research it

Look at the websites of the following two recruitment companies and examine some of the jobs that interest you:

- Jobs in Charities
- Leisure Jobs UK

Links to the sites are available at www.heinemann.co.uk/hotlinks.

1 To what extent do you think these sites are good at recruiting employees?

2 Do you think the sites and the jobs presented on them are likely to attract the right standard of applicants?

The two main ways of recruiting the right person for the job are internal and external recruitment. Internal recruitment involves employing someone already working for the organisation, which may involve promotion. External recruitment involves appointing someone from outside the organisation.

The benefit of employing an internal candidate is that the business will already have an idea of their strengths and weaknesses. However, an external candidate may bring new skills and experience into the organisation.

Just checking

What is recruitment?

Why is it so important that a business recruits the best person for the job?

Describe the two main ways of recruiting employees.

The advantages of internal recruitment	The advantages of external recruitment
There is less risk because the employer already knows the person and what they are capable of.	New ideas are brought into the organisation from outside.
It saves the cost of advertising and thus is cheaper.	There is a 'buzz' from a new person joining.
It saves on induction costs.	Internal jealousies are avoided, which can happen when someone gets promoted over someone else in a company.
The opportunity for promotion within the organisation encourages people to work hard.	

The right person for the job

Workforce planning is the process of identifying an organisation's likely future needs for people in terms of:

- numbers – how many?
- skills – what will they be required to do?
- locations – where will they be needed to work?

Creating a workforce plan enables an organisation to plan its recruitment and training.

Case study – Recruitment at David Lloyd

Let's look again at recruitment at David Lloyd Leisure, where jobs are advertised in different ways.

1 The company first looks at its existing employees to fill a vacancy, either at the same level or as a promotion. If there are no suitable people within the organisation, then it will be necessary to advertise externally.

2 For external recruitment, David Lloyd advertises vacancies via its website or through vacancy boards in its centres, as well as using Internet-based recruitment sites such as Leisure Jobs UK. Applications can be made online or directly to David Lloyd.

3 For harder to fill or specialist jobs, such as fitness trainers, David Lloyd advertises externally:
- through its website and offline media
- through local cinema and radio
- by placing advertisements in specialist magazines such as Running Fitness and Men's Health, or in a local paper.

It is important to consider the advantages of using different media for external advertising:

- A vacancy board would encouage users of a David Lloyd centre to join the existing team. Because they would be regular users of the centre, they would have a good idea of what the job involved and would be known to staff at the centre.

- The online website would attract a wider selection of people. It could attract applicants nationally who are interested in taking up work at leisure centres. At the same time, it would be a good way of attracting local people who are searching for local jobs.

- Local cinema and radio are also very good ways of attracting recruits, particularly in city areas. The people who work in leisure centres are likely to be sociable people who like to go out to the cinema as well as listen to popular local radio stations.

- Specialist magazines such as Running Fitness and Men's Health will be read by young men and women who are interested in sport and fitness. While browsing through these magazines they are likely to be attracted to and interested in job advertisements for leisure centre work.

Take it further

What other forms of media are there which might attract 'the right person for the job' for the position of fitness trainer?

Talk about it

A supermarket chain classifies its jobs according to work level. Level 1 jobs involve working directly with customers and include a variety of in-store tasks such as filling shelves with stock. Employees at this level are required to work accurately and with enthusiasm. Level 2 jobs involve more responsibility. Employees at this level might lead a team of employees who deal directly with customers. Level 2 jobs require the ability to manage resources and set targets, as well as managing and motivating others.

One of the chain's stores is in the process of recruiting a new team leader who will be responsible for a group of employees who work in the café cleaning tables, taking customer orders and cooking food. There are three candidates for the job:

- Seema is an internal candidate and has been working in the café for two years since leaving school. She is bright, enthusiastic and performs all of the tasks carried out in the café to a good standard. She is keen to take on more responsibility and got on well with the previous team leader. She has some good ideas for improving work practices.

- Lucy is an external candidate. She left school two years ago and for the last six months has been a team leader in a fast food restaurant. She has a very good reference stating that she is a hard worker and that she has made some positive changes at her current place of work. Lucy is a good team player with a detailed knowledge of the catering business.

- Simon is an external candidate who used to work at the supermarket. He worked in a Level 1 capacity, mainly filling shelves with stock and working on the checkout. However, after two years, he became frustrated because he wanted to take on a more senior position. He therefore looked for jobs elsewhere and was successful in his application for a Level 2 team leader role at a rival supermarket. He has developed into a popular team leader, with the willingness and ability to troubleshoot and motivate his team.

1 **What would be the benefits and drawbacks of: a) appointing Seema; b) appointing Lucy; c) appointing Simon?**

2 **What tasks and activities could Seema, Lucy and Simon be asked to carry out on the day of the interview which might help the store decide which of them to recruit?**

3 **How might the interviewing panel decide who to appoint if they are equally impressed by two of the candidates?**

Just checking

What is workforce planning?

What methods might a business use to recruit externally?

Employability skills

To do a job well, it is important to have the skills required specifically for that job: a hairdresser needs to know how to style hair, a bricklayer needs to know how to lay bricks and a nurse needs to know how to treat patients. However, in order to perform all of these jobs, and indeed most jobs, a range of skills called 'employability skills' is also required.

Apply it

1 **What specific job-related skills do you think are required for each of the jobs illustrated above?**

2 **What general 'employability skills' do you think are required for all of them?**

Employability skills are ones that employers, as well as teachers, trainers and other people involved in education, regard as being very important. A key aspect of employability skills is having appropriate qualifications.

The GCSE in Applied Business that you are studying is a good qualification to have because the skills it promotes all relate to employability.

The table below details employability skills. Look at each of the skills and think carefully about those you have, those you need to develop and how you can present them to an employer. Fill in the right-hand column of the table to help you.

Employability skill	Demonstrating the skill	How can I develop this skill and demonstrate it to potential employers?
Written communication	Assignments and materials that you produce for this course; letters and reports that you write; material set out in an interesting and well structured way; good clear presentation with accurate spelling, punctuation and grammar.	
Oral communication	Working with others and making presentations; showing that you can put ideas across in a persuasive and interesting way; showing that you have good listening skills.	
Team work	Working with and collaborating with others; examples of team sports; group projects; work experience; Duke of Edinburgh's Award etc.	
Flexibility	Modifying behaviour to better fit in with others' needs; taking on new responsibilities; working part-time while still meeting coursework requirements.	
Problem-solving	Finding solutions to problems; overcoming obstacles; generating new and original solutions.	
Planning and organising	Organising tasks and activities to meet objectives and deadlines; managing coursework; organising work experience tasks; organising sporting and social events.	
Initiative	Doing things and making decisions without having to be prompted; setting up a business or website; working independently on a work experience placement.	
Decision-making	Choosing from alternatives; creating an appropriate work/study balance; career planning.	
Negotiation	Arriving at agreements/compromises with others.	
Leadership	Leading others; team leadership; helping others.	
Business awareness	Understanding how businesses work; being enterprising; managing risk; work experience; setting up a business or charity.	
Creativity	Coming up with imaginative new ideas.	
IT skills	Being able to apply a range of IT solutions to your work; web design; good PowerPoint presentations.	
Numeracy	Having good basic numeracy skills and being confident with handling numbers; setting out business accounts; handling cash.	
Time management	Meeting deadlines and completing tasks in good time.	

It is very important to understand that employers are looking for the skills outlined above. They use a variety of approaches to check whether candidates can demonstrate them, for example:

- Interviews are good ways of checking communication skills.
- Team activities test teamwork skills.
- Problem-solving tasks allow candidates to demonstrate whether they can come up with creative ideas and solutions.

It is therefore very important to be aware of your employability skills and to identify ways of developing them as you work through your Applied Business GCSE. The tasks and activities suggested in this book provide you with lots of opportunities to build on your skills. Work experience and part-time work also provide excellent chances to develop employability skills, as do voluntary work, sports and other team activities.

Take it further

Find an advertisement or job description for a job that interests you. Make a list of the key employability skills you would expect to be associated with that job.

Just checking

What are employability skills?

13

The recruitment process

There are a number of stages involved in the recruitment process for a new job.

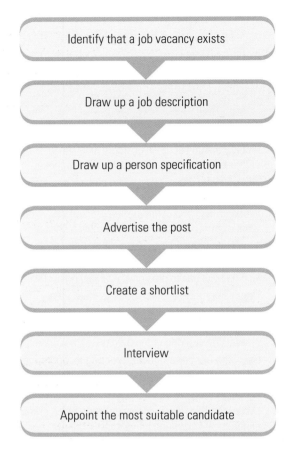

Describe it

A **job description** is a document that sets out the key responsibilities and tasks involved in performing a particular job.

A **person specification** details the personal qualities an individual will need to perform a particular job.

Apply it

Working in a group of six, select a job advertisement from the local paper that you are all interested in and request a job application form. Working as a group, fill in the application form after carefully considering the person specification that is supplied with the application form or in the advert.

When a business starts or is growing, it may need to employ new staff. A business may need to replace existing staff who leave or retire. Whenever a business recruits, it is essential to set out a clear description of what the job entails. A **job description** sets out:

- the title of the job
- to whom the job holder is responsible
- for whom the job holder is responsible
- a description of roles and responsibilities.

A **person specification** sets out the skills, characteristics and attributes a person needs to do a particular job. Together job descriptions and person specifications provide the basis for job advertisements. They help job applicants and post-holders know what is expected of them. As they are sent to anyone applying for jobs they should:

- contain enough information to attract suitable people
- act as a checking device for the business to make sure that applicants with the right skills are chosen for interview.

Apply it

Brights is a large department store chain in the south of England. The company has combined its job descriptions and person specifications into single documents. Each document shows how a job-holder fits into the business. They help Brights to recruit the right kind of person and help managers check that staff are carrying out their jobs to set standards. Below is an example of a Brights' job description and person specification.

Job: Department Manager

Reports to: Store Manager

Area of business: Homeware

Job purpose: To drive business improvements and performance within the department; to coach and develop the department team to give the best customer service and experience.

Person specification:
Skills: Leadership skills (such as influencing others and decision-making); operating skills (such as managing staff and stock management); general skills (such as communication, planning and problem-solving).

---

1 **Who at Brights would use this joint job description/person specification form and for what purpose?**
2 **Which of the skills shown in the person specification are job-specific and which are related to general employability?**
3 **Which of these skills do you think you already possess? Justify your response.**

Remember it

A person specification and job description are not only useful in the recruitment process. Once a job holder is in post, they can be used to check the areas of responsibility of the employee. If there are any disputes, the documents can be referred to.

Just checking

What is the difference between a job description and a person specification?

Identify at least two people within a business who might use these documents. Why might they use them?

Take it further

Get hold of a job description for a particular post. Create a person specification based on the job description.

Job advertisements

Once a business is clear about the job it is offering, it can go about advertising the post. How the advert is set out depends on:

- who the business is trying to attract
- where the advert is going to be placed, i.e. what media will be used (paper, radio, TV, website etc.)

A good job advertisement will include the following features.

Feature	Description
Job description	The major requirements of the job
What the business does	A brief description of the business and its activities
Location	Where the job will be based
Salary expectation	Figures are not always necessary, but an indication of salary level should be given
Address and contact	How to contact the recruiter, e.g. email address, postal address etc.
Closing date	This lets applicants know when they need to apply by
Qualifications	Certain jobs require a minimum entrance qualification. This should be clearly set out
Experience	What experience applicants are expected to have
Fringe benefits	The recruiter may wish to mention things that are additional to the job, e.g. free canteen meals, a company car etc.
Organisational identity	A logo or badge associated with the company

Apply it

 The Joker Theatre Company
Sales Manager
Birmingham
Basic Salary £25k + car

The Joker Theatre Company is looking for a new Sales Manager to increase the sales of theatre tickets for this exciting theatre company. The Sales Manager will receive an initial salary of £25,000 plus a performance bonus for meeting sales targets.

We are looking for someone with at least two years' experience of working in sales who has a proven record of success. The successful candidate will need to have familiarity with business practices and good IT skills.

For further details apply to:
Director of Personnel
The Joker Theatre Company
The Haymarket
Birmingham
BR2 0NG

Telephone: 0204 900 1234

Study the job advertisement shown above.

1 Does the advertisement give a clear picture of what the job entails?

2 Does the advertisement set out clearly where the job is located?

3 Do you think that the advertisement is focused enough to attract people with the right sorts of qualifications to fill the post?

4 What sorts of people do you think are most likely to apply for the post?

5 Would an applicant know how to apply for the job?

6 What improvements, if any, would you make to the advertisement?

Now create a job advertisement of your own. This could be for a job you, a relative or friend has, or a job you would like. Your advertisement should show that you have a clear understanding of what makes an effective job advertisement. It should be well structured and set out in such a way as to appeal to and attract appropriate job seekers.

Take it further

Find a job advert for a position that interests you. Identify the key features of the advert, e.g. the job title, salary etc. Which features of the advert are particular clear and which are unclear or even missing?

A job advertisement needs to be placed in appropriate media. Today many jobs are advertised on the Internet. They may be placed on the company's own website or on the site of a specialist recruitment agency or jobsite, such as Jobsite UK or Reed. When choosing the media, a business needs to think about the target audience. For example, if it wants to recruit locally, it could place an advert in a local newspaper, on the local radio or at a local job centre. If the job is to be advertised nationally then it is important to identify the appropriate media for this, for example a specialist magazine or a national newspaper.

Shortlisting

When a business has received all the applications for a job, it will make a **shortlist**. This is an important process that involves matching the applications with the job description, and particularly the person specification. The application form, CV, covering letter etc. that the candidate submits are vital in this process. The more the potential employee can demonstrate a match to the job description and person specification, the more chance they have of being shortlisted. Those applying who do not take notice of the job description and person specification in their application are unlikely to be shortlisted. This is why every job application must be treated individually.

Shortlisting is a very important process. When creating the shortlist, a business must make sure not to miss out candidates who have some really good qualities but perhaps have not presented themselves as well as they could have on paper. At the same time, some candidates might have exaggerated their 'good' points and it is important, therefore, to check thoroughly. Some estimates suggest that most people manipulate their CVs to make them look better. This can involve missing out important details or saying that they have a lot of experience of activities required in the person specification when really they have very little experience. When creating a shortlist, it is important to carefully consider whether it would be possible for an individual to have had the experience they claim to have. It seems that the problem of dishonest CVs grows in times of economic hardship such as the recession in 2009. Typical examples of dishonesty include people saying they left a job because they were made redundant, or worked somewhere they didn't. Because some employers expect to see details of up to ten years of employment, university, schooling and address history, it is inevitable that some people make mistakes. However, others cover up criminal convictions and fraud against previous employers.

Research it

Examine one or more of the job sites listed here. How easy are they to navigate when looking for the types of jobs that you and your friends are interested in? Links to the sites can be found at www.heinemann.co.uk/hotlinks.

Describe it

A **shortlist** is a list of the best applicants – those that most closely meet the requirements of the job description and person specification.

Just checking

What information should a job advertisement possess?

Name five different forms of media a business might use to advertise a job and identify why each might be chosen.

Describe it

Screening is a means of deciding which applicants should go forward to the later stages of the recruitment process.

A **curriculum vitae** (or CV) is a document that summarises a job applicant's background, qualifications, experience and interests.

Selection and interview

Selection involves choosing the most suitable people from those that apply for a vacancy, whilst keeping to employment laws and regulations (more on laws and regulations in the next section). **Screening** applicants is a very important part of the selection process. This ensures that those selected for interview have the best match with the job requirements.

The diagram below shows the typical selection process for a management post.

Vacancies advertised on website or other media such as national press

Screening of applicants to find the best match with the person specification

Successful candidates invited for interview

Successful candidates asked to complete job-related tests

Unsuccessful candidates notified

Successful candidates invited to second interview

Successful candidate(s) sent offer letter and contract

For many jobs, interviews are carried out by a panel, usually made up of two or more people. During the interview process, a number of documents will be used to make sure the process is carried out well:

• Copies of applicants' application forms, their **curriculum vitae** and supporting letters of application.
• Copies of the person specification, the job description and a list of questions to ask.
• Copies of references (although some companies only take up references after the interview process has been completed).

Generally speaking, interviewers will try to make the interviewee feel relaxed and comfortable so that the interviewee can show his or her best side. An opening remark might be to ask the interviewee about his or her journey to the interview on that day such as, 'Where have you come from?' and 'Did you find it easy to get here today?' When there are several interviewers, a starting point may be to introduce the interviewee to each of the panel in turn.

The interviewee is usually asked a set of predetermined questions. One of the reasons for this is to make sure that each candidate is treated the same and given the same opportunities. This helps the business to meet its responsibility under various employment laws. The questions asked should relate to the person specification and job description.

When you go for an interview, expect the interviewers to be taking notes. They will be checking to see that you meet the job criteria and will be comparing you with other candidates. They might use a score sheet to compare candidates' responses to questions and the extent to which they fit what the business is looking for.

Post: Junior Retail Manager

Candidate's name: Paul Bartlett

Requirements:
    Score 1=Poor
       5=Excellent

	Score 1–5	Notes
Previous experience:	5	Carried out similar work at electrical retailer.
Punctuality:	1	Turned up late for interview.
Intelligence:	5	Answered questions well with good attention to detail.

An interviewer's score sheet

Many job selection processes today involve **psychometric** or **aptitude testing** to find out whether individuals have the right sort of personality to carry out particular types of work. For example, a psychometric test might seek to find out an individual's willingness or ability to work in a team situation or how they handle stress. Some organisations place a great deal of emphasis on these tests because they believe they are:

- good indicators of the sociability/personality of individuals
- predictors of whether they will fit into the organisation.

The interview process is not just for the organisation to find out about the applicant, but also a chance for the applicant to find out about the organisation. It is therefore a two-way process. The organisation will want to make a good impression on the applicant. The interviewee will want to know whether the organisation is somewhere they would feel comfortable working, whether they feel they can work with the people in the organisation, whether the job is really what they expected and indeed want. Recruitment is an expensive process and it is important that both parties are happy with the outcome. An organisation does not want to appoint a person who then leaves after a month because they do not like the job or the people they work with!

Remember it

A **psychometric test** is a way of assessing an individual's personality, drives and motivations, either by means of a paper and pencil questionnaire or an online test. These tests have been devised by psychologists and are considered relatively accurate.

An **aptitude test** is used to find out whether an individual is able to do the required work and may involve them carrying out a work-related task. For example, in selecting new pilots, a number of airlines test applicants' speed of reaction to sudden movements as well as their performance in flight simulators. These test response times and the ability to cope with pressure.

Apply it

Produce a short word-processed leaflet setting out guidance to an employer on how to conduct an employment interview.

Then draw up a list of questions an interviewer might ask at an interview for a specific job. Create a short list of questions the applicant might ask during the interview.

Just checking

What methods could an employer use to find out about the personality of a potential employee?

Apart from candidates' letters of application, what additional documents should be circulated to inform panel members at an interview?

The law and recruitment

When recruiting employees, it is essential that businesses comply with the law. There are also ethical and moral considerations that a business has to take into account, especially if it wants to present itself as a socially responsible employer. Ethics are concerned with behaving in the 'right' way and relates to issues such as 'fairness', providing 'equality of opportunity' and promoting diversity (having different types of people and cultures in the workforce).

Case study – Unlawful discrimination

Pauline Alexander is deaf and the first person to successfully claim disability discrimination against a recruitment agency. Although Pauline is deaf, she had previously been the director of a property company. She applied to the recruitment agency for the position of Diversity Trainer. She was asked to phone in. She did this using TypeTalk (a relay telephone service for deaf people). The person Pauline spoke to said he thought her hearing loss would be an impediment to doing the job. He asked for a CV, but the following week contacted her to say that she would not be invited to interview because of her hearing loss. When Pauline pointed out that this was discriminatory, the agency backtracked inviting her for interview.

The Employment Tribunal awarded Pauline Alexander £5,000 in compensation plus legal fees to be paid by the employment agency.

An Employment Tribunal is an independent body responsible for making legal decisions related to employment disputes.

1 What is meant by the term 'discrimination'? Carry out a search on the Internet to find definitions of this term.

2 How do you think Pauline Alexander was discriminated against?

3 What message does the result of her Employment Tribunal send out?

4 Do you think that the award was sufficient in terms of:
   a) compensating Pauline for the damages caused;
   b) stressing the importance of not discriminating against deaf people?

Research it

Find out more about employment tribunals by visiting the Employment Tribunals website via www.heinemann.co.uk/hotlinks.

Take it further

Look out for other cases involving discrimination in recruitment in national newspapers. These don't hit the headlines every week, but there are plenty of cases that are reported in newspapers over a longer period of time. So keep an ongoing lookout for such articles. You can also do a search on the Internet to help you find examples of cases of discrimination. Identify the issues involved.

Remember it

A **Genuine Occupational Requirement** (GOR) relates to specific reasons why a person should be of a particular sex or race or possess some other skill in order to do a particular job. For example, in some faith schools it is a requirement that the applicant has some understanding and sympathy with the religion of the school. Think back to the Pink Ladies taxi service on page 127 – might they have a GOR when they recruit new staff?

It is important for employers to ensure they have procedures in place to meet their legal obligations and avoid discrimination when recruiting. An applicant can take an employer to an employment tribunal if they believe they were discriminated against during recruitment. When writing job descriptions and person specifications, employers need to set out clearly the tasks the person will have to do and the skills they need. Requirements should not be put in that are not directly related to the job. For example, for a position as a fitness trainer in a leisure centre, it is not necessary to know whether the person is married or what religion they are.

In job advertisements it is unlawful to specify that the applicant must be of a particular gender or race, unless it is a **genuine occupational requirement**/qualification.

It is unlawful to publish job adverts that imply that a candidate's success depends on them not having or not having had a disability.

In addition, publishers of such adverts (e.g. newspapers) are also liable in court if they publish such adverts. The Employment Equality (Age) Regulations 2006 require employers to be careful when wording advertisements to ensure that they do not contain words that may be linked to age, such as 'young and dynamic', 'mature' or 'lively'. Other examples include 'would suit someone who has just qualified' and 'minimum of ten years' experience'. This is because applicants must not be treated any differently because of their age.

Job application forms should only ask for the minimum of personal details. It is not lawful to ask for ages on application forms. When interviewing people there are certain questions that should not be asked, either directly or indirectly. These include whether a person is married, is in a same-sex civil partnership, or plans to have children. None of these questions have any bearing on whether the applicant can do the job they have applied for. For the same reason, there should be no questioning about sexual orientation or religion.

Tests and assessments given to candidates for a job should not be discriminatory. For example, a written English test would discriminate against those whose first language is not English. However, if the employer can justify that having good written English is necessary for the job then this is acceptable.

A recruiter may need to make adjustments to a test for disabled applicants, such as giving them more time to complete it or providing a text-to-speech reader for computer-based tests.

Finally, when making the selection, the employer needs to be able to justify the decisions they make. They could face a claim of unlawful discrimination if they select one person over another because of race, gender or sexual orientation, rather than basing their decision on qualifications and experience. The use of score sheets to record candidate responses and the extent to which they match the person specification and job description helps a business provide evidence that it has met these regulations.

Just checking

Why must businesses comply with the law when recruiting?

Give three examples of stages in the recruitment process where discrimination can occur and, for each example, state what businesses can do to prevent it.

Talk about it

Dennis is a 45-year old gay man who has been working in finance for the last 20 years. Recently he applied for a job in the bank where he works. The job was a team leader post and was advertised both internally and externally. It asked for 'a young and enthusiastic employee who is keen to learn new skills'. Dennis filled in the application form for the job which asked him about his age, education, previous experience, hobbies and interests. It took him a long time to fill in the application because it asked for lots of details, including whether he was willing to work flexitime and his views about equal opportunities at work. Dennis was pleased when he was shortlisted.

He was interviewed by a recruitment consultant, a senior manager from the bank and the person who previously held the post. Dennis was disappointed to find that the old team leader was involved in the interview as on a previous occasion at a party this person had made disparaging remarks about what he referred to as 'gays'. The initial questions related to aspects of work set out in the person specification. However, the interview then covered a range of more personal issues. Dennis did not get the job.

1 **From reading the case study, do there appear to be any areas where discrimination might have occurred?**

2 **How could Dennis find out if he had been discriminated against?**

Describe it

Training is the process through which an employee acquires the right sorts of knowledge and skills needed to do their job well. Because modern jobs are continually changing, employees usually need to receive training throughout their working lives.

Employees – training

Once a business has recruited the right person for the job, they will need to be trained. Through individual or group **training**, employees learn new information and skills, as well as updating existing skills and knowledge. Training is not something that should just happen once – an employee will continually need to keep up with changes and developments, for example new laws and changes in technology.

There are two main types of training:

- 'On the job' training involves training in the workplace. The trainee learns from being given responsibility to carry out real work tasks. They will typically be supervised while they are learning and given feedback by a mentor or coach. The coach works with the trainee to identify targets and goals and the sort of training that is required.

- 'Off the job' training happens away from the place of work. For example, a trainee accountant may spend half of their time studying accounts at a local college or university.

The main purposes of training are:

- **Induction** This involves introducing an employee to a new job. Typically it will include an overview of the company and important details to prepare for working in the organisation, such as health and safety training. An important part of induction is getting to know other people and being introduced to company routines.

- **Understanding job requirements** Initial training should focus on making sure that an employee is able to do the basic requirements of the job.

- **Development of job skills** Specialist skills will need to be developed which enable an employee to do a job well, e.g. skills of interacting with customers, the use of important IT applications etc.

Case study – Training

In 2005 Jason started working for Hairstylists International, an international hairdressing business with salons throughout Europe. Jason shadowed Patricia, an experienced stylist, for the first few weeks at the London salon. She told him about the company, settled him in and gave him some literature about job opportunities within the company. For much of the time Jason was doing fairly routine work like making tea, tidying and answering the phone, but he learnt a lot watching Patricia and she also told him all about the company and job opportunities within it. Jason soon started a hairdressing course at the local college where he learnt hairdressing techniques and skills.

After a year, Jason was cutting hair and being mentored by Patricia. She gave him advice and was always prepared to step in when he lacked confidence. Jason was very proud when he received a Level 3 NVQ Certificate in Hairdressing from his local college. Soon after, Jason was given his own chair at the salon. The company encouraged him to attend international training events where he learned some of the latest techniques. He hopes to eventually set up his own salon.

1 Identify the different types of training Jason received.

2 What was the reason for each aspect of his training?

- **Broadening knowledge of the business** The more a trainee knows about the wider activities of the business and the nature of work in the organisation, the better they are able to help the organisation meet its objectives.
- **Changing attitudes and skills** In the modern world, organisations frequently have to make changes. Training therefore needs to be designed to help individuals learn to adapt to new attitudes which move the organisation forward.

Identifying training needs

Most organisations have an employee appraisal process, sometimes referred to as a **performance appraisal** or review. These are usually carried out by a line manager or team leader (the appraiser). The individual being appraised (the appraisee) and the appraiser will sit down together to establish targets to work towards in the coming period. These targets will normally be based on a review of performance in the previous period and targets for the organisation or team as a whole.

Common stages of staff appraisal are:

- The line manager meets the job-holder to discuss performance. Targets are set and agreement is arrived at on how the job should be done in the next period. Training needs are identified.
- The outcome of the meeting is recorded and signed by both parties. A training plan is set out.
- The job holder performs the job for the next period and engages in the agreed training.
- At the end of the period another performance review is held and so on.

Training is a very important process because:

- it enables companies to be successful by having highly skilled people
- employees feel valued because they are being invested in by their organisation.

Training awards

The National Training Awards are designed to celebrate organisations and individuals that show excellence in their commitment to training. Anyone can nominate organisations and individuals for these awards.

In addition, organisations that look after their employees by providing training and other opportunities are able to display an Investors in People (IiP) badge at their workplace. IiP is an organisation that sets standards and monitors how organisations look after their employees. They set tough requirements and tests before they will issue the IiP certificate to an employer. Over 30,000 organisations in the UK have met the IiP standards.

Remember it

Performance appraisal involves making a judgement about and providing feedback on how well an individual is doing their job. At the appraisal meeting new targets are set for the coming period, which often include training needs. These are agreed by both the employee and their line manager.

Assessment tip

You can use evidence from a period of work experience or a part-time job to describe the different types of induction and training available in a specific business. If this is not possible, your teacher may ask a trainer from a local organisation to come into your school or college to describe the induction and training process in their place of work.

You should also evaluate the effectiveness of this induction and training, in other words, come up with some suggestions for improving it.

Hotlink

To find out more about the National Training Awards and IiP, you can find links to both websites at www.heinemann.co.uk/hotlinks.

Just checking

Identify and describe the two main types of training.

What are the main purposes of training?

Curriculum Vitae

Name: Prakesh Patel
Date of Birth: 1.3.1992
Address: 50 Palmerston Road, Reading, RG31 9HL
Telephone: 01604 76321

Education:	Waingel's Copse School, Reading (Sept 2004–July 2008)
Training:	Orientation Call Centre, Reading (2008) – Team Leader
Qualifications:	Edexcel Double Award in Applied Business
	Mathematics GCSE
	English Language and Literature GCSE
	Sports Studies GCSE
	French GCSE
	History GCSE
Work history:	I am now a team leader at a call centre providing support services to a leading service provider. My work involves coaching others. I recently won an award for the most promising new recruit.
Interests and activities:	Captain of school football team; house captain and prefect (2008). Venture Scout. Gold Award Duke of Edinburgh.
	This year I led a small group of students from three schools all of whom successfully completed the Three Peaks Challenge climbing the highest mountains in Britain in under 24 hours.

Referees: Mr D. Martin
Waingel's Copse School
Denmark Ave
Woodley
Reading RG3 8SI

Rev. R. Babbage
St Jude's
Church Street
Reading RG4 7DQ

Is this a good CV?

Applying for a job

Many of you will already have applied for part-time jobs. Modern students are faced with a very competitive market place when looking for jobs so it is important to get it right. You may already have experience of applying for a job or work experience placement and have an understanding of how you should set out a record of your qualifications, experience and achievements to date.

The best way of presenting yourself when applying for a job is with a Curriculum Vitae (or CV). There are three stages you should complete when creating your CV:

- Collect together all the facts about yourself you want to include.
- Create a draft version of the CV.
- Edit and refine the document several times before using it.

Always keep in mind that your CV needs to pass the '30 second test', which is the amount of time an employer may take to look at your CV to decide whether to look at it in greater detail! It will help to keep the following in mind:

- Keep your CV short – no more than two A4 pages.
- Use good quality paper; maybe use a pastel coloured paper to make your CV stand out from the crowd.
- Lay out information using clear headings to make it easier for the reader to navigate.
- Use bullet points to describe things like duties, responsibilities and achievements.

The following is a list of good 'action' words to use in a CV:

Achieved, Analysed, Assisted, Broadened, Collaborated, Communicated, Conducted, Controlled, Co-ordinated, Demonstrated, Designed, Developed, Devised, Directed, Enabled, Executed, Facilitated, Generated, Harmonised, Identified, Improved, Increased, Initiated, Installed, Launched, Managed, Marketed, Negotiated, Organised, Oversaw, Participated, Performed, Pioneered, Presented, Promoted, Proposed, Provided, Reorganised, Researched, Resolved, Restructured, Reviewed, Scheduled, Secured, Selected, Set-up, Shaped, Tested, Trained, Upgraded, Visualised, Won, Wrote.

Of course, if you use them you must be able to prove that you have done what you say you can do!

When applying for jobs, as well as creating a CV you will usually also be required to write a letter of application for the job. The letter should have a clear structure, with a beginning, a middle and an ending. It should state:

- your reasons for applying for the job
- the contribution you can make to the organisation
- how you have developed your capabilities through training and education
- the skills and knowledge you have acquired that would help you to do the job well.

The letter also needs to address the person specification and the job description. It needs to be interesting too as you are trying to 'sell' yourself to the business. It should contain just enough information to support your application form and CV. You will know that you are writing effective letters if they lead to interviews. Here are some important rules to remember.

- Use good English with accurate spelling.
- Use your own words rather than copying those in the advertisement.
- Do not try to be too clever by using long words.
- Keep the paragraphs short.
- Try not to use 'I' too much.
- Word-process your work.
- Keep a copy of what you have written.

It is also essential that you fill in your job application form well, which could be a paper form or an electronic one (i.e. online). Always read carefully any instructions provided with an application form before you start writing or typing as this will help you to avoid making mistakes. Follow these useful tips:

- Make sure that you provide all of the requested information. If you leave any sections blank, make it clear that you meant to or you may be thought of as careless. If the information requested is not relevant to you write/type 'Not applicable'. This shows you have considered the information requested and not simply ignored it.
- Write clearly and neatly when filling in a paper form. Use black ink as the form may be photocopied. If appropriate fill in the form using your computer.
- Make sure to send a passport photograph if this is requested.
- Check for spelling and grammatical errors. If you are filling in your form electronically, make sure you save it regularly and print it off to check it.
- List your most recent jobs first. Employers are interested in what you can do now rather than what you did in the past.
- List your most recent education and qualifications first.
- Make sure that the people you put down as referees are reliable and will show you in a positive light.
- Don't forget to sign and date the application form.

Take it further

Produce your own up-to-date CV. Ask someone else to evaluate your CV against the following checklist:

- Have you given a good impression of your skills, knowledge, experience and personality?
- Are these set out in a concise and readable fashion?
- Do significant achievements stand out?
- Have you eliminated confusing terms, jargon and obscure abbreviations?
- Are all words spelt accurately? Have you used correct grammar?
- Is the layout clear and organised?
- Does your CV have a good 'feel'?
- Would the person reading it understand it?
- Would the person reading it want to find out more about you?

Apply it

Using the Internet or the local press, find a job that you would like and think you could get. Create a CV and a letter of application for the job. If you are able to get hold of the application form for the job, complete that too. Use all of the tips and advice on these pages to help you. This will be good practice in developing the skills of searching for jobs and in completing application forms.

When you have completed the form, print it off and show it to others in your class. Get them to comment on what they think. Is it neat and tidy? Is it completed fully? Are there any mistakes?

Just checking

What information should appear on a CV?

What is the difference between a letter of application and an application form?

Roles and working arrangements of employees

Job roles

Customer Assistant Roles

Our groundbreaking new store at White City isn't just the place to go for an outstanding retail experience. It's also the place to go for an outstanding retail career. And we're on the lookout for enthusiastic, talented people to join our new team and make sure our flagship store opens with a bang.

We're currently looking for enthusiastic people to join our in-store café team as Customer Assistants and ensure our customers enjoy the great service just as much as they love the delicious food. We're also after people to keep our shelves stacked and our store gleaming in one of our out-of-hours roles (late nights or early mornings). Whether you've honed your talent in a retail environment or any other service industry, if you can put a smile on each customer's face as they snap up our fantastic range of products, then you'll fit in perfectly here.

For a business to be successful, everyone must know what they and others should be doing. Everyone has a role to play. These roles need to fit together into a clear structure. The advert opposite is for part-time jobs at Marks and Spencer at White City in London. The jobs advertised are part-time ones.

From the advert, we can see that the job roles require the employee to work in a team. The team would have a team leader who would be responsible for each member of the team and, in turn, the team leader would report to a customer service manager who would be responsible directly to the store manager. We could set this information out as an organisation chart.

Research it

Create an organisation chart for your school, college or place of work showing the various job roles. Draw up a job description for one of the job roles in that organisation detailing how that particular job fits into the overall structure.

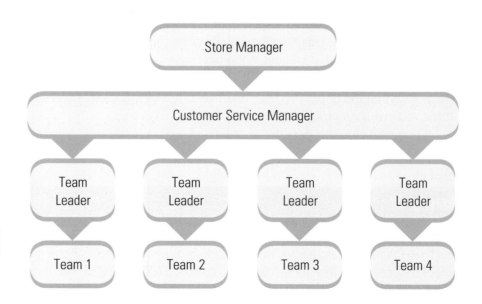

An organisation chart shows how various job roles fit together. A job description then gives a clear description of what an individual needs to do in a job role.

Case study – **Work levels at Tesco**

Tesco has identified six work levels within the organisation:

Work level 1 – frontline jobs working directly with customers. For example, working on the checkouts or stacking goods.

Work level 2 – leading a team of employees dealing directly with customers.

Work level 3 – running a unit. Requires management skills, including planning, target setting and making reports.

Work level 4 – supporting operating units and recommending strategic change. Requires good knowledge of the business, the skills to analyse information and make decisions and the ability to lead others.

Work level 5 – responsible for the performance of Tesco as a whole. Requires the ability to lead and direct others.

Work level 6 – creating the purpose, values and goals for Tesco. Responsible for Tesco's performance.

As you can imagine, pay and bonuses increase with higher work levels. More experience and higher qualifications are required to perform the top level jobs.

1 **Which level and its associated roles could you see yourself performing now? Explain your answer in terms of your current skills, interests and qualifications.**

2 **Which of the roles could you see yourself performing in five years' time? Relate your answer to the qualifications and training you expect to have acquired by then.**

3 **How could you progress from Level 1 to higher levels?**

4 **Which of the roles do you see as being management roles? What is it about these roles that fit them into the management category?**

There are a number of key job roles in medium and large sized businesses. These include managers, supervisors, operatives and support staff. As you can see from the Tesco case study, there are several layers of management in large organisations.

* Senior (strategic) managers work at levels 5 and 6. They make the big decisions about Tesco, for example developing new Tesco retail outlets in the United States and Tesco's stance on organic products. The decisions they make set out what Tesco stands for in the market place.

* Level 4 managers at Tesco also make strategic decisions. They are there to support the various operating units, for example deciding how goods will be delivered to the stores and the IT networks that will be used for stock control.

* Level 3 would be referred to as middle managers. They have a very important role to play in organising and controlling how resources are used. They include store managers. They have a big role to play in making sure that the individual supermarkets run well on a day-to-day basis and that all necessary systems are in place.

* At level 2 we have supervisors or, as they are more commonly called today, team leaders. They make sure that a part of the organisation, for example the café or the fruit and vegetable section, are run well. They take responsibility for all of their team members. Team leaders are the backbone of an organisation. They are people who know how things should be done at 'ground level'. Team leaders know the capabilities of all the resources (machines, equipment, people and materials) because they work with them every day.

In addition to managers and team leaders, there are a number of support roles. People in support roles work across an organisation, for example providing IT or administrative support.

Apply it

A job role is the part that an individual plays within an organisation and fits into an organisation chart. Create all or part of an organisation chart for a chosen business to show how a particular role fits into it.

Just checking

Why is it important to define job roles?

What is an organisation chart?

Flexible working can make life easier for families

Flexible working

The world of work has changed dramatically in recent years. At least half the workforce is female and the number of **part-time** jobs compared to full-time ones has increased enormously. One of the major changes in working conditions has been the growth of flexible working. Fifty years ago, organisations had a large core of full-time employees who expected a job for life. Today this core has shrunk and more and more workers are agency temps, sub-contractors and part-time workers. This has had an enormous effect on job roles, pay and conditions. The illustration below shows the development of what is referred to as the 'flexible firm'. A flexible firm can cut its labour cost to a minimum by limiting its number of core workers.

Core workers

Shrinking

Core workers

2000 and beyond

1980s

Remember it

A **part-time** worker is someone who works fewer hours than a full-time worker. There's no specific number of hours that makes someone full- or part-time, but a full-time worker will usually work 35 hours or more a week.

Core workers tend to be multi-skilled, full-time workers who enjoy good pay, working conditions and benefits. They are essential to the basic operation of the business.

Peripheral workers are temporary or part-time workers and usually receive less favourable pay, working conditions and benefits. They are very useful in providing greater flexibility to meet the organisation's needs, for example employing extra staff at Christmas or during the summer.

External workers are not employees of the business but are agency temps or workers in contracted-out sevices.

Talk about it

How many of your friends and family have full-time jobs working for an employer? How many work part-time or flexitime or have temporary contracts? How many are sub-contractors?

Produce a chart showing the proportion of people that you know who fit into each of these categories. Compare your results with other groups. What differences/similarities are there?

The financial crisis at the end of 2008 caused many workers to lose their jobs. Large numbers of full-time employees were made redundant because they cost too much for banks, service providers and manufacturers to employ. Troubled businesses seek to cut costs and are therefore more likely to employ part-time and casual labour.

Part-time workers have the same employment rights as other employees. The law states that a part-timer must be treated at least as well as a full-timer doing similar work. They must get at least the same hourly pay rate as a full-timer doing a similar job. They must not be excluded from training and career development opportunities and are entitled to the same rights to sick pay and maternity, paternity and adoption leave and pay.

An employee's working arrangement is set out in an **employment contract,** which should include the following details:

- name of the employer and the employee
- job title or job description
- date employment started, the place of work and the address of the employer
- amount of pay and how often it will be paid
- hours of work
- holiday pay entitlement
- sick pay arrangements
- pension arrangements
- notice periods
- for temporary jobs, the date employment will cease
- disciplinary rules.

Contracts of employment also cover overtime work. Overtime is when you work outside of your normal contracted hours. For example, if an employee is contracted for 35 hours a week, they may be entitled to one and a half times their normal pay rate for each extra hour they work. Sometimes the multiple is much greater, maybe two or three times the normal rate. These may be put in place if a worker is expected to work 'unsociable hours', for example at weekends, at night or during public holidays.

Contracts also cover shift work. For example, some factories work 24 hours a day and divide the day into shifts, such as:

- Morning shift: 8am–4pm
- Afternoon shift: 4pm–12pm
- Night shift: 12pm–8am

Rates of pay will vary according to the shift worked.

In addition, there may be special arrangements to pay employees for weekend working. Some factories work six days a week, with essential maintenance work then being carried out on a Sunday. The 24/7 way of working is common to many types of business, including some airlines and energy plants. Some workers may expect to be called out in the middle of the night, including police, fire and ambulance workers, doctors and nurses, and gas, water and electricity repair workers.

Describe it

An **employment contract** is a legal agreement between an employer and an employee, setting out the terms on which one agrees to employ the other. It also details the responsibilities of both the employer and the employee to each other.

Just checking

Identify and describe some of the more flexible working arrangements that exist in the modern workplace.

What is a contract of employment and what details should it contain?

Talk about it

Working in groups, set out what you think might be the drawbacks of flexible working on a piece of flipchart paper and then make a presentation of your findings to the class. Perhaps you could draw a picture at the centre of your sheet to show what a 'typical' flexible worker might look like.

Research it

Interview one person you know who would be considered a flexible worker. What do they see as being the main benefits and drawbacks of working in this way?

Remember it

Teleworkers are people who work with computers and telecommunications from home.

Flexibility for the 21st century

Flexibility has become a big part of working life in Britain in the 21st century. There are a number of key benefits of flexible working, both to employers and employees.

Main benefits to employers	Main benefits to employees
Can use a wider number of employees by offering flexible contracts	Can create a better work/life balance. Part-time work can be combined with child care, for example
Part-time contracts are a way of reducing costs	Employees are able in some cases to work for part of the week at home
Easier to cut down on flexible labour when the going gets tough	It may be possible to combine more than one job

There are many different types of flexible working. **Home-working** illustrates both the good and the bad aspects of flexible working. According to the Office for National Statistics there are over a million people in Britain working from home doing low paid work that would otherwise be done in factories. The most common type of work, done mostly by women, involves sewing; the next most common involving packing and print finishing. Almost half of these people are earning less than the minimum wage.

On the plus side, there are at least two million people who work from home for say three days a week and then go into an office for two or more days. This type of flexibility can enable a better work/life balance than working full-time. The government encourages employers to adopt working arrangements that create a better work/life balance.

The following table shows the growth in home-working and **teleworking** in the UK (in millions and percentage of the UK workforce).

	1997	2001	2005	2009 *estimate based on continued growth
Home-workers	2.3 (9%)	2.6 (10%)	3.1 (11%)	3.6 (13%)
Teleworkers	0.9 (4%)	1.5 (5%)	2.4 (8%)	2.8 (10%)

Source: Labour Market Trends

Research it

You can access a very useful report about home-based working from the Office for National Statistics. The report is by Yolanda Ruiz and Annette Walling and can be accessed by visiting www.heinemann.co.uk/hotlinks.

Flexitime is an arrangement whereby employees can decide the hours they work within limits set by the employer. They are required to work a certain amount of hours per week but can choose when they work these hours. There is usually a 'core period' when employees are expected to be at work, for example between 10am and 2pm. However, the employee is free to decide when they start and finish work. There are all sorts of advantages to this including enabling the employee to organise childcare, look after elderly relatives, and attend educational courses.

Job sharing is an arrangement that has become increasingly common and involves two or more part-timers carrying out the work of a full-timer. Typically the two workers will work at the same desk in an office, just at different times.

Hot desking is where an employee doesn't have to work from a fixed position at their place of work. Instead their workplace provides a range of workstations that are linked together with access to broadband Internet facilities. When combined with home-working, it is possible for businesses to require much less office space than in the past. This arrangement can also improve the work/life balance. For example, Sun Microsystems, a computer business based in California, decided to change the way in which workers carry out their tasks. A far greater degree of flexibility has been given, from home-working to flexible access sites called iWork Cafés. The company claims that it can save $71 million on office space alone. About half of the 70,000 staff took up the initiative. Time and money saved from not having to commute proved a big incentive.

Contracting out is where an employer assigns work to someone outside the business.

It seems likely that the trend towards flexible working will continue to grow. Home-working in particular is likely to benefit both employers and employees through reduced requirements for office space and employees enjoying a better work/life balance. There are also unexpected benefits such as less traffic on the roads. Flexible working has only been made possible by revolutions in technology such as:

- rapid electronic communications such as broadband
- the development of light portable communication systems such as laptops and mobile phones.
- Wi-Fi and other connections. Today there are Wi-Fi hotspots all over the country where people can gain access to the Internet.

It has also been made possible due to recognition by businesses that they can become more competitive through flexibility and Government encouragement for flexible working conditions.

Apply it

Find out about job sharing within your school or college or among friends and relatives. Are there teachers or administrative workers involved in a job share? How does this work out in practice in terms of hours worked, sharing responsibilities and sharing information?

Just checking

Describe the ways in which employers and employees can benefit from flexible working patterns.

List some of the most important types of flexible working arrangements.

3.2 How do businesses develop?

Protecting the customer and the business

Every product or service that is bought or sold must meet certain **standards**. Some of these standards are laid down in law, some in voluntary codes of practice within an industry, and others are set by businesses themselves. The legal system sets out a fair framework for trading and also helps to settle any disputes that might arise.

Remember it

Standards are expectations, often set out in writing, which identify the acceptable characteristics or use of products, materials or services. For example, in the UK we have Food Safety Standards. These standards set out the acceptable contents of foodstuffs (including animal feed). They also set out how foodstuffs should be handled and packaged. The Government plays an important role in setting and monitoring standards, for example through the Food Standards Agency. Other standards are created voluntarily by businesses working together, for example Advertising Standards.

Apply it

How do you think the law would help in each of the following instances?

At Christmas last year, shopping turned out to be a disaster!

1 **I bought my Aunt Sienna a dress, but she spilled some wine on it and when she washed it, it shrank. She couldn't wear it again. The label said shrink-proof!**

2 **I also bought my sister Juniper a pair of gloves which had one of the fingers missing on the right-hand glove!**

3 **I gave my brother Dylan a multi-purpose football pump adaptor, but it wouldn't fit any of his footballs.**

The Sale of Goods Act says that goods must be:

- 'Of satisfactory quality', which means free from significant faults except defects which are drawn to your attention by the seller (for instance, if goods are declared to be 'shop-soiled').

- 'Fit for the purpose', including any particular purpose mentioned by you to the seller. For example, if you ask for a jumper that is machine-washable, you should not be sold one that has to be hand-washed.

- 'As described' on the package or sales literature, or verbally by the seller. If you are told that a shirt is 100% silk, then it should not turn out to be a mix of silk and something else.

Any product that you buy from any sort of trader (e.g. shop, street market, mail order, door-to-door sales-person) should meet these requirements. They also apply to food and goods bought in sales.

Case study – **What to do if things go wrong**

If there is something wrong with what you buy, you should tell the seller as soon as possible. Exactly what you are entitled to depends on how serious the fault is and how soon the goods are returned.

If you take faulty goods back straight away, you should be able to get your money back. You have not legally 'accepted' the goods and this means you can 'reject' them (i.e. refuse to accept them). You can still reject goods even if you have taken them home, provided that you have examined them and try them out as soon as possible.

When you take faulty goods back to the seller, you may be offered a replacement or a free repair. You do not have to agree to this. You can insist on having your money back. If you agree to a repair, you may have problems getting all your money back later if the fault is not sorted out because, in law, you will have accepted the goods. If you accept a credit note, you will not usually be able to exchange it for cash later on.

Buyers should not be put off by traders trying to talk their way out of their legal responsibilities. The law says that it is up to the seller to deal with complaints about defective goods, so the seller should not try and lay the blame on the manufacturer. As a buyer, you have the same rights even if you lose your receipt. A receipt, however, is useful evidence of where and when you bought the goods.

1 **In your view, do the laws about 'acceptance' put the buyer or the seller in the best position? Justify your answer.**

2 **Have you ever had to return goods? What did the seller do about it? Do you think that they were operating within the law? Justify your answer.**

The law also protects consumers when buying a service, for example from a dry cleaner, travel agent, hairdresser, or personal trainer. You are still entitled to certain standards. A service should be carried out:

- with reasonable care and skills. For example, you would not expect a personal trainer to put you on a fitness programme for an Olympic athlete.

- within a reasonable time. If you have your iPod repaired, it should not take weeks and weeks. You are entitled to agree upon a definite completion time with the supplier of the service.

- at a reasonable charge, if no price has been fixed in advance. However, if the price is fixed at the outset, or you have agreed some other way of working out the charge, you cannot complain later that it was unreasonable. Always ask a supplier how much they will charge for a particular service. If they give you a fixed price in a quotation this will be binding.

Apply it

What should a consumer do if they are sold goods which are not in a condition that should be reasonably expected? Produce a leaflet for consumers telling them about their basic consumer rights.

Just checking

Identify three things the Sales of Goods Act states about the condition of goods sold.

What rights are consumers entitled to when they buy a service?

The real thing?

Other consumer laws

Businesses need to be aware of a number of other consumer laws and meet their requirements. Some of the most important consumer laws are:

The Trades Descriptions Act 1968

The description given of the goods forms part of the contract between the buyer and the seller. This act makes it a criminal offence for a trader to describe goods falsely. A type of case frequently prosecuted is where street sellers pretend that they are selling a branded good.

The Weights and Measures Act 1963

This act aims to ensure that consumers receive the actual quantity of a product they believe they are buying. For example, pre-packed items must have a declaration of the quantity or weight contained within the pack. It is an offence to give 'short weight'.

The General Product Safety Regulations 2005

These Regulations cover the general safety of products. The law states that 'no producer shall supply or place a consumer product on the market unless the product is a safe product'. This law was implemented by the European Union and replaced previous UK Government legislation. Producers and distributors are required to inform consumer protection authorities if they become aware that they have supplied a dangerous product, which may require the product to be recalled (you may have seen product recall notices in shops which ask customers to return certain items). A safe product is one that will not cause harm during its use and installation.

Case study – Only Smarties have the answer!

In 1988, Nestlé launched the blue Smartie to complement existing colours red, yellow, orange, green, brown, pink and violet. However, when Nestlé removed artificial colours from the sweets in 2006, no immediate solution could be found for blue, as this is a difficult colour to find a match for in nature. Blue Smarties were therefore removed. As a result of intensive research and development work, Nestlé found that it could use Spirulina, a type of seaweed, to give a blue colouring to Smarties ensuring that this favourite shade could re-appear in 2008 without compromising the 'No Artificials' claim.

1 Can you think of other examples of products that have been changed to make them healthier?

The Food Safety Act 1990

This act gives Environmental Health Officers powers to shut down premises where food is not being prepared in a hygienic way. Regulations cover such things as refrigeration and cooking temperatures.

In 2000, the Government set up the Food Standards Agency (FSA) to monitor food safety in order to protect customers. The FSA created a traffic lights system to help customers make healthier food choices.

The green-, amber- or red-coloured labels on packaging indicate whether a product is high or low in certain components such as fat, carbohydrate and salt. This helps the customer and allows retailers to show that they are taking a responsible approach.

Red shows high amounts of fat/saturated fat/sugar/and or salt. It's fine to eat this food occasionally or as a treat, but think about how often you choose it and how much of it you eat.

Amber shows medium amounts of fat/saturated fat/sugar and/or salt, making it an OK choice, although going for green is better.

Green shows low amounts of fat/saturated fat/sugar and/or salt, which makes it a healthy choice.

Traffic light signalling has four main benefits to both consumers and businesses:

- It makes it easier for consumers to eat more healthily.
- It encourages consumers to look for and demand healthier food.
- It provides businesses with an incentive to provide healthier food. Customers will increasingly prefer these.
- Businesses can show that they are considering the needs of customers and taking their responsibilities for the health of the nation seriously.

However, there are costs involved to a business including additional costs associated with meeting guidelines on fat and salt content and re-designing packaging. In some cases this additional cost has to be passed onto the consumer in the form of higher prices.

Take it further

Next time you are unhappy with a product or service you have bought, write a letter of complaint using the following advice.

- Keep the letter brief and to the point. You could use bullet points like these.
- Describe the item or service you bought.
- Say where and when you bought the item or when the service was carried out and how much it cost.
- Explain what is wrong, any action you've already taken, who you have spoken to and what happened.
- Say what you want done to remedy the situation, for example a refund or repair.
- Send the letter recorded or special delivery, or deliver by hand if possible.
- Keep copies of any letters you send. Don't send original documents, send photocopies.

1 **How would you expect a business to respond to such a letter? Justify your answer.**

Assessment tip

You may find it useful to talk to somebody from a particular business to find out which laws have the most impact on that company and the way in which it operates. You should also carry out some extra research to find out more details about those laws.

Hotlink

You can find out lots of information about consumer protection, both from a consumer's and a business' point of view, by visiting the following websites:
- Consumer Direct
- Trading Standards Central
You can find links to both these sites at www.heinemann.co.uk/hotlinks.

Just checking

Identify and describe at least two important consumer laws that affect businesses.

How is each likely to affect business activity?

Market trends

Business success depends on satisfying customers' needs. Over time a business will want to increase its customer base and this may involve developing existing goods and services or brand new ones.

Case study – Success stories

Two businesses that have done particularly well in recent years are Innocent and Dorset Cereals. Both companies were pioneers in responding to the growing demand for healthy foods. Innocent started out by producing a small range of smoothies. Dorset Cereals started by producing one or two muesli products. In the early days, these products had to win the confidence of the supermarket chains and were initially only given small amounts of shelf space. However, the market has grown and both of these companies have been a great success.

Today, Innocent produces a wide variety of drinks and has now branched out into healthy meals. Dorset Cereals produces nine different mueslis, cereal bars, porridge and light flakes. Most leading supermarket chains are now pleased to give substantial shelf space to these two brands.

1 **Why do you think Innocent and Dorset Cereals have been so successful?**

2 **What other companies can you identify that have made a success of the trend for healthy living? Think further than just healthy foods.**

You can find out more about the history of both these companies by visiting their websites. Links to the sites are available at www.heinemann.co.uk/hotlinks.

Describe it

A market **segment** is a sub-group of people or organisations sharing one or more characteristics that lead them to have similar product needs. For example, the toothpaste market consists of segments of children with milk teeth, low income households that may want to purchase budget toothpaste, old people with dentures, and so on.

Some markets grow over time, others are static and some shrink in size. The table below shows some markets along with which category they are currently in.

Growing	Static	Declining
Health foods	Umbrellas	Newspapers
Health and fitness	Standard ballpoint pens	Cassette tapes
Organic food	Standard toothpaste	Scooters

Note that the term 'standard' has been used to describe some markets because there will be some **segments** of a market that are growing. For example, whilst the sale of ordinary toothpaste remains relatively static there has been an increase in the sale of 'whitening' toothpastes.

Apply it

1 Try and add some markets of your own to the table above, remembering to specify particular segments. Why have some of the markets you have identified grown while others have fallen? The reasons may relate to the development of new technologies, e.g. online news services, broadband etc.

2 See if you can find out the growth in the size of a market of a particular product. The best way of finding out about increases in sales is to study the business reports in a newspaper for a couple of weeks. Look carefully and you are likely to find reports about a specific type of product or industry where sales have been rising recently. Often there will be a diagram illustrating these changing sales figures over time.

3 Investigate whether a business of your choice is part of a growing, static or shrinking market. Can you explain why?

Research it

When investigating market trends, one of the most interesting areas you can look into is food sales in the UK. The best source of information when researching this area is the Food Statistics Pocketbook, which is published by the Department for Environment, Food and Rural Affairs each year and is available online. There is information about market demand for ethical food, ethnic food and a range of other types of food. Another useful source is Dairy Statistics – an insider's guide, published by MDC. Links to both documents are available at www.heinemann.co.uk/hotlinks.

It is important to realise that some trends may be short-term, whereas others are long-term in nature. For example, over a long period there has been an increase in demand for many goods and services such as petrol, housing, restaurant meals and so on. However, in the short-term there may be a sharp fall in demand in some of these markets caused by price rises or falling incomes. As a result of the financial crisis in 2008, the demand for houses started to tumble, people reduced their expenditure on clothes and spent less money on eating out.

Remember it

It is helpful to distinguish between a **fad** and a **trend**. A fad is very short-term, for example this season's fashion 'must have'. However, a trend will have a longer term effect on the market, e.g. the trend to eat more healthily or to drink bottled water. For a fad there will be a sharp increase in sales followed by a sharp fall. For upward trends there may be some ups and downs in sales figures but the long-term picture will be upwards. (A downward trend would show a long-term decrease over time).

Apply it

Make sure you are clear about the difference between a fad and a trend. Can you identify businesses that are growing because there is a market trend encouraging the growth of these businesses?

Just checking

Define the following words: trend; market; segment; fad.

Trends in economic activity

Businesses are often classified according to particular market sectors. The table below shows some examples of businesses along with the sector in which they operate.

Businesses	Sector
Tesco, Sainsbury's, ASDA	Supermarkets
Hello!, OK!, Bella	Women's magazines
The Star, The Sun, Daily Mirror	Tabloid newspapers
Costa Coffee, Starbucks	Coffee shops
Rolex, Swatch	Watches

An important part of business success comes from:

- being in a market sector that is growing
- gaining more sales and **market share** than other businesses in that sector.

Describe it

Market share is the percentage of the total sales of a product or service accounted for by one company.

For example, the fitness equipment industry in the UK, which supplies equipment such as bikes, treadmills and weights to gyms, fitness clubs and home-users, is growing in size and has enjoyed high growth rates, although growth is slowing down. Life Fitness UK is the largest business in the market with a market share of over 27%. The second biggest company in this sector is Technogym UK, which has a market share of about 25%. There are a number of other smaller firms also operating in the market.

Case study – Read all about it?

Women's weekly magazines are very popular but they have experienced a recent fall in sales. However, this varies between magazines. In the first half of 2008, *OK! Magazine* defied the downward trend by increasing its circulation by 9%. Sales were 607,048 compared with 557,014 for the same period the previous year. Rival magazines *Reveal*, *Real People* and *Bella* all registered drops of more than 20%. *OK!*'s arch-rival *Hello!* roughly maintained its market position, climbing just 1.7% year on year to 427,054.

1 **Why do you think *OK!* is so popular?**

2 **How are *OK!* and *Hello!* able to keep ahead of the competition?**

3 **Explain two advantages to a business like *OK!* of having the highest share in a market like women's magazines.**

4 **Why are market trends important to study for the publishers of women's magazines?**

Case study – Responding to trends

Businesses have to compete with each other. This is well illustrated by the supermarket industry where the big supermarkets compete very strongly with each other. Tesco is the market leader. However, figures produced in late 2008 showed that despite accounting for £1 out of every £3 spent in supermarkets Tesco is not having it all its own way. The financial crisis had a big effect on spending patterns, as shown in the table below.

Supermarket	Trend in sales growth	Market share
Aldi	22.1%	3%
Lidl	9.8%	2.3%
Morrisons	9.6%	11.2%
ASDA	9%	17.1%
Sainsbury's	5.6%	15.7%
Tesco	5.5%	31.4%

Market share and sales growth of the six leading supermarkets in the 12 weeks to October 5th 2008 (Source: TNS: Worldpanel data)

1 Identify the main change in the trend in sales growth.

2 Explain one possible cause of the change you identified in question one.

3 Discuss one way in which one of the larger supermarkets like Tesco or Sainsbury's could respond to this change.

Certain types of business are fashionable. For example, the Aston Martin, James Bond's favourite car, is top of the UK's list of 'cool' brands. Other cool brands include Apple's iPod music player, the website YouTube, hi-fi manufacturer Bang and Olufsen and search engine Google. Other businesses supply goods for which there is a steady demand like Boots, Marks and Spencer and WH Smith. Other businesses are less successful and don't last long. You may have noticed shops on your own high street that were only open for a short while before closing down.

Take it further

Investigate market trends in your local area. Which businesses seem to be popular? Can you find out what is happening to their sales? (You could ask the manager of the business – explain what you are researching and why!) Which businesses seem to be having growing sales and which have falling sales? Which businesses have been around for a long time and are likely to stay in the immediate future? Which businesses seem to come and go? Can you think of some reasons for the trends you identify?

Assessment tip

You need to use your own experience of what is happening in your local town, as well as articles in national newspapers, to identify businesses that are in growing, static, or declining markets.

From researching a local business, you should look at figures for sales and for sales revenue to identify whether the business has a growing, static or declining market. Use other statistics to explain what is happening to the business, e.g. number of employees, range of products/services it provides.

Just checking

What is a market sector and how can a business be successful in its sector?

Location

One of the most important decisions a business has to make is where to locate its premises. A business owner will set up where they believe the business will have its best chance of success.

Case study – **Moving to a better location**

In July 2006, Premier League football club Arsenal moved to The Emirates Stadium from its previous ground Highbury, which is less than a mile away. The old stadium had a capacity of 38,419, whilst the new stadium has a capacity of 60,355.

Arsenal needs to be able to compete with rivals such as Manchester United, whose ground Old Trafford has a capacity of 77,098. The bigger your ground's capacity, the more sales revenue you can make per match. The size of your sales revenue helps to determine the profit you make and hence the sort of players your club can afford to buy. This simple example shows the importance of getting your location right!

There are a number of factors that affect the location of a business.

Apply it

Listed below are some of the factors that influence the location of a newsagent.

- Other shops close by
- Plenty of space in shop for customers
- Easy access to suppliers for delivery purposes
- Passing trade
- Ease of parking
- Proximity to housing
- Availability of paper boys and girls

Produce a similar diagram of your own showing the factors that influence the location of another type of business.

Distance to markets Many businesses need to be located close to their market, i.e. their customers. Think of a coffee shop at a railway station or motorway services. Service industries, such as entertainment and banking, also have to locate near their markets to be available for their customers. Many manufacturing industries locate close to their markets, particularly if they produce bulky or fragile items which are expensive to transport.

Availability of raw materials Some businesses use a lot of heavy and bulky raw materials to make their products. However, these products may be a lot smaller and lighter than the ingredients or components which have gone into making them. For example, finished steel is a lot lighter than the ore, limestone and other materials it is made of. If the raw materials are bulky and expensive to transport, it makes sense to locate near to them. These industries are known as 'bulk-decreasing industries'.

Transport costs Different industries have different transport needs. Two major influences are the pull of the market and the raw materials. These depend on whether the industry is 'bulk-increasing' or 'bulk-decreasing'. Many businesses set up close to good transport links, for example Holiday Inn hotel outlets are close to airports, train stations and busy roads.

Availability of land Land costs vary a lot from area to area. Some firms require a lot of space to make or sell their goods. They will choose sites which are out of town where costs are lower, e.g. manufacturing plants and superstores.

Availability of labour The right sorts of labour and skills are easier to find in some areas than others. If businesses want a large pool of cheap labour they might set up in centres of population where there aren't many employers. If they want skilled labour they will set up where they are most likely to find those skills, e.g. a pharmaceutical company may set up near a university with a good science department.

Safety Some industries have to locate their premises well away from heavily populated areas, e.g. nuclear power stations, munitions factories and some chemical companies.

Utilities A business must consider five standard utilities: gas, electricity, water, disposal of waste and drainage. Industries such as food preparation and paper production use large quantities of water. Food-processing creates waste and the cost of waste disposal will affect the location.

Communications Many businesses need a strong core of IT communications systems. It is therefore important to set up in areas where communications are clear and reliable. This might exclude some mountainous or highland areas. Cities with excellent wireless and broadband facilities are a real attraction.

Regional factors Locating in the same area as similar businesses, suppliers and markets may be considered an advantage. The quality of local schools, housing, leisure and recreational facilities can also help to encourage high quality staff to join and stay with the business.

Government incentives The government provides financial support for businesses to set up in some regions. These will usually be areas of higher unemployment.

Assessment tip

You will need to be able to evaluate why a business has chosen its location. Make a list of locational factors and then try to rank them in terms of importance in affecting the location of the business. Explain why each of the key factors is important. Perhaps you could ask someone from the business to describe which of the factors the business sees as being most important.

Just checking

What factors can affect where a business chooses to locate?

Describe how these factors can vary in importance depending on the type of business.

3.3 What are external factors?

To a certain extent, a business' success depends on how well it is run. However, there are some factors over which the business has very little influence. These are referred to as external factors because they are 'outside' the business. There are three important external factors which have an effect a business' success:

- Business competitors
- Economic conditions
- Environmental constraints.

Business competitors

Most businesses face some form of competition. Some of this competition may be **direct**, for example two newsagents selling the same magazines, newspapers and sweets. Other competition is **indirect**, say, your local cinema competing indirectly with your local video shop for the money you spend on entertainment.

Describe it

Direct competition is where the competition offers the same good or service as you.

Indirect competition is where businesses compete for customers but do not offer identical goods or services.

Apply it

1 **What are the main direct and indirect competitors in the following industries?**

Industry	Company	Direct competitors	Indirect competitors
Petrol retailing	Shell		
Supermarkets	Waitrose		
Book selling	Blackwells		
Economy hotels	Travelodge		

2 **Identify and explain at least three ways in which the competitors you have listed above compete with each other.**

Competitors often compete with each other on price. For example, supermarkets will compete with each other to provide cheap everyday items such as boxes of matches, soap powders, bin liners, pet food etc.

Another way in which firms compete is on quality. For example, airlines like British Airways and Singapore Airlines seek to compete with each other to provide the best personal service from flight attendants, the best possible comfort and in-flight entertainment etc.

Another aspect of competition is availability of the product. For example, one of Coca-Cola's slogans is 'Within an arms reach of desire'.

Case study – Luscious!

Lush is a popular producer of homemade cosmetics. Lush produces all its cosmetics and ingredients itself, including perfume. A Lush store is like an old-fashioned grocers, with heaps of products, and signs and messages written on blackboards. Lush cuts out packaging costs by not having packaging. The company identifies its customers as being 'SEGOR', which stands for people who have 'sustainable, ethical, green, organic or responsible' attributes.

Based in Poole, Dorset, Lush has almost 400 stores worldwide. It believes that it doesn't have any direct competitors. Its nearest rivals are companies like The Body Shop, which has nearly 2,000 outlets worldwide. However, Lush believes that The Body Shop is more like established cosmetics companies because its products are packaged, and today the company is owned by L'Oreal.

Other indirect competitors for Lush include chemists and supermarkets selling perfume, soap and other cosmetics. Supermarket chains are much larger than Lush, operating thousands of outlets. They deal directly with cosmetic manufacturers and are often able to sell cosmetics at very low cost. Chemists offer a range of low price cosmetics, as well as exclusive high price brands.

The supermarkets, the chemists and chains like The Body Shop therefore all provide competition for Lush. However, Lush sees itself as being different as their products are organic and handmade.

1 **Why might customers prefer to buy from Lush rather than from a competitor? Explain your answer.**

2 **Do you agree that companies such as The Body Shop, Boots and supermarkets are not direct competitors with Lush? Justify your answer.**

3 **In what ways do you think that Lush competes with rivals in terms of price and quality?**

This means that they aim to make Coca-Cola available wherever people want it across the globe: in stores, vending machines, cafés and restaurants, sports centres etc. Of course, today the Internet has made it easier for firms to make products available to customers; we can order goods online whenever we like. For example, book retailers like Amazon make hundreds of thousands of books available that can be ordered at the click of a mouse.

Apply it

In March 2007, a survey of 6,000 UK customers carried out by the Customer Satisfaction Index showed that the UK's ten favourite shops were:

1	Waitrose	6	H&M
2	John Lewis	7	Play.com
3	IKEA	8	Dunhelm
4	Amazon	9	Primark
5	T K Maxx	10	JD Sports

1 **For each of these shops, state whether you think they compete mainly in terms of price, quality, availability or a combination of these?**

Assessment tip

You will need to know who the main competitors are for the business you have chosen to study for the assessment for this unit. What are the main ways they compete with your business, e.g. price, quality, availability, location, after-sales service, other factors?

Just checking

What is direct competition?

What is indirect competition?

In what ways can businesses compete with each other?

Apply it

Can you identify goods and services that are targeted specifically at the following groups?

a) Males; b) Females; c) Teenagers; d) Elderly people; e) Rich people; f) Poor people; g) Sporty people; h) Fashion-conscious people; i) Elderly males; j) Teenage females; k) Rich teenagers; l) Poor females.

Remember it

Psychographics segments people according to their lifestyle. A person's lifestyle is their individual pattern of behaviour made up of their attitudes, interests and habits.

Demographics segments people according to facts about them as members of the population, e.g. their sex, their age, the size of their family, their income, where they live, the type of work they do etc. For example, there are magazines targeted at males and females, people who live in London, grocers/hairdressers/bankers, and so on.

Linking products to customers

Products and services are linked to particular groups of customers. This is called 'target marketing'. To find out the target market for products and services it is first necessary to carry out market research (see page 128–9 for more on market research).

Market segmentation is the process of dividing a market up into groups of similar customers in order to provide products that meet the needs of different customers.

- Primary segmentation is dividing customers into groups that buy completely different products. For example, Colgate-Palmolive makes soap and toothpaste for different markets.
- Secondary segmentation takes place based on **psychographic** and **demographic** factors.

Businesses need to 'position' their goods and services to capture and retain the interest of the targeted segment of customers. The 'position' of a product is the image that is created by marketers in the minds of customers. For example, Red Bull is positioned as a 'pick you up' that will re-energise the drinker, perhaps after a long night out or before a period of exercise. Innocent Smoothies are positioned as a very healthy drink option.

Talk about it

In groups, discuss what sort of 'position' is created for the following drinks?
- Bottled water   • Cola   • Tea bags   • Cappuccino

Assessment tip

What sort of positioning is used by the business you are studying for your coursework in this unit? How does the business go about creating this positioning?

Case study – Red Bull

Red Bull is a mixture of caffeine, vitamins, carbohydrates and taurine, a substance that jump-starts the body's metabolism. It is a very popular drink and was adapted from a product from Thailand called Krating Daeng (Thai for Red Bull). It was sold in a brown bottle and was popular among workers in Thailand wanting to keep awake in order to work long hours. It was developed by Austrian businessman Dieterich Mateschitz, who altered the formula to make it acceptable in the West and changed the packaging. Today it is sold as an energy drink and has won 65% of the market for this type of product.

1 **What type of customer do you see Red Bull as being primarily linked to? It might help you to keep the following in mind:**

   What age do you think typical customers of Red Bull might be? Are they male or female? Young or old? Are they rich or poor? What sorts of lifestyles do they lead?

New technologies and e-business

New technologies in business have allowed new ways of producing goods and services and making them available to customers. The last twenty years have been revolutionary in the speed of change and the development of new ideas. Some of the new technologies include cleaner fuel in cars, lighter bicycle frames, flat-screen televisions, iPods and digital cameras. Not only have these developments made life better for consumers, but they have also made it possible for businesses to become competitive in different ways. Today all businesses use new technologies, such as electronic databases to store customer data, spreadsheets to perform business calculations, and electronic communications to link up the different parts of the company and to link with suppliers.

Research it

Identify examples of ways in which your school or college and/or the business you are studying for this unit has adopted new technologies. What are the new technologies? How do these opportunities help the school/college or business to become more attractive to customers? For example, your school/college may use electronic registers, swipe cards, a school learning intranet, interactive whiteboards etc.

Case study – Shop till you drop!

A survey carried out by the market research company Nielsen in January 2008 showed that 85% of the world's online population has used the Internet to make a purchase. More than 50% of Internet users had made a purchase within the month of the survey being carried out. The survey stated that the convenience of using the Internet had made it an essential part of the way people make purchases. The survey found that in the UK, 97% of Internet users make purchases in this way.

The most popularly purchased items across the globe are:

1 Books (41% of purchases)
2 Clothing/accessories/shoes (36%)
3 Videos/DVDs/games (24%)
4 Airline tickets (24%)
5 Electronic equipment (23%)

1 **What items do you purchase online?**
2 **What makes a website you purchase from attractive when compared with the competition?**

A product-related website can:

- educate customers about new or existing products and their use
- provide information, for example about new product developments, what to do if things go wrong with a product and so on
- provide recreational activities such as games, competitions and fun activities
- enable customers to make purchases.

In terms of making a business website competitive, it is important to develop what are referred to as the 3Cs:

Content
drives users to a website and includes news, interviews, product information etc.

The 3Cs of a good website

Community
Visitors to a site need to feel they are valued by the site provider and the brands it represents

Commerce
is a way of generating income, through shopping, advertising, sponsorship etc.

Just checking

Identify different ways in which businesses can target customers.

How have developments in technology created new ways for businesses to compete with each other?

Economic conditions

The 'economy' consists of consumers and producers of goods making millions of buying and selling decisions every day. The Government plays an important part in the economy by buying and selling goods, as well as making laws, such as those concerning consumer protection. The Government also taxes businesses and individuals. When the economy is doing well, businesses sell lots of goods and provide lots of employment. When economic activity (buying, selling and production) slows down, then businesses suffer.

In the summer of 2008, Marks and Spencer, one of Britain's most famed retailers, reported a sharp fall in sales. They said this was caused by falling consumer confidence. They were worried that consumers were spending less and that the pricing policies and promotions offered by competitors were cutting into profits. The chairman of the company stated, 'If there's nobody that thinks there's a price war going on, then I'm a Dutchman'. His view was that stores like ASDA and Tesco were cutting prices to win customers at a time when customers had started to spend less.

Business success or failure is influenced by what is happening in the wider economy and changes take place in the economy all the time. So what are these changes and how do they affect business?

Economic stability

The second half of 2008 showed that the economy can become very unstable very quickly. In the period leading up to 2008, banks had lent lots of money to their customers to buy things like houses and cars. But then a large number of borrowers were unable to pay back their loans. This started in the United States and spread rapidly to Britain and across the globe.

People with savings in the banks began to worry that the banks had lent out their money and might not be able to get it back. They started to withdraw their savings and some of the banks quickly ran out of cash. As a result, all of the banks cut back on their lending and businesses and customers suddenly found it difficult to borrow. In turn, they had to cut back their spending.

Once spending starts to fall it affects us all. Businesses sell less and are then forced to cut back on their number of employees. Fewer people in work means less spending in restaurants, coffee shops, cinemas, clothes stores and so on. Businesses start to close down. By the start of 2009, Britain was in the grips of a **recession**.

Of course, just as the economy can go into recession, it can pull out. When we come out of a recession, people start to spend more, businesses make more sales, create more jobs and so on.

Talk about it

Why do you think retailing is likely to become more competitive when the economy moves into a downturn (i.e. consumers start to cut back on the amount they spend)?

Describe it

A **recession** occurs when for two quarters (a quarter is three months) in a row the value of all the goods sold in an economy falls. This is called 'negative economic growth'.

Inflation

Inflation is a major headache for businesses. It occurs when there is a general rise in the price of goods in the whole economy. Of course, not every price will be rising but *average* prices will. In the UK, average prices are measured by the Government using a measure known as the Consumer Price Index (CPI).

Inflation hurts business because it creates uncertainty. A rise in the rate of inflation might reflect a rise in the costs they have to pay: employees will want more wages, costs of materials will go up and the cost of fuel and energy may also rise. Rising costs eat into profit margins. Businesses then have a choice:

- Keep prices constant and see profits fall.
- Raise prices and perhaps lose out to competitors.

Apply it

You own a high street clothes shop. For the last few months, the CPI has been increasing. Your business rates have gone up, your electricity bill has increased, the cost of stock has increased by 10%. You have two employees, but they are grumbling that they could earn more working in other shops.

1 **What factors would you need to consider before deciding whether to raise your prices or to keep them steady?**

Take it further

Identify ways in which the businesses you have selected to study in this unit have been affected recently by changes in economic conditions.

Research it

Carry out a search on the Internet for:

- the UK Consumer Price Index (CPI)
- UK consumer spending

Both of these searches should take you to the Office for National Statistics website. On this site you will be able to see what the current rate of inflation is in the UK and the current state of consumer spending. You can also get up to date information on the CPI using the Biz/ed website. Compare these figures with previous months to find out whether these figures are rising or falling and the likely impact on UK business.

Just checking

Define the following words and terms: economy; recession; inflation.

Describe it

The **interest rate** charged by banks in the UK is determined by how much they have to pay in interest if they want to borrow from the Bank of England.

Controlling business costs

Businesses need to minimise their costs if they are to be competitive. As we have already seen, some of these costs are outside their control. One of the most important costs for any type of business, whatever its size, is the **rate of interest**. The interest rate is the cost of borrowing money and is expressed as a percentage (%). For example, if a business borrows £1,000 for one year at a 5% interest rate, it would expect to pay back £1,050.

> **£1,000** (the sum originally borrowed)
>
> + **£50** (the interest charge, 5% of £1,000)
>
> = **£1,050**

Case study – **What interesting rates**

The Bank of England changes interest rates to influence inflation. In doing so, it also influences economical activity. For example, if prices are rising quickly it will raise interest rates to discourage borrowing. However, if the economy is in a recession it will cut interest rates to encourage spending and make it cheaper for businesses to borrow money.

Study the illustration on the right which shows changes in the interest rate up until November 2008.

1 What was happening to interest rates?

2 Why do you think the Bank of England was changing interest rates in this direction?

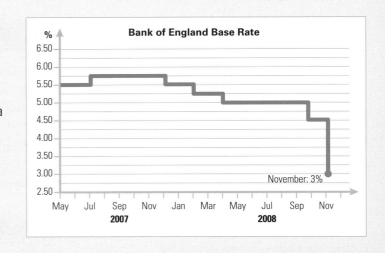

Research it

Find out what the current Bank of England interest rate is. All you need to do is to carry out an Internet search using the search terms 'UK interest rate', along with the month and the year when you do your research.

Nearly all businesses borrow money. They hope that when they come to repay the money the interest rate will be as low as possible. Rising interest rates harm business profits. Sometimes high interest rates can ruin a business. This is because they have to pay a lot of interest on money they have borrowed, which adds to their costs. If they are only just managing to break-even, the rise in costs can cause them to go into loss. If they are not able to increase their revenue, the rise in interest rates can be the last straw: cash flow dries up and they may be forced to close.

Other important costs for a business are **commodity** prices and costs of raw materials. The most important commodity price affecting all businesses is energy costs. Petrol and diesel are required for transport, and gas and oil are required for fuel, lighting, heating and the powering of machines.

Another important business cost for businesses that buy and sell abroad is buying currency. The cost of this is determined by the exchange rate of one currency for another, for example the pound for euro or dollars. If lots of people want to buy British goods and services, the pound becomes a popular currency and people are prepared to pay more for it. It will therefore exchange for larger quantities of foreign currencies.

However, a rising pound doesn't always help business. If they sell a lot of goods overseas then the cost to foreigners of buying British will rise if the pound rises in value. This is because they have to give up more of their own currency to acquire the amount of pounds they need. The exchange rate can make it seem like prices have risen! However, British businesses find that their goods become more competitive when the value of the pound is falling. Foreigners are then better placed to buy cheaper British goods. This is because foreign buyers have to give up less of their currency to buy the same amount of pounds they need. British exporters, therefore, benefit from a fall in the value of the pound. The exact opposite of both instances would be the case for UK importers.

Describe it

Commodities are basic items that are mined, extracted or farmed that go into making most other goods. They fall into four main categories: energy (e.g. oil and gas), metals (e.g. gold, silver, copper), livestock (e.g. sheep and cattle) and crops (e.g. wheat and rye).

Remember it

A business that sells goods or services to a buyer in another country is called an **exporter**.

A business that buys goods or services from a seller in another country is an **importer**.

Talk about it

In small groups, discuss the following:
- Who gains most when the value of the pound rises? British exporters or British importers?
- If British exporters were finding it difficult to sell their goods overseas, would they want the pound to fall or rise in value? Explain your answer.

Assessment tip

Study the local paper to find out how changes in the economy are affecting businesses generally in your region. You can be pretty sure that these wider changes will have the same sort of effect on any business that operates in your area.

Just checking

What is the current Bank of England rate of interest?

How can it affect businesses, both for good and for bad?

The role of the Government

The Government plays a big role in managing the economy.

It is a major employer and spender of money on goods and services.
A very useful website to explore is ukpublicspending.co.uk. You can get a very detailed view of how the Government spends the money it gets in taxes and other sources of income.

The table below shows Government spending as a percentage of all spending in the UK over time. You can see, for example, that in 2008 the Government accounted for 42.908% of all spending (bottom right). In other words, about 43 pence in every pound spent in the UK was spent by the Government on our behalf. The chart also shows Government spending in individual areas, for example about seven and a half pence in every pound was spent by the Government on health care.

	1997	2001	2005	2008
Pensions	6.060%	6.807%	6.998%	7.308%
Health care	4.976%	5.408%	6.721%	7.515%
Education	4.553%	4.522%	5.126%	5.615%
Defence	3.091%	2.878%	2.721%	2.819%
Welfare	7.895%	6.173%	6.366%	6.610%
Law and order	1.891%	1.880%	2.294%	2.372%
Transport	1.225%	0.908%	1.294%	1.448%
General Government	0.796%	0.952%	1.587%	1.869%
Other spending	4.611%	3.999%	5.065%	5.492%
Interest	3.444%	2.624%	1.971%	2.248%
Balance	0.476%	0.426%	−0.268%	−0.388%
Total	39.019%	36.578%	39.874%	42.908%

Source: HM Treasury, HMSO. Reproduced under the terms of the Click–Use Licence

Talk about it

In 2009, the Government was spending more money to try and combat the world credit crunch and the recession. Why do you think Government is spending more money in this way? What is likely to be the effect on future taxes for people in Britain?

You can see how important Government spending is to businesses. For example, road builders like McAlpine and defence contractors like BAE Systems rely heavily on contracts to supply the UK Government.

It creates the rules and laws which affect how businesses are allowed to compete with each other. The Government seeks to make sure that businesses don't become too big. It seeks to prevent monopolies, which is where one firm dominates a market. For example, if all the energy companies in Britain were joined together to form one large company, it would then be able to charge much higher prices than before when there was competition. But the Government doesn't allow this and businesses are not allowed to fix prices.

It makes laws that set out how businesses can be set up and what they are allowed to do. Businesses must comply with many laws. These govern things such as choosing a company name, producing annual accounts, and health and safety. They protect customers and employers, as well as suppliers and shareholders providing money for business.

It taxes businesses and gives subsidies to encourage business activity. For example, businesses pay a tax on profits called corporation tax. They also help the Government to collect income taxes on employee wages, as well as Value Added Tax (VAT) which is a tax on spending. The Government also pays subsidies to some businesses. These are the opposite of tax. For example, the Government gives money called subsidies to farmers to help them produce important crops and to invest in new farm equipment. Farmers also receive subsidies if they make improvements to their land and farming methods that help protect the environment.

It tries to make sure that the economy runs smoothly. For example, when the economy is in recession the Government can raise its own spending. This pushes more spending into the economy. Those that receive Government spending as incomes will re-spend it, pushing further spending into the economy. Alternatively, if inflation is rising, the Government may seek to slow down spending. It could do this by raising taxes so that consumers have less to spend.

Apply it

Study national newspapers over a one week period. Then make a list of ways in which Government activities have affected specific businesses in that week. Use two columns. One column should identify the business affected. The other column should set out what the Government activity is and how it is likely to affect the business.

Assessment tip

Find out how Government activity in managing the economy affects the business you have selected to study for the assessment in this unit. How does Government activity enable the business and customers to plan their spending and saving activities?

Just checking

Describe five ways in which the Government has a part to play in managing the economy.

Case study – The Government and the environment

The Government is playing a major part in encouraging businesses to become 'greener'. This includes taxing businesses for harm they cause the environment. An example of this is the landfill tax, where businesses are charged for waste material that has to be deposited in landfill sites. The rates of tax are much higher on toxic and 'special wastes' which require more treatment. The Government is also providing incentives to businesses to become 'green'. This includes subsidies for businesses involved in creating 'green' energy such as wind farms, and a low vehicle excise tax for energy efficient cars.

Environmental constraints

Many business activities can have damaging effects on the environment. For example, with increasing air travel the capacity of UK airports, such as Stansted and Heathrow, has been expanded with new terminals. This benefits passengers wanting to travel abroad, as well as the airlines and other businesses. However, it is harmful to local people and wildlife and nature surrounding the airports.

Case study – Terminal 5, 6, 7, 8...?

The plan to build Terminal 5 at Heathrow started in 1985. The permission to go ahead with the project was finally agreed in November 2001 after a planning enquiry that lasted almost four years. The cost of the enquiry was shared between British Airports Authority (BAA) (who owns the airport) and British

Airways. In 2007 it was announced that there would be a sixth terminal, as well as a new runway which will be started by 2020. It cost £4.3 billion to build Terminal 5 and took 60,000 workers six years to build. It is estimated that the number of passengers passing through Heathrow will increase by 27 million a year. The airport currently employs 68,000 people and this number will be increased substantially. The new Terminal 5 includes 150 retail units, including 25 restaurants and 3,250m² of duty free shopping.

There has been a lot of opposition to the expansion of Heathrow from local residents and environmentalists. They argue that the expansion of the airport increases noise and air pollution. It also increases traffic congestion and is harmful to local wildlife. They argue that it is a huge waste of money at a time when aircraft emissions are causing a lot of damage to the ozone layer, contributing to global warming.

1 **Copy and complete the table below. The table should set out who stands to benefit and who will lose out from the expansion of Heathrow Airport.**

Winners	How they will benefit
British Airports Authority (BAA)	Will gain more revenue from charges to airlines who use the airport and shops who lease premises there
British Airways	
Air travellers	
Shops and restaurants	
Employees	
Losers	**How they will lose out**
Motorists travelling near the airport but not using the airport	Traffic congestion and extra petrol costs from queuing
Local households	
Users of amenities near Heathrow	
Birds and animals	
The global environment	

Assessment tip

Find out what impact the local or national business you are studying for the assessment for this unit has on the environment. Who benefits from the activities of your chosen business and who loses out from its activities?

It is expected that the number of people using cars, taxis, buses and coaches in and out of Heathrow will more than double now that Terminal 5 has opened. In addition, there are extra lorries bringing goods to the airport. The extra traffic will increase noise and air pollution.

Those who are in favour of the expansion of the airport argue that it brings a lot of trade and earnings to Britain – at least an extra £600m a year in exports. They argue that modern aeroplanes are much less noisy than in the past and that Terminal 5 would not lead to any increase in night flights from the airport. They say that modern planes are much bigger (e.g. the A380 superjumbo carrying 555 passengers) so there is less air congestion and noise pollution per passenger.

Apply it

Find an example from your local newspaper of a local business which may be having an adverse effect on the environment. Set out a table showing who stands to gain and who will lose out from the business activity which the article focuses on.

External stakeholders play an important role in pushing businesses to be more environmentally effective. They include:

- environmental pressure groups such as Friends of the Earth
- green incentives
- green stakeholders in a business
- the Government (through taxes, fines and incentives)
- green employees
- competitors producing rival green products.

Just checking

Give an example of a how business activity can negatively affect the environment.

What could be done to stop or reverse the effects?

Business and environmental law

One of the most rapidly growing areas of business law in recent years relates to the environment. Laws have been made to prevent, wherever possible, damage to people and natural resources. It makes sense for business to comply with these laws. If they don't:

- the business gets bad publicity
- there are fines and penalties for breaking environmental laws.

Examples of environmental laws include:

- **Packaging and packaging waste regulations** Businesses can be fined for putting too much packaging on their products.
- **The Waste Electrical and Electronic Equipment (WEEE) Directive** This sets out to reduce waste going to landfill sites. Every item with a mains plug must be collected and where the electrical equipment contains hazardous substances these must be treated. For example, many computers contain a poisonous substance called cadmium. When a business decides to get rid of its computers it can't just dump them in a landfill site. Instead it must make sure that the computers are collected and processed to remove the harmful substances. Failure to comply leads to heavy fines.
- **The Water Resources Act** This act relates to water pollution. It states that a person breaks this law if: '…they knowingly permit any poisonous, noxious or polluting matter or any solid waste matter to enter any controlled waters'. Controlled waters mean things like rivers or canals. If a person breaks this law they can be sent to prison for three months or face a fine of up to £20,000, or both.

Forward-looking businesses realise that they need to do more than just follow what the law sets out. They need to be ahead of the law and introducing new environmental standards that appeal to customers.

Businesses need to find out what their customers expect and make sure they respond. For example, Marks and Spencer recently responded to environmental pressures from consumers and the Government. It introduced a £200m 'eco-plan' in 2007 which aims to stop sending waste from its stores, offices and warehouses to landfills and to cut its use of packaging by 25%. It is also increasingly using recycled plastic and cardboard. Shoppers are now charged for plastic bags and long-lasting shopping bags are also available.

Remember it

Recycling is the conversion of waste products into new materials or products. For example, waste paper can be converted into new paper products.

Research it

Carry out some Internet-based research to find out two other recent laws which control business activity by preventing the release of harmful waste products. Use search terms such as 'air pollution laws' and 'water pollution laws'.

Case study – Recycling at Innocent

Drinks company Innocent wants to lead the world with its environmental record. It says:

'First step – we don't use new stuff unless we have to. We have just introduced the first ever 100% recycled plastic drink bottle, and we use 100% recycled boxes and distribution packaging. Second step – we try and use less. It's the simplest and the most often overlooked step, but very important. We have reduced the amount of plastic in our bottles by 20% and we are now looking to do the same with our kids' cartons. Third step – we tell our drinkers about the best recycling and other end-of-life options.'

Innocent believes that it is important to contribute to 'global cooling' rather than 'global warming'. It states that the best way to do this is to reduce the business' use of natural resources. It aims to reduce its **carbon footprint** from farm to fridge. Steps Innocent is taking to reduce its carbon footprint include:

- Refusing to air freight fruit.
- Using green energy in its offices.
- Wherever possible, getting ingredients from local suppliers.

1 **Describe two benefits to a company like Innocent of having a strong recycling record.**

2 **Describe one possible benefit to a business of going beyond the legal minimum standards in how its operations impact the environment.**

3 **Apart from its current packaging policies, identify and explain one possible method that Innocent could introduce to reduce the waste it generates.**

Remember it

Share of public services 12%
Financial services 3%
Recreation and leisure 14%
House – buildings and furnishings 9%
Car manufacture and delivery 7%
Clothes and personal effects 4%
Food and drink 5%
Home – gas, oil and coal 15%
Home – electricity 12%
Private transport 10%
Public transport 3%
Holiday flights 6%

Source: carbonfootprint.com

A **carbon footprint** is the measure of the impact an activity has on the environment. It is based on the amount of greenhouse gases produced by doing things like burning fossil fuels to heat our homes. A carbon footprint is measured in tonnes (or kg) of carbon dioxide equivalent. The chart opposite shows a typical breakdown of carbon output for someone living in the UK.

Just checking

What laws has the Government passed that are likely to impact on the way that businesses behave with regards to the environment?

What actions are businesses taking to respond to these laws?

Assessment tip

Make sure you can identify and evaluate what your chosen businesses are doing to manage waste and recycle materials.

Unit 3 Make the Grade

How does your assessment work?

This unit is assessed by a **controlled** task. You will need to examine two businesses: one local business and one national or international business. You will have eight weeks of curriculum time (approximately 24 hours in total) to research the tasks for the assessment and four weeks (12 hours in total) to write up your work in class. The write-up will be carried out under the supervision of your teacher, so there will be restrictions on what you can use in these sessions to help you.

Remember it

A **controlled assessment** means that your coursework is monitored by your tutor and you will do all your written work at school or college, not at home.

There will be questions based on three activities which will be written by Edexcel that you will need to complete for the assessment of this unit.

Activity 1 (30 marks)	Evaluate why people are so important to business
Activity 2 (30 marks)	Investigate how businesses develop
Activity 3 (30 marks)	Analyse how external factors affect business

Nic

I work part-time at BT so it seemed sensible for me to research this company as an example of a national/international business. There is lots of information about its activities on the Internet and my manager provided lots of information about people at work, including information on recruitment, training and so on. As I live opposite an organic fruit and vegetable shop it was sensible to study this as my local business.

Getting ready for your assessment

There are a number of ways in which you will be able to gather information for the assignment. They include:

- leaflets and other publications/promotional materials produced by your chosen businesses
- the Internet – the website of your chosen businesses and other related websites
- articles in magazines and newspapers about your chosen business
- information in books about your chosen business
- visits to your chosen business
- speakers from your chosen business visiting your school or college.

Alice

My first thought was to look at Coca-Cola when choosing my national or international business. But my teacher suggested that it would be better to look at businesses with a base in Nottingham where I live, like Paul Smith the famous upmarket clothes shop.

However, because I want to be a hairdresser, I decided to compare a large Nottingham-based hairdressers called A Cut Above with Tony and Guy, the international hairdressers and Internet-based hair products retailer.

Pritesh

When carrying out my research, I spent a lot of time planning what I wanted to find out when I visited my local business, which is a department store. I took a notebook with a heading for each of the questions I wanted to ask. I tried to make sure I had at least one page of writing below each of the headings, although sometimes I used charts and diagrams. This way I hoped to have enough information on which to base my write-up. When I interviewed the store manager, I took a small pocket tape recorder with me. I could also have borrowed a Dictaphone from my mum's work. I wanted to use something like this as it is often difficult to remember everything that is said and not easy to write it all down at the time.

Keep all of your notes and documents together in a portfolio. This should include, leaflets, brochures, and material downloaded from websites. **Make sure that the information you collect is relevant and useful.** Simply printing off masses of information without thinking about how it will be useful to you is a waste of time – and paper! It will also make it difficult to find what you want during the write-up. Organise your portfolio into headings and sub-headings with an index. When you come to write up your work, you can use this portfolio in class. If it is messy it will be difficult to find what you want in a hurry. So keep it organised.

So what do you need to find out and what tasks will you need to carry out? We will now look at each of the three assessment activities for this unit in turn.

Activity 1: Evaluate why people are so important to businesses

You need to consider the following:

- How does your larger chosen business maintain, monitor and improve its customer service to meet the expectations of customers? Show how it does this for:
  o internal customers
  o external customers.

- Evaluate how well it does this from the business point of view. This means making a judgement – does it provide excellent customer service, reasonable customer service or not very good customer service? You must provide justification for your judgements and these must be based on the evidence you have collected in your research.
- For an appropriate advertised role in one of the two businesses:
  o create a CV and letter of application, addressing all the points in the job description and person specification
  o produce suitable questions for both the interviewer and interviewee to ask.
- For one of the two businesses:
  o describe the different forms of induction and training available
  o suggest improvements which the business could make to its induction and training processes.

Michael

I was able to base the research for the first part of this assessment activity on my work experience. I was working as an IT assistant for a large confectionery company. During this time I was able to talk to the marketing and sales managers about how the company goes about measuring customer satisfaction, for example by comparing sales figures from month to month, as well as any customer complaints. I was able to look at the way the company trains employees to treat each other as internal customers. I found out why this was seen as being so important to the way the company worked.

Before starting the work experience, I had to write a letter of application and create a CV. I did this by carefully studying the job description and person specification to make sure that I covered everything. When I started the work experience, I was given a two-day induction programme and the training manager told me about the training opportunities I could take up if I worked for the company after my work experience.

Activity 2: Investigate how businesses develop

You will need to compare and contrast the two businesses you have chosen, considering the following:

- What is happening to the market for these two businesses? Are they growing, static or in decline? State your reasons and back them up with evidence such as statistics.
- For just one of the businesses:
  o explain the two most important consumer laws that affect the business and show how they are important
  o evaluate the reasons why the business has selected its current location.

Activity 3: Analyse how external factors affect business

You will need to compare and contrast your two businesses, considering the following:

- For one business:
  o Who are its main competitors? How does competition from them affect the chosen business?
  o How important are flexible working arrangements, both to employees and the business?
- For both businesses and their customers:
  o What effect does the Government's management of the economy and changes in economic conditions have on the businesses?

Gemma

I compared Tesco with my local Co-op supermarket. Researching figures on the Internet, I was able to set out detailed figures which showed that Tesco had increased nationally and internationally in terms of number of outlets, the countries it operated in, retail shop floor space, number of employees, turnover and profit. In contrast, my local Co-op store manager showed me that the Co-op's figures have been more or less static over the last three or four years. The number of customers and employees is static, although sales have increased a little but profits have fallen slightly. My research showed that important consumer laws for Tesco include the Sale of Goods Act. The Food Safety Act is also very important, with foods needing to be kept at the right temperatures. I also looked at why Tesco had set up at the edge of our town. The location is near to important roads, as well as centres of population. The rates that it pays are much lower than some other town centre supermarkets.

Suliman

My brother works in the Showcase Cinema in Bristol, whereas my sister works at Cineworld. I looked at how they compete with each other and other local cinemas by comparing things such as number of showings, range of films, quality of cinema facilities, convenience of location etc. In addition, my brother arranged for me to talk to the cinema manager about flexible working. Most employees are part-time and a number job share too. The important thing for the cinema owner is to arrange shift work patterns so that there are always enough people working. Employees get different pay and conditions according to their contracts. It was very interesting looking at how Government taxes profits from cinemas and the support the Government is giving to the British film industry. While I was doing my research, the economy moved into a difficult period and cinema attendance fell considerably as people switched to home entertainment.

Developing skills

In this unit, you will have read about employability skills (see pages 134–5) and thought about ways in which you can develop these skills. As you complete the three activities for the assessment of this unit, you will need to reflect on the skills you are employing to carry them out as these skills will be assessed. Whilst you are completing the tasks, you should keep a record of when and how you have developed the skills listed in the table below.

What the skill is	When you employed the skill	How you employed it
Time management, personal organisation and action planning		
Using data and problem-solving		
The role that you played in group work when working together on the tasks		
Making presentations – consider how suitable the methods were that you used		

Assessment tip

A number of examples of student work have been given in this Make the Grade section. Look at the assessment objectives for the course. Do you think these examples meet the assessment objectives? Are they analytical? Do they demonstrate knowledge and understanding? Are they applied to the businesses? Do they evaluate effectively or are they too descriptive? You must make sure your work meets the assessment objectives.

Unit 4 Financial Planning and Forecasting

Describe it

Income is the money businesses receive from customers and other sources such as bank interest.

Expenditure is the money paid out by a business.

Profit is made if income is greater than revenue over a period of time – it is not the same as cash flow!

A **loss** occurs if the expenditure of a business is greater than its income over a period of time.

Cash flow is the movement of money into and out of a business.

Creditors are the people and other businesses that are owed money by a business.

Break-even is the point at which income from selling an item covers the costs of supplying it.

All businesses need **income** to survive. The money they receive (usually from customers) is used to pay for items such as staff wages, materials and business rates. This is called **expenditure**. In Unit 2, you learned that businesses need to record accurately every single transaction. If the records show that income is greater then expenditure over a period of time then the business is making a **profit**. If the reverse is true, it is making a **loss**. If a business continues making a loss for a time it will probably have to close – the business is said to be insolvent.

For this reason, businesses should always be thinking about the future in financial terms. This is known as **financial planning**. There are several ways to carry out financial planning. One is to forecast **cash flow**. This simply means that future income and expenditure is forecast to try to make sure that there is always enough money in the bank to pay the **creditors**. Businesses also produce budgets. These allow managers to make decisions about items that require expenditure. For example a marketing manager might be allowed to spend up to a certain amount on advertising.

When businesses first start up they will have had to pay out money to begin with, but they may not have many customers and so make a loss. As they attract more and more customers, the business reaches a stage where it becomes profitable. When a business sells enough to cover its costs this is known as the **break-even** point. Businesses use break-even analysis to help them plan when looking at a new idea,

The income and expenditure figures for a business are always changing

such as introducing a new product. Finally, when the financial future of a business is being considered, decisions must be made about where to obtain any extra money needed for investment. Some examples are loans from banks, selling shares and using money saved from profits.

This unit describes four ways in which businesses can plan for their financial future so that they can reduce the risk of problems or difficulties. These are:

4.1 Investigating business cash-flow forecasts
4.2 Investigating business budgets
4.3 Investigating break-even analysis in business
4.4 Investigating sources of business finance and financial planning

For each topic, you will also learn how ICT can be used.

Case study – Airbus A380

In March 2008, a giant Airbus A380 flew into London Heathrow for the first time. The plane is capable of carrying 853 people but its operators, currently Singapore Airlines, Emirates and Quantas, have opted for fewer seats and more luxury. There were 455 seats on Singapore Airlines' first flight to London to make space for people to walk around and allow for 'suites' where passengers can relax in their own cabin.

Many people now look forward to travelling on one of these new huge planes. Unfortunately, this project has not been without its problems. The original development **budget** was £6 billion. However, due to a major technical problem, which meant the whole wiring system had to be re-designed, the budget was exceeded by several billion pounds. Originally the **financial plan** was that the plane would **break-even** when 250 aircraft had been sold. This figure is the number of planes that have to be sold before the whole project makes a **profit**. However, because of the problems that were experienced – and the delays involved – the break-even figure keeps being revised. It now stands at 420, but may change again!

Another effect of the delays was that the first aircraft to be delivered was two years late. This meant that Airbus did not receive income as early as it expected, which caused a **cash-flow** problem. A major **source of finance** was loans from European governments.

How you will be assessed

Your learning from this unit will be assessed by examination. The examination lasts for one hour and will include different types of questions. Some will ask you to choose the correct answer from options given while for others you will be asked to write one or two paragraphs. All questions are compulsory, and for one or more questions that require an extended written answer you will be assessed on your written communication skills. You do not need to remember any formulas (for example break-even) as these will be provided. You can also use a calculator, but not a dictionary. At the end of this unit, a section called Make the Grade has been included to help you do your very best in the examination.

Apply it

In a group, discuss the meaning of all of the words in bold. Check your ideas with your tutor.

4.1 Investigating business cash-flow forecasts

Cash-flow statement

You may be surprised to learn that businesses with good products and healthy order books can still get into financial difficulties. This could be because their cash-flow situation is poor. Failure to manage cash flow is one of the main reasons why businesses fail. The term bankrupt is used for sole traders and most partnerships. Limited companies become insolvent and go into liquidation.

Businesses need to check their cash flow carefully on a daily basis, therefore, to make sure that enough money is coming into the business to allow them to be able to pay all their bills. To help them do this a business prepares a cash-flow forecast which is an attempt to estimate when cash will come into the business and when it will go out in payments. They can then monitor this forecast using a cash-flow statement that records actual cash flow in and out of the business.

Summary cash-flow statements

Look at the example of a cash-flow statement in the table below. This is a cash-flow statement for a business for the month of May. The table beside it explains the terms used in the statement.

Remember it

A business becomes insolvent when a creditor who has not been paid takes it to court to get their money. If the debt cannot be paid the business will usually be forced to stop trading immediately.

	May £
Total receipts	20,000
Total payments	18,000
Net inflow/outflow	2,000
Opening balance	5,000
Closing balance	7,000

Item	Meaning
Total receipts	This is the total amount of money received and actually paid into the bank account during the month.
Total payments	This is the amount of money actually leaving the bank account to pay creditors.
Net inflow/outflow	This is the difference between the two figures above, i.e. inflow minus outflow.
Opening balance	This is the amount of money in the business' bank account at the start of the month.
Closing balance	This is the total amount of money in the bank account at the end of the month. It is calculated by adding the figures in the previous two rows.

The closing balance figure is very important. If it is negative (in other words if the account is overdrawn) the business cannot automatically meet its debts and could be in trouble.

Remember it

Total receipts means the same as **inflow**.

Total payments means the same as **outflow**.

Apply it

There are two calculations in this sample cash-flow statement. The first calculation results in the 'net inflow/outflow' figure of £2,000 and the other gives the 'closing balance' figure of £7,000. Check these calculations to make sure that you agree with them.

What is a cash-flow forecast?

Businesses try to forecast cash flow accurately for weeks and months ahead. The main aim is to identify potential problems where there may not be enough money in the bank to cover normal bills and any other planned expenditure. On the other hand, if the forecast shows that there would be a large surplus, the business may want to invest the money to earn interest. It may even consider investing in new projects.

There are two types of figures that need to be forecast.

- An **inflow** means the amount of money forecast to be paid into the business. Most businesses operate on a credit payment basis. This means that customers are given a period of time, for example 28 days, in which to make payment after receiving goods, so predicting exactly when payments will be made is not always easy.

- **Outflows** are more predictable, because a business can be more certain when it pays money out, for example it knows it will have wage bills to pay every month.

Describe it

A **cash-flow statement** shows the amount of money coming into a business, the amount being paid out and the difference between the two.

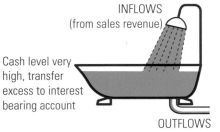
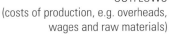

INFLOWS (from sales revenue)

Cash level very high, transfer excess to interest bearing account

OUTFLOWS (costs of production, e.g. overheads, wages and raw materials)

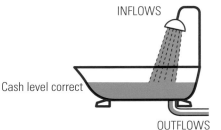

INFLOWS

Cash level correct

OUTFLOWS

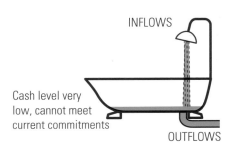

INFLOWS

Cash level very low, cannot meet current commitments

OUTFLOWS

The principle of cash flow

Apply It

Bill Bates runs a garden centre. At the start of February he has £2,000 in the bank. He has forecast sales of £8,000 and has to pay invoices of £5,000 from different suppliers. If his figures are correct, what will be his closing balance? Do you think he may have cash-flow problems? Give a reason for your answer.

Take it further

Bill's wife has her own jewellery business. At the start of February she had £4,000 in the bank and had forecast sales of £3,000. She also had an outstanding bill to her major supplier of £6,000 due for payment that month. Do you think her financial position is better, or worse, than her husband's? Give a reason for your answer.

Just checking

What is the difference between a cash-flow statement and a cash-flow forecast?

Identify two reasons why a business may have a problem with cash flow.

Describe it

A business' **liquidity** at any moment in time is a measure of its ability to pay debts due.

Her Majesty's Revenue and Customs (HMRC) is the Government department that collects tax payments such as income tax, corporation tax and VAT.

Liquidity

In business, the term **liquidity** is used to describe a business' ability to pay its debts when they are due. For example, if a company is due to pay three suppliers a combined total of £3,000 on 21 August and only has £2,000 in its bank account, it has a liquidity problem. You learn more about liquidity in section 2.4 (see page 110) where liquidity ratios are discussed. Here we are concerned with measuring cash flow and a business' ability to pay its suppliers and other debtors (for example, **Her Majesty's Revenue and Customs**) on time. An example of a particular business will be used to explain this set of ideas.

Case study – Printright Ltd

Printright is a small printing firm owned by Iain Torrance. Iain's administrator has just given him a cash-flow forecast for the next three months.

	January (£)	February (£)	March (£)
Total receipts	20,000	12,000	21,000
Total payments	18,000	30,000	17,000
Net inflow/outflow	2,000	-18,000	4,000
Opening balance	5,000	7,000	-11,000
Closing balance	7,000	-11,000	-7,000

Iain makes some notes as he looks at the forecast.

- Three months have been forecast – January to March.
- The inflow for January is £2,000 greater then the outflow so the business appears to not have liquidity problems, at least for that month.

- The closing balance of £7,000 in January looks quite healthy.
- This January closing balance becomes the opening balance for February.
- The closing balances for February and March are both negative, but the problem stems from February where receipts are reduced and payments have increased dramatically compared with the January figures, resulting in a net outflow.

Iain is concerned with the negative closing balances forecast for February and March. He must take action. His first reaction would probably be to look for ways of increasing revenue in February and at the same time try to reduce the £30,000 planned expenditure figure for the same month. If he still thinks that he will have a negative bank balance then he must decide where the money should come from. Obtaining a bank loan or an overdraft are two possibilities. These, and other sources of funding, will be explained in section 4.4 on page 218.

Apply it

Copy out the cash flow table above but change the following two figures for February:

Total receipts: £16,000

Total payments: £20,000

Re-calculate the other figures and comment on Iain's probable reaction.

Assessment tip

Study the Printright cash-flow forecast carefully. In the exam you may be asked to complete a cash-flow forecast by labelling rows or filling in missing figures. You may also be asked to check calculations. It is good practice to try to draw the outline (with headings) from memory.

Differences between businesses

Different types of business will have different patterns of cash flow. Some examples of this are given below.

- Some businesses are in the primary sector, such as arable farming (producing crops such as wheat and barley) and are seasonal. In these cases, the cash flow (both inflow and outflow) will vary depending on the time of year.
- Some businesses have only a few customers, such as businesses who supply products to Tesco. In this case, their cash flow is dependent on the supermarket's policy on debt payment.
- Many manufacturing businesses, which are in the secondary sector, allow their customers to buy on credit. This means they allow a period of time after delivery of the goods before payment has to be made. They need to allow for these delayed payments when they calculate their cash flow.
- Many businesses in the tertiary sector have customers who pay immediately, such as restaurants, retail stores, petrol stations and hairdressers. In this case, the inflow part of the cash flow is almost instant.

Apply it

At Bill Bates' garden centre, trade is **seasonal**. Which months do you think will be busiest, and why? In small groups, identify four more types of business that have seasonal trade. Compare your ideas as a class.

Take it further

What actions can businesses take to improve sales during quiet periods to boost cash flow? Think of as many examples as you can. Remember it is no good if an idea costs more to implement than it will earn!

Talk about it

In 2008, it was estimated that small and medium sized firms were owed an average of £30,000 each by late-paying customers who bought on credit. These are often large firms. If you owned such a business, what could you do about it? Discuss your ideas in small groups and compare your suggestions as a class.

Describe it

Seasonal markets occur when there is a variation in sales levels at different times in the year. An extreme example would be Christmas trees.

Just checking

What does the term 'liquidity' mean?
What kind of liquidity problems might a supplier of Christmas trees have?

'The warehouse roof needs mending, or...'

Remember it

Working out the return on capital employed (ROCE) is one way of finding out how well a business is using the money that is invested in it. Look back at page 108 to remind yourself how this is calculated.

Apply it

Sophie and Rizwan have £1,000 each in savings. Sophie says that her money is earning 5% interest from the bank and she is quite happy with that. Rizwan wants to invest his money in a business. He wants to offer a service looking after people's pets in their own home when they are on holiday. He reckons he will need most, if not all, of his money for some basic training in animal care (for himself), advertising and insurance. He reckons that he will soon be earning £2,000 per year.

Decide for yourself whether you would follow Sophie's plan or Rizwan's. Discuss your decision in a group.

The importance of cash-flow forecasts

Cash-flow forecasts are prepared by business managers so they can plan to have enough cash to maintain their operations. In this section you will learn how managers use cash-flow forecasts to make important decisions about the business. These include whether or not to:

- produce new goods or services
- invest in new resources
- carry out new activities
- expand existing activities
- reduce existing activities.

Later in this section you will learn about cash-flow forecasts where both income and expenditure are divided into different categories – for example, expenditure could include wages and materials. Finally, you will look in more detail at this type of forecast to identify possible problems or opportunities. This could include deciding what to do about cash surpluses or deficits.

When a business is thinking about increasing or cutting back on investment, it should first look at the cash-flow forecast for several months ahead. If the forecast closing bank balance shows a large increase month-on-month, then the business must decide what to do with the money.

The surplus cash could be put into a bank savings account to gain interest. However, most businesses think that they can produce a better return on capital by investing in business activity to make a profit. If the business needs more money than the cash-flow forecast predicts, then it may look at other possible sources of funds – as you will see in section 4.4.

Produce new goods or services

Businesses often produce additional goods to add to their existing product lines – such as toiletry manufacturers who produce complete ranges from bath and shower gels to shampoos and different types of toothpaste.

A business that offers a service may add to these. Amazon started in business selling only books. Now it sells a wide variety of products, including children's toys, electronic goods and kitchenware. Blockbuster, which originally started by renting out videos and DVDs, soon started hiring out computer games and now offers a door-to-door rental service, too.

Invest in new resources

Important resources for all businesses are equipment and buildings. Investment in these areas can be to repair or update existing resources.

For example, a garage could replace 15-year-old equipment (used for MOT testing) with new equipment. Alternatively, the same business could build an extension for valeting customer's cars. This is an example of investing in a resource that, in the short term, is a drain on cash but in the long term can produce an improvement in cash flow.

Carry out new activities

Another way of developing a business is to diversify. This means carrying out new or different activities. For example, a business that produces cooked meat may decide to produce packaged sandwiches for supermarkets. A cattery owner who was interested in horses or dogs could expand by starting a livery yard or opening a kennels. Whatever the plan, extra money would be needed to pay for new equipment and supplies, as well as staff recruitment and training.

Businesses may also develop by carrying out associated activities or services, such as gas suppliers like British Gas and E.ON which offer policies against gas leaks and boiler breakdowns.

Expansion and contraction

Instead of using surplus cash to make different products or carry out new activities, the money may be used simply to expand the existing business. For example, a shoe manufacturer could increase output by 20% by investing in more machines. On the other hand, if a negative cash flow is forecast, a business may have to reduce costs by contracting or investing less.

> ## Just checking
>
> Give at least two examples of actions a business might take if it is forecast to have a large positive cash-flow.
>
> Give two examples of actions a business could take if a large negative cash-flow is forecast.

Case study – Solving a sticky problem

In the last few years Cadbury has made several changes to its product lines. It has disposed of its popcorn manufacturing unit and sold its beverages unit for £8 million. It is now developing its ranges of health and wellness sugar confectionery and has also diversified into chewing gum.

Chewing gum is attractive for two reasons. First, it is more profitable than confectionery. Second, the British spend £250 million a year on chewing gum. However, the benefits were not immediate because of the costs involved in the project. £10 million was spent on marketing and advertising to challenge Wrigley, the market leader. Cadbury has also invested £70 million building a new chewing gum factory in Poland and is also recruiting staff and investing in facilities to focus on new product development. One of its latest innovations is chocolate-flavoured chewing gum that tastes similar to after-dinner chocolate mints.

1 **Identify three changes Cadbury has made to its products and/or the activities it undertakes.**

2 **Why did Cadbury decide to start producing chewing gum?**

3 **Identify three ways in which it invested money after it made this decision.**

4 **At the end of 2007, Cadbury had 12.5% of the chewing gum market. Using the information in the case study, calculate the value of its sales for the year.**

5 **Suggest two benefits Cadbury gains by reviewing and changing its product lines regularly.**

Compare all your ideas as a class.

More about cash-flow forecasts

The example of a cash-flow forecast shown on page 186 is a simplified version. In practice the inflow and outflow figures would be broken down into several items each. This section gives more information on this, using an example of a business. This is described below.

Case study – Alpha Alarms

Alpha Alarms is a small business that specialises in installing and maintaining domestic burglar alarm systems. The business is owned and run by Lee Wozniak who employs a technician. The business owns a van and has a rented lock-up garage where detectors, control panels etc. are stored. Lee's customers often pay immediately, but Lee allows a month's credit if required.

Lee provides a maintenance service for customers by carrying out an annual test and inspection. The fee for this also includes an emergency call-out service.

Study the cash-flow forecast for Alpha Alarms carefully and note the following:

- The forecast covers a four-month period but only the figures for the first two months are inserted.

- The total inflows/receipts figure (A) is made up of two items. These are income from alarm installation and income from maintenance contracts.

- The total outflows/payments figure (B) is made up of five items. These are:

  - wages for Lee and the technician

  - van running expenses (mainly diesel for most months including January, but this is increased in February due to the need for a major service of the van)

  - insurance premiums for the van and other property. These are paid in monthly instalments

  - alarm materials that Lee normally orders on a monthly basis

  - garage rental which is paid monthly.

- The remaining components (C–E) are identical to the outline forecast already illustrated on page 186.

	January (£)	February (£)	March (£)	April (£)
INFLOWS/RECEIPTS				
Alarm installation	2,500	3,000		
Alarm maintenance	1,500	1,700		
Total inflows/receipts (A)	4,000	4,700	0	0
OUTFLOWS/PAYMENTS				
Wages	2,500	2,500		
Van running costs	200	800		
Insurance	50	50		
Alarm materials	500	1,500		
Garage rental	100	100		
Total outflows/payments (B)	3,350	4,950	0	0
Net inflow/outflow (C)	650	-250	0	0
Opening balance (D)	300	950	0	0
Closing balance (E)	950	700	0	0

Alpha Alarms cash-flow forecast

The reason for breaking down the inflow and outflow totals into sub-headings is so that any potential problems can be more easily identified. The greater detail also allows a business such as Alpha Alarms to compare the forecast cash flow with the actual to see where the differences in cash inflows and outflows are occurring. This helps Lee to manage the business more effectively and also to plan ahead.

Take it further

Use a calculator to check that you agree with the calculations for each of the two months.

Completing a cash-flow forecast

Lee is pleased that there is a positive figure for the closing balance for the two months, but is concerned that the balance falls by £150 from January to February. He decides to jot some figures on a piece of paper before completing the chart for the next two months.

Cash-flow, March and April

Maintenance contracts: March £1,800, April £1,500

Wages – same as for first two months except that the technician is due a bonus of £300 in April

Van running cost: £200 for both months

Insurance: no change

Monthly garage rental increases to £120 in March

Alarm installation: March £3,200, April £2,200

Materials: £1,000 for March, £2,000 for April

Lee's notes

Apply it

Use the figures Lee has jotted down to complete the last two columns of his cash-flow forecast. You will need to copy out the forecast using all the headings and figures already provided. When you are sure that you have all the figures in the right boxes, complete the calculations to fill in the following boxes:

- Total inflows/receipts
- Total outflows/payments
- Net inflow/outflow
- Opening balance
- Closing balance

When you are happy that you have done everything correctly, ask your tutor to check your work.

Assessment tip

In the exam you may be asked to complete a blank cash-flow forecast chart using figures provided separately. Remember to check carefully that you have entered the correct numbers in the correct place. Then check any calculations at least once.

Take it further

Look at the figures you have produced. What do they tell you about the financial health of Lee's business? Do you think Lee will be happy with them? Give a reason for your answer.

Just checking

List at least two types of cash-flow for a typical business.

Explain what is meant by the term 'closing balance'.

Interpreting cash-flow forecasts

The basic approach

In this section you will learn more about how businesses interpret cash-flow forecasts. The basic rule is to start with the closing balance figures. Some of the main factors are:

- Any negative closing balance may be a cause for concern.
- What are the trends in the closing balance figure from month-to-month? If it is increasing, then the business would appear to be in good health. A constant decline may be a cause for concern.
- A sudden dip giving a negative balance (perhaps due to **capital expenditure**) may show the need for a short-term loan or a temporary increase in the overdraft facility.
- When a problem with the closing balance figures has been identified, the next step would be to look closely at the individual income and expenditure items to find the cause.

This approach is illustrated by looking at the cash-flow forecast for a business called Patel Printing.

Describe it

Capital expenditure occurs when a large amount of money is spent on an item (e.g. a machine or a building extension) which will last a long time.

Case study – Patel Printing

Patel Printing is a business that is owned by Shabir Patel. It can produce a range of printed documents, such as leaflets, handbooks, brochures etc. It is located in an old warehouse that was bought by Shabir outright some years ago with a bank loan. The loan was paid off within three years. The printing business only occupies part of the building and the remainder is rented out to a car parts supplier. A cash-flow forecast for the business is shown below. Note that deliveries are undertaken by a sub-contracted firm. The miscellaneous heading is for small items of expenditure, such as light bulbs and pens. Study the forecast carefully and then carry out the task that follows.

Do you see any problem(s) with the closing balances? If so, what are they and what would you suggest could be done to improve the situation?

Patel Printing

	January (£)	February (£)	March (£)	April (£)
INFLOWS/RECEIPTS				
Printing revenue	22,000	17,000	21,000	24,000
Rental income	3,000	3,000	3,000	3,000
Total inflows/receipts	25,000	2,0000	24,000	27,000
OUTFLOWS/PAYMENTS				
Labour	12,000	12,000	12,000	12,000
Electricity	950	950	950	950
Materials	8,000	10,000	7,000	8,500
Delivery	2,400	2,400	2,400	2,400
Miscellaneous	40	50	30	40
Total outflows/payments	23,390	25,400	22,380	23,890
Net inflow/outflow	1,610	-5,400	1,620	3,110
Opening balance	0	1,610	-3,790	-2,170
Closing balance	1,610	-3,790	-2,170	940

Take it further

1 Shabir now amends his cash-flow forecast to give the following final balances from January to April: £1,650, £3,000, £3,700, £4,200. Do the amendments that Shabir has made improve the forecast cash flows? Justify your answer.

2 Shabir is thinking of spending £4,000 on a new machine. When would you advise him to do this? Give a reason for your decision.

Cash-flow forecasts and stakeholders

As you have already seen, the closing balance of a cash-flow forecast can show as a surplus or a deficit. If these figures are large then the various stakeholders linked to the business could have an interest in the situation as the following table shows.

Stakeholder	Surplus	Deficit
Owners	Pleased, as the extra money could be used to give them more income or would allow them to invest the money in the business to produce further improvements.	Worried, because a sustained deficit means that the business is not doing so well and it would be difficult to pay suppliers on time. In the short term, a bank loan may be needed. In the longer term costs, such as staffing, may have to be cut.
Employees	Job security as the business is doing well. May be prospects of a pay rise!	Worried as overtime may be restricted and even jobs cut. Pay may be frozen.
Customers	May not be very aware of financial situation. Possibly ensures good, well-funded after-sales service and better customer facilities.	Deliveries may be delayed due to cut-backs. Demands for prompt payment of money owing. Orders may not be fulfilled at all if the business is in deep trouble.
Financiers	Pleased as any outstanding loans can easily be repaid. Financiers would normally be happy to lend money to businesses with a healthy cash-flow surplus.	Worried that loans would not be repaid. Would be reluctant to lend money. May insist on early re-payment of any outstanding debts. Also could withdraw overdraft facilities.
Suppliers	Pleased since they know that there is plenty of money to pay them.	May find that payments are delayed, or even non-existent. Could demand payment on delivery or even refuse to supply goods/services at all.

Talk about it

In 2009, many retailers had difficulties staying in business when sales dropped sharply because of the economic situation. What do you think the cash-flow forecast of a small retail business would have looked like at the time? How many different types of stakeholders were involved and what might have been their main concerns? Discuss your ideas with your tutor.

Just checking

Explain what effect a proposed future payment on a large item of capital expenditure might have on a cash-flow forecast.

Explain why suppliers would be interested in the cash-flow situation of a business they deal with.

Patel Printing

	January (£)	February (£)	March (£)	April (£)
INFLOWS/RECEIPTS				
Printing revenue	22,000	17,000	21,000	24,000
Rental income	3,000	3,000	3,000	3,000
Total inflows/receipts	=SUM(B3:B4)	=SUM(C3:C4)	=SUM(D3:D4)	=SUM(E3:E4)
OUTFLOWS/PAYMENTS				
Labour	12,000	12,000	12,000	12,000
Electricity	950	950	950	950
Materials	8,000	10,000	7,000	8,500
Delivery	2,400	2,400	2,400	2,400
Miscellaneous	40	50	30	40
Total outflows/payments	=SUM(B9:B13)	=SUM(C9:C13)	=SUM(D9:D13)	=SUM(E9:E13)
Net inflow/outflow	=SUM(B6-B15)	=SUM(C6-C15)	=SUM(D6-D15)	=SUM(E6-E15)
Opening balance	0	=SUM(B18)	=SUM(C18)	=SUM(D18)
Closing balance	=SUM(B17+B16)	=SUM(C17+C16)	=SUM(D17+D16)	=SUM(E17+E16)

Cash-flow forecast for Patel Printing showing spreadsheet formulas

Use of spreadsheets

Spreadsheets are a useful way of compiling and working on a cash-flow forecast and statement. In this section you will learn how to do this. You will also learn that this technique has several advantages, but that there are also some disadvantages.

Building a cash-flow spreadsheet

Study the cash-flow forecast for Patel Printing carefully. You will note that the inserted figures are identical to those in the chart on page 192. The difference is that, wherever there is a calculation needed, the appropriate formulas are shown in the spaces. Even if you have not learned about spreadsheets, after a few minutes you should be able to see the logic of these formulas and how the formulas work. If you are still not sure, ask your tutor for help.

Case study – Jan's Florists

Jan runs a flower shop and is learning how to use a spreadsheet. She decides to produce a simple one to begin with so that she can build up her confidence.

As well as selling flowers, Jan also sells greeting cards. Help Jan by copying out the table and writing formulas into the appropriate boxes. Ask your tutor to check your results.

	A	January (£) B	February (£) C
1	**A**	**B**	**C**
2	**INFLOWS**		
3	Sale of flowers		
4	Sale of greeting cards		
5	**Total inflows**		
6	**OUTFLOWS**		
7	Flowers purchased		
8	Wages		
9	Electricity		
10	**Total outflows**		
11	**Net inflow/outflow**		
12	**Opening balance**		
13	**Closing balance**		

Advantages of using spreadsheets for cash-flow forecasting

- Calculations can be done quickly and accurately – provided that the formulas are correct! This also allows more time to study the information rather than carrying out tedious calculations.
- Re-calculations can be made quickly. This allows for **'what…if'** situations to be explored.
- Spreadsheets can be used to produce charts and line graphs.
- They can also be cut and pasted into other documents or presentations.
- Forecast cash flows and actual cash flows can be compared more easily. This allows the business to be able to see what is actually happening and make adjustments to their forecasts.

Disadvantages of using spreadsheets for cash-flow forecasting

- Spreadsheets can be too large to be seen on one screen or printed on one sheet of paper.
- A small mistake, such as a slight error in a formula, can be hard to detect and could lead to a major problem.
- Learning how to set out a spreadsheet does take time and effort. In some situations a pen, a piece of paper and a calculator could be quicker.
- Changes are easy to make but, unless each version is saved as a separate document, historical records may not exist.
- As with any task carried out on a computer, work can be lost. It is important to make back-up copies at regular intervals – and preferably in more than one memory system.

Cash-flow forecasts, cash-flow statements and liquidity

Remember that there is a difference between cash-flow forecasts and cash-flow statements, no matter how they are produced.

- Cash-flow forecasts are prepared using predicted income and expenditure. Cash-flow statements are completed using actual income and expenditure figures.
- Cash-flow forecasts enable managers to ensure they have enough cash available to operate the business and to take action promptly if they foresee a possible problem.
- Cash-flow statements show the situation which actually exists and identifies the actual liquidity position of the business at that point in time.

Describe it

Businesses should always be looking to the future to identify possible problems and opportunities. This is called **'what…if'** thinking. For example, '**What** would happen **if** we reduced costs by 10%?'

Talk about it

A major disaster for anyone preparing a spreadsheet is to lose all or part of their work because of a computer problem or because of their own carelessness! Suggest the actions you could take to prevent this happening.

Just checking

Give at least two advantages of using spreadsheets for cash-flow forecasts.

Suggest two potential problems when spreadsheets are used for cash-flow forecasts.

4.2 Investigating business budgets

Budgets and budgeting

A **budget** is an estimate of the amount of money planned to be spent in the future on an item or a list of items. Budgets are another example of a planning tool to help a business manage and control its finances more effectively.

Budgets range in scope and complexity. Major projects, like the London Olympics in 2012, can be very difficult to prepare budgets for because of the length of time involved and the nature of the project. For a small business, budgets can be much simpler and sometimes much more accurate as a result.

In planning for the 2012 London Olympic Games, the original budget was estimated at £2.4 **billion**. This figure has had to be revised and some people claim that in the end the total cost will be £20 billion.

This section explains how budgets and budgetary control are used in business. Various types of budget are examined as well as the way they allow managers to take action before problems get out of hand. You will also learn how a budget system can also help to **motivate** managers to perform better.

Why are budgets necessary?

In this unit and in Unit 2 you learned that there are several ways of measuring financial performance, such as cash flow, break-even analysis, balance sheets, and profit and loss accounts – so why do we need budgets? The simple answer is that all the other statements give information about the business as a whole. They are of little use in helping individual managers in the business make day-to-day decisions.

How are budgets produced?

Budgets are normally written for a year in advance, broken down into monthly stages. In medium-sized and large businesses, each department will have its own budget. The starting point would normally be the previous budget and what changes should be made to produce the next one. The main things to consider are:

- How well did the previous budget work? Was it overspent or under-spent? What lessons can be learned?
- What level of activity is expected? For example, in a production department, how many items do they expect to produce?
- Budgets cannot be set in isolation. For example, production and marketing must agree on how many goods are to be made and sold.

Describe it

A **budget** is a plan that identifies, estimates and itemises future spending.

A **billion** is a thousand million, so just one billion pounds is a lot of money. If your first car costs you £2,500, how many could you buy for a billion pounds?

Motivation is an incentive that inspires workers to work hard and attempt to achieve the goals and aims of a business.

Talk about it

Jack and James are brothers. Jack has always found it easy to live within his income. If times are hard he simply spends less. James is forever writing out a budget for himself, but never sticks to it.

Are you a Jack or a James? And if you are a Jack, what would you advise any 'James' in your group to do? Debate the issue and decide!

Apply it

Seatright is a small business that makes reasonably cheap chairs for conference halls and restaurants. The production budget for one month is shown below.

Item	Planned monthly expenditure (£)
Cloth for seat covers	12,000
Sheet metal	9,000
Steel tubing	7,500
Wages	16,500
Electricity	2,000
Machine maintenance	3,000
Total	50,000

Study the sample budget carefully. You will see that the expenditure section is itemised with a planned amount of money to be spent each month against each item.

- Who decides on the budget? It may be senior managers in a business who decide on the overall budget for a business and from this decide the individual budgets that departments within the business have to work to.
- Can any savings be made? For Seatright, can cheaper steel be used or less scrap produced?
- The new budget should be seen as a challenge to the manager who is also known as the **budget holder**. The target should be hard, but achievable. Budgets should not be imposed on managers – ideally they should be agreed beforehand.

Feedback on budgets

Information on what money is spent under each heading is collected and presented every week or month so that any problems that may be developing can be identified quickly and the manager can take action to put them right.

Revenue budgets

As you have seen, most budgets concentrate on expenditure. However, someone has to keep an eye on the income so that, at the end of the day, income is planned to be greater than expenditure. In private businesses, income or revenue comes mainly from customers. There are other possible sources, such as Government grants, sale of equipment or buildings or rental income. A revenue budget could list all of these with amounts of money written against each heading.

Talk about it

In a group, discuss how easy or difficult it would be to prepare a personal budget listing all your items of income and expenditure for the next month. Then say how easy or difficult it would be to keep to it!

Describe it

A **budget holder** is the manager responsible for trying to ensure that expenditure is kept within the budget.

Take it further

Working in small groups, identify the similarities and differences between budgets and cash-flow forecasts. Compare your ideas as a class.

Case study – The vandal budget!

Budget items will depend upon the type of business and what it spends money on. At Harry Ramsden's fish and chip shop in Blackpool, vandals broke the front window so often that they allowed £500 per week in the budget to pay for repairs!

Just checking

Explain in one or two sentences what the term 'budget' means in a business context.

Why are budgets an essential part of the financial planning process?

Describe it

Financial discipline means controlling business expenditure to the levels required by the budget.

Variance is the difference between the planned and actual amount in a budget.

'I wish I'd known we were in so much trouble six months ago.'

Remember it

Budgets, cash-flow statements, profit and loss accounts and balance sheets are all different documents that tell a business different things. This information helps to improve decision-making.

Budgetary control

The main purpose of having budgets is to *control* business expenditure and provide employees in the business with a guide to what is available to be spent in a particular time period. Having this **financial discipline** is important in decision-making where choices have to be made. We say that drivers are in control of a car when they see what is happening on the road ahead and then brake, accelerate or change direction accordingly. Budgetary control means the same thing. Actual expenditure is compared with the amount that was planned in the budget and then appropriate action is taken if necessary.

Budget reports showing variances

Below you can see an extended version of the Seatright budget to which two columns have been added – actual expenditure and variance. These two columns are completed at the end of the budget period. For a production budget, this means the items have actually been made. For a sales budget, this means the items have now been sold. The completed budget report provides feedback to the budget holder.

Variance is the difference between the planned expenditure and the actual figure. Note that when actual expenditure is bigger than planned expenditure the figure is negative, indicating a potential problem.

Item	Planned monthly expenditure (£)	Actual expenditure (£)	Variance (£)
Cloth for seat covers	12,000	15,000	–3,000
Sheet metal	9,000	8,500	500
Steel tubing	7,500	7,800	–300
Wages	16,500	14,000	2,500
Electricity	2,000	1,900	100
Machine maintenance	3,000	3,000	0
Total	50,000	50,200	–200

Seatright budget feedback

Assessing budget reports and feedback

The manager who is responsible for the budget needs to look at the budget report very carefully and think about the following points:

- What is the total variance? The main worry is if it is a high negative figure.
- Any individual large negative variances should be a cause for concern. Action must be taken to investigate and improve the situation in the months to follow.

- Large positive variances are good news, but need to be investigated because planning should ideally be more precise.
- Small variances are not too important, but if they persist for some time for any given item, they may need investigating.
- Any significant variances that recur month after month may mean that the budget has to be adjusted the next time round.

Motivation and budgets

Motivation in business relates to how keen and eager an individual is to work hard and do a good job. Businesses can encourage a worker to behave in a particular way that helps achieve the businesses goals. Most people are motivated if they feel that they are doing well. You probably know yourself that if you are given praise and encouragement you are more likely to put in increased effort to achieve a higher standard.

The budget process can motivate employees in two ways – at the budget setting stage, and when receiving budget feedback.

Motivation when budgets are agreed

Everyone likes a challenge and most people like to feel they are good at something. For a manager, setting and agreeing a budget should result in targets that are challenging, but achievable. If this works, the manager is then motivated to meet or even improve on the targets that were set. In some ways, this is similar to putting managers in the position of being entrepreneurs because it allows them to make their own decisions about how to run their own part of the business.

> ### Talk about it
> In a group, in turn, talk about a situation where you feel that you really achieved something special. It could be in sport, getting a high score in a computer game – or even achieving a good grade for an assignment.

Motivation by budgetary control

Managers can be motivated by budgetary control because they receive feedback on their performance when they receive the budget report. This can encourage the budget holder to work harder or differently in the future to achieve the target.

> ### Talk about it
> In some businesses, successful budget holders may find their targets have increased for the following year. How sensible do you think this is and how might it affect motivation? Discuss your ideas as a class.

> ### Apply it
> Use the checklist to assess the Seatright budget report. Make a comment against each item of expenditure. Then compare your ideas as a class.

> ### Just checking
> Explain the use of the term 'control' in the budget process.
>
> Explain what is meant by the term 'variance'.

Different types of budget

The budget process

In medium-sized and large organisations, the managers of most **functional areas** have a budget for the area they control. These organisations therefore have several budgets and these have to complement each other like the pieces of a jigsaw that have to fit together.

Remember it

Functional areas are departments, such as production and sales, which you learned about in Unit 1. The managers of these departments are responsible for making sure that their budget targets are met.

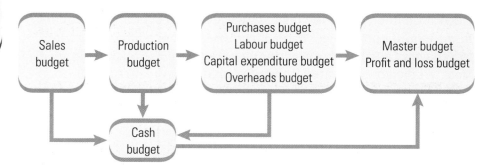

How budgets are linked

The diagram above shows the budget process. You should bear in mind that this process often starts several weeks or even months before the start of the budget year. For example, if a firm's budget year runs from the start of June in one year to the end of May the following year, the process of setting the budget could be started in March.

- The starting point is to agree the sales budget. This forecasts the number of products or level of service the business plans to achieve in the following year. The sales budget gives the plan for the level of activity that the business expects to achieve for the budget year. This means, for example, the number of products that the business should make and sell over the twelve-month period. This is the starting point for all of the other budgets.

- Once the level of activity has been set, the next step is to compile the production budget. For this, the production manager and staff have to decide how they plan to produce the goods.

- When this has been decided, the purchasing department has to set targets for the price and quantity of materials needed.

- The labour budget is set by deciding on how many people will be needed and how much they will be paid. The labour budget is the total cost of wages, normally for the people directly involved in production.

- The overheads budget relates to costs not directly linked to the production of goods or services.

- At the same time, the capital expenditure budget – which sets expenditure on large items of equipment and buildings – is also agreed. For example, if the level of activity is planned to increase by 30%, the production department may need extra machinery which means building an extension onto the factory.

- A cash budget forecast, which is very similar to a cash-flow forecast, is produced which takes all of these factors into account. For example, the sales forecast will provide information on the income expected and the labour budget will provide one component of the expenditure expected.

All of these budgets are put together to create a master budget that summarises all of the income and expenditure planned for each month in the budget year. This is often shown as a budgeted profit and loss account. These follow a similar format to the actual profit and loss accounts that you learned about in Unit 2, but are based on estimates and planned sales.

Remember it

The starting point of the budget process is to set the level of activity. This can also be called **projected sales**. In the manufacturing industry, this is the number of products expected to be made and sold.

Apply it

The sales department for a mobile phone manufacturer forecasts that sales will fall by 25% in the next 12 months. Look at each type of budget identified in the budget process and suggest how it could be affected by this information. Compare your ideas as a group.

Take it further

Some people say that a budget should be a **plan**, not a **forecast**. Why do you think that they say this?

Other differences between types of budgets

There are several other differences between budgets that are useful to know and understand.

Sales budgets

The main budget that concerns the sales department is the one that forecasts the level of activity for the 12-month budget period. The main things to consider are:

- What happened last year? Can we do better?
- What are the trends in the market?
- What is the current economic climate like?
- What do we know about competitors' activity?
- Would an aggressive promotional campaign boost sales?
- Is this a seasonal market (see page 187)?

The sales department has two main decisions to make. It has to decide upon the target level of sales and the price of the products. But one of these usually affects the other! A low price can lead to a high volume of sales whereas increasing the price can reduce sales levels.

The figure for forecast income from sales is also used in the cash budget. For one product (remember that many businesses sell more than one product) the formula is:

Income = number of products sold x price

The sales or marketing department will also have a budget for expenses, such as advertising and promotions, staff costs and market research.

Budget challenges = To maximise overall sales income whilst keeping sales expenses as low as possible.

Just checking

Explain why all senior managers are involved in the budget process.

Identify which budget plan is normally the first to be produced.

Remember it

Zero-based budgets are budgets compiled when a business is starting up. There is no historical information to help, for instance, to forecast a sales figure.

Describe it

In manufacturing terms **quality** means producing a product that is fit to sell. Those that are not fit to sell are called rejects.

In most manufacturing processes, mistakes are made which result in products that are not up to standard. These either have to be repaired (re-worked) or **scrapped** because they are not fit to be sold.

Assessment tip

In the exam you may be asked to calculate simple sales and production budget figures and comment on the results. This usually means identifying whether the business will benefit or not based on the figures you have calculated.

Production budgets

For many manufacturing businesses, such as car makers, this is the largest budget in terms of total cost. Typical items in a production budget are:

- Labour costs (see also below)
- Production materials (raw materials and components)
- Energy (gas and electricity)
- Maintenance of equipment
- Stock and storage.

Budget challenges = To produce maximum **quality** output whilst using the minimum number of resources, such as labour, materials etc. This means, amongst other things, keeping the amount of waste or **scrap** material to an absolute minimum.

Purchases (materials)

The purchases budget is set to work out the cost of the materials used in production. Manufacturing companies often have a department that specialises in purchasing these materials. Once they know the number of products to be sold, they have to plan to purchase the materials required at the minimum cost, bearing in mind the quality they need. They also have to find reliable suppliers who will deliver the goods on time.

Budget challenges = To buy high quality goods at reasonable prices and with reliable deliveries.

Labour

A labour budget is set because most businesses need employees to produce goods or provide a service. The cost of labour is also part of the production budget. Labour costs will increase if extra workers are needed or if staff are paid higher overtime rates. Businesses often try to reduce their labour costs. This may be possible by automating a process with machinery, using modern technology or setting up a facility overseas where labour costs are cheaper, such as factories in China and call centres in India.

Budget challenges = To retain high quality staff whilst keeping the wage bill to a minimum.

Overheads

Overheads are costs that are not directly connected to production. They are sometimes known as 'indirect costs'. Examples of overhead costs are management salaries, heating and building maintenance. Quite often, the overhead budget is divided between the various departmental budgets, for example on the basis of floor area.

Budget challenges = To keep overheads to a minimum whilst providing a reasonable level of service.

Cash budget

This is the same as the cash-flow forecast you learned about in the last section. It shows how money will be moved to and from the firm's bank account. It will also include planned expenditure from the capital expenditure budget described next.

Budget challenges = To keep a small, but positive amount in the current bank account.

Capital expenditure budget

Capital expenditure is money spent on large, durable items such as machinery, vehicles and buildings. Quite often, capital expenditure is planned more than a year ahead. However, the portion to be spent in one year is included in that year's budget. Note that capital expenditure is linked to decisions about sources of funds, which is explained on page 219.

Budget challenges = To make sure that the total cost of owning capital equipment (purchase, maintenance, disposal) is kept to a minimum.

Profit and loss

In Unit 2, you learned that businesses produce a profit and loss account for a financial year. As its name suggests, it shows the overall performance of the business for that year. A forecast profit and loss budget is first produced from the master budget and can then be updated as the business progresses through the year.

Talk about it

Identify the routine items of expenditure you have at home, why bills can increase and how this can affect household budgets. Then list those items that would also apply to a business. Discuss your ideas as a class.

Assessment tip

In the exam you may be asked about the purpose of budgets in general, or of a particular type of budget, such as the production budget.

Just checking

Identify at least two expenditure items which would normally appear in a production department's budget.

Apply it

You are investigating a small manufacturing business that makes jeans. Last year the business sold 20,000 pairs of jeans at £30 each. 2,000 jeans could not be sold because of faults during cutting and finishing.

1   **Calculate the cost to the business of the faulty jeans.**
2   **What type of production materials might this type of business use?**
3   **The owner is considering increasing the price of jeans this year to customers. What is the danger of doing this?**
4   **What other items, besides production materials, will you find in the production budget?**
5   **The owner wants to automate the process for cutting the material into the outline shape for jeans. (a) Suggest two benefits to the business of doing this. (b) What budget will contain the planned expenditure on the new machine?**
6   **The owner wants to increase his profit next year. Suggest how he could budget to do this.**

Discuss your ideas in small groups and compare your suggestions as a class.

Interpreting budgets and the application of ICT

As you have already learned, budgets are designed to give feedback to managers about their departments – and therefore their own performance. Managers must therefore study budget feedback reports carefully and be able to interpret them so that they can take the best action possible.

Remember it

Favourable variances occur when expenditure is less than planned.

Adverse variances occur when expenditure is greater than planned.

In this section you will learn that different types of business will have different types of budgets. You will also be shown how to do simple budget calculations. In addition you will learn about how managers interpret variances – both **favourable** and **adverse**. Finally the use of ICT in the budget process will be explained.

The range of budgets used in different businesses

So far in section 4.2 you have learned about the budget system of manufacturing businesses. Read about the following two businesses and then complete the tasks listed below that follow them.

Assessment tip

Different types of organisation have different budget structures. In the exam any budgets will relate to the business described in the scenario at the start of the paper.

Apply it

A Vitality is a hotel, leisure and fitness complex. It comprises a hotel with 50 bedrooms, a restaurant with 100 covers (a 'cover' is a table setting for a customer), a golf course, six tennis courts and a gymnasium. There is also a conference centre with four seminar rooms.

B Universal Horticulture Ltd is a business that is based on a garden centre. As well as supplying plants to domestic customers, it also offers a service that maintains domestic and business customers' gardens. In both cases, this means cutting lawns, planting bedding plants, weeding and trimming hedges and shrubs. In addition the business offers a service that provides potted plants for exhibitions, weddings and other major events.

1 **For each of these businesses, suggest two departments that could hold separate budgets. Note that there are no fixed rules about this! The main point is that you can justify your choice of departments.**

2 **For each of these budget areas, list one item of income and three of expenditure that would be likely to appear in the budget.**

Sales budget calculations and variances

Metalica is owned by Jack Holt. The business makes wheelbarrows and metal pressings for a local kit-car manufacturer. All scrap metal is sold to a local merchant. Part of the factory yard is rented out to haulage contractors. The rental varies from month-to-month depending on the number of lorries parked. The sales budget for May is shown below. When the budget is completed the variance is calculated by finding the difference between the planned sales and the actual sales.

Sales budget for May			
Sales	Budgeted sales for May (£)	Actual sales for May (£)	Variance for May (£)
Wheelbarrows	58,900		
Kit-car parts	25,700		
Scrap	4,000		
Yard rental	1,900		
Total	90,500		

Apply it

Copy out the budget table above and enter the actual sales figures. These are: £53,000 for wheelbarrows, £32,000 for kit-car parts, £6,000 for scrap and £1,500 for yard rental.

Complete the table by calculating the variances and totals in each column.

Work in small groups to examine the completed budget and to decide your answers to the following questions.

1 **How do you think the budget holder will react to each of the variance figures and why?**

2 **Suggest possible reasons for each variance figure.**

3 **What would be the total variance for the year if this degree of variance was repeated for the rest of the year (i.e. for the next 11 months)? How might this affect the profit and loss account?**

Production budget calculations

A production budget at Metalica takes into account the number of items to be made as well as the cost of making them. Each wheelbarrow costs £30 to make and sells for £50 and each kit-car pressing costs £15 to make and sells for £25. Therefore the number of items that must be produced in May is calculated from the budgeted sales (£58,900 divided by 50 and £25,700 divided by 25).

A summary of the output for the next three months is shown below. Jack wants to work out the total costs of producing wheelbarrows and kit-car pressings over the three months. To do this he must multiply the total number of each item by the cost of producing them.

Apply it

Help Jack by calculating the total cost of producing (a) wheelbarrows and (b) kit-car pressings over the three months (May to July).

Month	Number of wheelbarrows to be made	Number of kit–car pressings to make
May	1,178	1,028
June	1,200	1,100
July	1,200	900
Total	3,578	3,028

Production budgets and variances

A production budget can also be produced on a monthly basis and variances calculated at the end of the period – just like you saw for the sales budget. Below is Jack's planned wheelbarrow production budget for the month of May.

Production Budget for May			
Items made	Budgeted production (£)	Actual production (£)	Variance (£)
Steel	8,000		
Wheels	5,700		
Tyres	6,500		
Wages	11,500		
Maintenance	2,000		
Fuel	1,640		
Total	35,340		

Apply it

Copy out the budget. Then enter the actual production figures for May. These are:

£12,000 for wages, £2,600 for fuel, £8,500 for steel, £5,000 for wheels, £6,500 for tyres, £1,500 for maintenance.

Complete the table by calculating the variances and totals in each column.

This time work on your own to choose the two variance figures that you think would be of most interest to the production manager. Be ready to justify your choices. In both cases, identify two reasons that could explain the cause of the variances. Compare your ideas with those of other members of your class.

Assessment tip

In the exam it can be useful to work out the totals for each column and use these as a check on your other calculations. In this example the total variance figure should equal the difference between the planned and actual totals.

Favourable and adverse variances

Favourable variances occur when the amount of money spent is *less* than that planned in the budget. **Adverse variances** happen when *more* money is spent than planned. Small variances within two or three per cent of the budget figure would not receive too much attention. This is because it is almost impossible to precisely achieve any budget target.

Large variances, whether favourable or adverse, need to be investigated.

Large favourable variances are good news in the sense that they contribute to the overall profitability of the business. However, they still mean that there has been an unexpected change of some kind. So the budget holder must still investigate to discover why this change took place. If the change is permanent then the budget itself may have to be adjusted.

Large adverse variances are a more serious problem. If there are too many or if they are repeated month after month, the business could make a loss. Again, if the problem cannot be solved, the budget itself may have to be changed in the future or serious decisions may need to be taken about the future viability of the business.

ICT and budgets

As you know, ICT is invaluable when many routine calculations have to be made quickly and accurately. It therefore has a part to play in the budget process. The main aspects are:

- Once budget planning data is input into the computer it can be easily retrieved.
- Amendments to the plan can be tested on a 'what … if' basis.
- Once budget performance figures are input, the variance and other calculations can be carried out almost instantly.
- The budget information can be accessed by a wide range of people – provided that they have clearance to do so.
- Budget software packages can be bought 'off the shelf'.
- More sophisticated packages can use data directly from other financial databases to provide almost continuous feedback.

Take it further

If you are familiar with using a spreadsheet package like Microsoft Excel, use this to work out the variance and total calculations for the production budget on page 206.

Just checking

Why would it be useful for managers to be able to look at the budget performance for their department on their computer?

What two figures would be multiplied together to give total sales income?

4.3 Investigating break-even analysis in business

Break-even analysis and break-even point

You have learned already that businesses receive money as income and pay out money as expenditure. The aim is to have more income than expenditure so that the business makes a profit. If the reverse is true, the result is a loss. If the income is the same as expenditure, the business is said to be **breaking-even**.

Describe it

Break-even is when income and expenditure are the same. There is no profit, but no loss either.

Case study – Gas boiler efficiency

Tom has a domestic gas central heating boiler. He reckons that it costs him £1,000 a year for gas to run it. An engineer tells him that new boilers are much more efficient and over 90% of the energy in the gas is turned into useable heat. Tom is told that the price of a new boiler is £2,000 but it will only cost him £700 each year in gas. He divides £2,000 by £300 (which is the difference between the current gas bill and the new one) and reckons that he will recoup the cost of installation in six or seven years. In other words, in no more than seven years he should break-even on his investment.

Apply it

Carry out the calculation Tom did yourself to make sure that you understand Tom's reasoning.

The example of Tom's boiler is just one way in which break-even is calculated. In this section you will learn how businesses calculate and use break-even analysis. You will learn how the break-even point can be found both by using a graph and by applying a formula.

You will also see how businesses use break-even analysis to help make decisions and, at the same time, realise that the method has its limitations. Finally you will see how ICT can be used to assist break-even analysis.

Take it further

What other factors should Tom think about when making his investment decision?

At least we broke-even!

Types of costs

In this section you will learn how to carry out break-even calculations. First you need to know about the various components of the calculation. An example, Noha's burger van, will be used to illustrate the various points.

Case study – Noha's burger van

Noha has a van that he drives to outdoor events, such as music festivals and funfairs, to sell burgers. He knows that he is doing reasonably well because every year he has enough money in the bank to have a week's holiday in Spain. His friend Judy has just finished a business studies course and tells Noha that he should analyse his business more carefully. She warned him that things could go wrong without him realising and also that there could be opportunities to improve the business.

Judy tells Noha that carrying out a break-even analysis should help him to understand his business better and help him to plan more effectively. She says that the first stage is to write down all of the items he spends money on. Opposite you can read the list Noha produced.

> Noha's costs
> Onions
> Van maintenance (including servicing and tyres)
> Margarine
> Gas for cooking
> Road tax
> Bread buns
> Petrol
> Raw burgers
> Sauces

Judy then tells Noha that he needs to divide these items into two lists – one called 'fixed costs' and one called 'variable costs'. **Fixed costs** are those that are not dependent on the amount of burgers he sells. For example, when he drives to a festival, he spends money on petrol even if he does not sell a single burger.

Judy then explains that **variable costs** are those that increase directly in proportion to the number of burgers he sells. For example, if Noha doubles the amount of burgers he sells, he doubles the money he spends on buns.

Noha then produces the list opposite.

Judy asks Noha why he has put the gas he uses as a fixed cost. Noha replies that this is because he tends to leave the hot plate on all of the time even when he is not cooking for a few minutes.

> Fixed cost
> Van maintenance
> Gas for cooking
> Road tax
> Petrol
> Variable costs
> Onions
> Margarine
> Bread buns
> Raw burgers
> Sauces

Describe it

Fixed costs are those that do not depend on the amount of goods produced or sold.

Variable costs are those that change in proportion to the level of production.

Talk about it

A haulage company carries out contract work for other companies. Working in small groups, identify as many fixed and variable costs for such a business as you can. Check your ideas as a class.

Just checking

What two figures are equal at the break-even point?

Explain the meaning of 'fixed costs' and 'variable costs'.

Break-even charts

Judy tells Noha that the next thing he needs to learn is what a break-even chart looks like. These can be produced like a graph, as you will see in the example below.

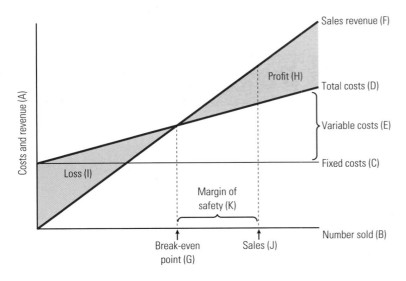

Judy says that although the chart may look complicated at first, if it is studied one step at a time it is logical and straightforward. Each step is given below.

A Costs and revenue The vertical axis of the graph shows the amount of money which is both spent as costs and received in revenue.

B Number sold The horizontal axis shows the number of items produced/sold – in Noha's case these are his burgers.

C Fixed costs The fixed costs line shows the total amount of fixed costs. The fact that the costs are fixed is shown by the straight horizontal line that does not change however many (or few) items are sold.

D Total costs The next line to find is the total cost line. This shows the fixed costs *plus* the variable costs. It starts at the left hand side at the point where the fixed costs line meets the vertical axis. At this position there is no production so the variable costs are zero. The line is then drawn to show how the variable costs increase in proportion to the number of items sold. The line then shows the total cost for any particular level of sales.

E Variable costs The difference between the fixed costs line and the total costs line shows the variable costs. This gap always widens to the right as variable costs increase for each item produced.

F Sales revenue The sales revenue line shows the total income for any particular level of sales. It starts at zero because if there are no sales, there is no income! The sales revenue line is found by multiplying the price charged by the number of items sold.

G Break-even point The point where the total costs line crosses the sales revenue line is the break-even point.

H Profit To the right of the break-even point, the difference between the two lines shows the amount of profit possible at all levels of sales.

I Loss To the left of the break-even point, the difference shows the amount of loss that would be made at all levels of sales.

J Sales If the amount of sales is as shown at (J) on the graph, then more items are being made than are needed to break-even.

K Margin of safety This is the difference between the sales figure shown at (J) and the break-even point. It shows the amount by which sales would have to fall before the business was about to make a loss.

Apply it

Work through the steps with your tutor. Refer to the chart as you do this. You might find it useful to do this two or three times. Then ask questions if there is anything you still don't understand.

Remember it

A **break-even chart/graph** is a pictorial way of illustrating a break-even situation. It is often easier to understand a graph than a page full of numbers.

Constructing a break-even graph

Judy tells Noha that he now needs to construct a break-even graph for his own business. To do this he needs to work out his fixed costs and his variable costs per week. He also needs to know his selling price and the maximum number of items he expects to sell in a week. Noha's information is shown here.

Fixed costs for one week		Variable costs for one week (per burger)	
Van maintenance	£30	Onions	5p
Gas for cooking	£5	Margarine	2p
Road tax	£10	Bread buns	12p
Petrol	£55	Raw burgers	50p
		Sauces	1p

Selling price of each burger is £1.20

Maximum possible weekly sales = 400 burgers

Completing an activity table

Judy tells Noha that a useful first step is to put the information into an activity table. This shows what the costs and sales income would be at different levels of business activity. She says it makes it much easier to draw the graph afterwards.

- Judy starts by totalling Noha's fixed costs. She enters these into the fixed costs cells in the table.
- Then she totals up his variable costs. She has to multiply this total by the number of burgers sold and enter the information into each cell.
- She adds these two figures together to obtain the total cost information.
- Finally, she calculates his income from sales to complete the top row.

Apply it

Judy's partially completed activity table is shown below. Copy this out and check you understand all the figures that have been entered. Then complete the blank cells using the information above and check your work with your tutor.

Number of burgers sold	0	200	400
Sales revenue			480
Variable costs	0	140	
Fixed costs	100		100
Total costs	100		

Assessment tip

In the exam you may be advised to complete an activity table before you draw a break-even graph. This is sensible because you then have all the figures you need. You will also need to label your chart properly so it is wise to practise doing this from memory.

Take it further

1. Use the activity table to draw a break-even chart for Noha's business. Label both axes, draw the costs and revenue lines, and find the break-even point. Label this and show the profit and loss areas.

   Assuming that Noha sells 300 burgers a week at £1.20 per burger, plot this on your graph and then show his margin of safety. Use the partially completed activity table Judy drew to help you if necessary.

2. Use your chart to find out how much profit Noha will make if he sells 400 burgers, and how much he will lose if he only sells 100 burgers.

3. Noha tells Judy that he is thinking about increasing his price to £4.50. Add the new sales line to your chart. What happens to the break-even point?

4. Write a note to Noha explaining what the break-even and margin of safety figures mean for his business.

Talk about it

Noha wants to improve his business so that he makes more profit. How might he do this? In a group, suggest as many ideas as possible.

Just checking

Name the three lines (not the axes) which are drawn onto a break-even chart.

Between which two lines do the profit/loss areas appear?

Apply it

Use the break-even formula to calculate the break-even point for Noha's burger business if he charges £2.50 per burger. Then check it agrees with the figure you found when you plotted the graph.

Assessment tip

You don't need to learn the formula. If you are asked to use it in the external assessment then the formula will be shown on the examination paper.

Take it further

Tess wonders what will happen to the break-even level of sales if she reduced the selling price of her T-shirts to £5. Can you tell her?

Using a formula to calculate the break-even point

As well as producing a break-even chart, you can also use a formula to find the break-even point. This is shown below. In this section you will learn how to use it.

$$\text{Break-even point} = \frac{\text{Fixed costs}}{\text{Selling price per unit less Variable cost per unit}}$$

Tess has decided to start her own T-shirt business, producing customised T-shirts for children and adults. She wants to see how profitable it will be and can work this out using the break-even formula. Tess's expected costs and revenues are shown below.

Fixed costs (which include rent, business rates, gas, electricity and wages for a part-time assistant) = £1,200 a month

Variable cost of each T-shirt (which comprises plain T-shirts plus ink) average £5.00 per shirt.

The average selling price is £7.00 per shirt.

Tess applies the formula in the following way:

$$\text{Break-even point} = \frac{£1,200}{£7-£5} = \frac{£1,200}{£2} = 600$$

Tess now knows that she needs to sell 600 shirts a month to break-even.

Note: the selling price per unit less variable cost per unit is sometimes called 'the contribution'.

Apply it

Practise using the formula by copying out the table below. Then complete it by calculating the break-even point for each of the eight sets of figures. Round your results to the nearest whole number if necessary.

	Fixed costs (£)	Selling price per unit (£)	Variable cost per unit (£)	Break-even point
A	100,000	26	10	
B	26,000	107	81	
C	13,000	11	7	
D	20 million	500,000	300,000	
E	68,275	187	56	
F	87,000	199	106	
G	26,300	1,721	864	
H	1.8 million	21	17	

Case study – Busy Builders Ltd

Busy Builders is a small privately owned building firm that specialises in building low-cost houses aimed at first-time buyers. It borrows money from a bank to buy land to build on and uses the proceeds of sales to pay the interest. It employs mainly permanent staff such as bricklayers, joiners and labourers. It also hires some tradesmen, such as electricians and plumbers, when they are needed. Equipment required, such as cement mixers and diggers, are leased. The costs involved are:

Fixed costs each year Labour £1,500,000, interest on loan £300,000, lease of equipment £120,000, insurance and other fixed costs £80,000.

Variable costs for each house Fuel £1,000, bricks £10,000, timber £6,000, concrete £4,000, sand and cement for mortar £3,000, roof tiles £6,000, contract labour £14,000, other materials (wire, pipes etc) £6,000.

The houses will sell for £100,000 each and Busy Builders is planning to build a maximum of 60 houses.

1 **Use the information on Busy Builders to complete the activity table shown below. Remember that before you do this, you will need to calculate the total fixed costs and the total variable costs.**

Number of houses sold	0	20	40	60
Sales revenue	£'000	£'000	£'000	£'000
Variable costs				
Fixed costs				
Total costs				

Note that the columns are headed '£'000'. This means that the figures underneath should be multiplied by £1,000, so the figure of £2,000,000 will now be written as £2,000. You can use this idea on the vertical axis when you draw the graph in your answer to question 2. It is often used to save writing down very long numbers.

2 **Now construct a break-even chart. Label all the features clearly and make a note of the break-even point. Use the break-even formula to check your result. From your graph read off the following information:**

   (a) **The sales revenue, total cost and profit if 50 houses are sold.**

   (b) **If 45 houses are sold, what is the margin of safety?**

   (c) **If only 20 houses are sold, how much money would Busy Builders lose?**

3 **Busy Builders is worried because the housing market has slowed down. If it lowered the house price to £75,000 can the firm still break-even? Use the formula to find out.**

Just checking

Use the formula given on page 212 to calculate the break-even point when the fixed costs are £3,000, the selling price is £5.00 and the variable cost per item is £4.00.

Give at least two reasons why using a chart to calculate break-even is better than using the formula.

Talk about it

There are two ways of calculating break-even. Discuss the relative strengths and weaknesses of each.

Uses and limitations of break-even analysis

Break-even analysis is an extremely useful technique, but it also has its limits. This section looks at both of these aspects, first of all from a general view and then in relation to each component of the graph. You will also learn how ICT can be used to help to calculate break-even.

General uses of break-even analysis

There are several types of situation when break-even analysis can be used:

- Usually break-even analysis is used to look at possible future situations and to help planning. This could be an overall picture of the business. It is often argued that break-even analysis is most useful when it is used to look at a single product.

- It can help managers to decide whether to produce more goods as this will mean an increase in costs as well as in sales revenue.

- It can help managers to decide whether it would be worth borrowing money to produce a completely new product, as the business would have to pay interest on any loans.

- Break-even analysis can be used with other techniques such as cash-flow analysis. These are often incorporated in a **business plan** (see page 224).

- It can help a business to decide whether to invest money to improve an existing product.

- It can help a business to decide on its price for a product and to show what might happen to the break-even level of sales if it decided to change the price.

Analysing the results of a break-even analysis

Each part of a break-even graph or formula can be examined individually to look for opportunities or threats. In particular, the effect of changes to the selling price or any increases or reductions in costs can be calculated.

- The total revenue line shows the forecast income from sales. This can be changed by increasing or lowering the selling price of the product. The new level of sales can be predicted giving the new income level. Similarly the effect of additional advertising (which would also increase the fixed cost) could be seen.

- Normally fixed costs should be kept to a minimum. An exception would be where additional expenditure, for example on advertising, could more than pay for itself with extra sales. Examples of reducing fixed costs would be moving to cheaper premises and sub-contracting non-specialist work, such as distribution.

Describe it

A **business plan** is a document that is prepared as an overall prediction of the business' potential performance. It is normally prepared for potential investors, such as banks, who will want this information if they are asked to provide a loan.

- Fixed costs can change and this can affect the break-even analysis. For example, the cost of business insurance or business rates might increase.
- Similarly variable costs should be reduced wherever possible. Examples would be looking for cheaper suppliers of materials and negotiating better deals with energy suppliers.

Limitations of break-even analysis

Any form of analysis has its strengths and weaknesses. It is important that anyone using break-even analysis is aware of what it can and what it cannot do. Otherwise poor decisions could be made which result in the business losing money. The main areas to be aware of are shown below.

- A business could forecast a sales level well above the break-even point – and therefore appear to make a profit. In reality, sales could fall far short of this because of aggressive competition or products that lack sales appeal.
- Fixed and variable costs could change, both for better or worse. For example, in 2008 the price of crude oil increased sharply. This led to an increase in transport and other costs for many businesses.
- Sometimes it is difficult to decide whether a cost should be categorised as fixed or variable. For example, in a factory, electricity is used for lighting (fixed) and also to run production machinery (variable). Normally some sort of allocation is made between fixed and variable cost levels.
- Sales income is normally based on a standard selling price that does not allow for discounts or special offers.
- Break-even analysis is easier to apply to businesses that produce products compared to those that supply a service. The main reason is that fixed costs are usually higher for businesses that supply a service. For example, a hairdresser employed by a salon is normally paid whether or not there are any customers. This makes the application of break-even analysis more difficult, but not impossible.
- Break-even analysis is more complicated when it is applied to more than one product. In this case, the balance of costs and revenue between the products must be constantly reviewed.

Talk about it

It has been reported that the cost of running the traffic warden system in an English county is greater than the income from fines. Do you think the issue of parking tickets should be a self-financing system? Decide your opinion as a class.

Just checking

Suggest at least three situations in business when break-even analysis could be used.

Give two reasons why a break-even analysis might prove to be inaccurate.

The application of ICT to break-even analysis

As with many routine financial analysis/calculations in business, ICT can provide an efficient and accurate way of achieving the task. This is because you can set up a spreadsheet quite simply to work out the break-even point using the formula shown on page 212.

Tess has used ICT to produce the spreadsheet below. It is the same calculation that was carried out on page 212. She has used it to find out the break-even point for her T-shirts. The spreadsheet is shown twice, first with the numbers in the cells and then with the formulas instead.

Work through both examples and check that you understand all the entries.

- The starting point is the fixed costs figure.
- The next entries relate to the variable costs. These need to be added together to obtain the total variable costs.
- The next entry is the sales revenue or income per item.
- The final entry gives the break-even figure. This line contains the same formula you saw on page 212, i.e. fixed costs divided by the sales revenue minus the variable costs.

	A	B	C
1	Fixed costs	1200	
2			
3	Variable costs		
4	Plain T-shirts	4.5	
5	Ink	0.5	
6			
7	Total variable costs	5	
8			
9	Sales price	7	
10			
11	Break-even number	600	
12			

	A	B	C
1	Fixed costs	1200	
2			
3	Variable costs		
4	Plain T-shirts	4.5	
5	Ink	0.5	
6			
7	Total variable costs	=SUM(B4:B5)	
8			
9	Sales price	7	
10			
11	Break-even number	=SUM(B1/(B9-B7))	
12			

Assessment tip

You may to be asked to calculate a break-even point in the exam, but will not be provided with a computer! It is therefore sensible to check that you are confident doing this.

Take it further

Spreadsheets are ideal for carrying out 'what … if' calculations. Set up Tess's spreadsheet yourself and then find out what would happen to the break-even point if each of the following events occurred in sequence:

1 **Electricity increases resulted in Tess's fixed costs rising to £1,300 a month.**

2 **Tess negotiates the price she pays to suppliers for her plain T-shirts down to £4 each.**

3 **Her T-shirts are so popular she is overwhelmed with orders and so she increases the price to £10 each.**

Note: Tess needs the information as a whole number each time, so set the final cell to give you an integer (the nearest whole number) as your answer.

Just checking

Which type of computer software would be used to carry out a break-even analysis?

Suggest two ways in which a 'what… if?' analysis could be used in a break-even analysis using a computer.

Case study – Katy's cakes

Katy has been taking a cake decorating course and now wants to make some extra income by making and decorating cakes for special occasions. She has some idea about ICT but not very much.

Katy has worked out that her fixed costs will mainly be the electricity she uses to bake the cakes. She has estimated this at £50 a month.

Her variable costs are cake ingredients, cake decorations and a cake stand. These vary depending upon whether she makes a sponge cake or a fruit cake.

Katy has decided her costs are as follows:

Sponge cake: Ingredients £2.50, decorations £1, stand 50p
Fruit cake: Ingredients £6.50, decorations £2.50, stand 50p

Katy is thinking of selling the decorated sponge cakes for £10 and the decorated fruit cakes for £15.

1 **Show Katy how to set up a spreadsheet to find out the break-even point for her cake business. Tell her, too, how to get her result as a whole number.**

2 **Create the spreadsheet yourself and tell Katy the break-even point for the sponge cakes and for the fruit cakes.**

3 **Katy is asked to produce a three-tiered fruit cake for her friend's wedding, but Katy has no idea how much to charge her. How could using ICT to produce a break-even chart help Katy to come to a decision? Compare your ideas as a class.**

You can read more about the benefits and drawbacks of using ICT in business finance on page 195.

4.4 Investigating sources of business finance and financial planning

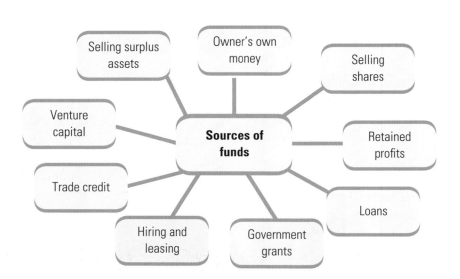

Sources of business finance

All businesses need money when they first start up and often later when they want to expand or update equipment. Even someone starting a window cleaning business needs to invest in cleaning materials, equipment and transport.

There are many sources of finance and these are shown in the diagram.

Case study – Don't bank on it!

Banks are one source of business funds, but in the autumn of 2008 many of them were in danger of running out of money themselves! Why? This is easy to understand if you know where banks get their money from. They get it from customers who have accounts with them, like you and me. They also get money from shareholders who have bought their shares. People buy shares because they expect to be paid a dividend twice a year as their reward. They also hope their shares will increase in value. Unfortunately, anyone with shares in a bank in 2008 saw their investments fall in value when banks lost money on loans they had made to the US housing market.

Some banks tried to raise money by issuing more shares. Some people bought them, but many people didn't and others sold the shares they had. This further reduced bank finances. Then some customers panicked and took their money out or moved it somewhere safer.

Another source of bank funds is other banks. This is called the 'inter-bank market'. Quite simply, banks lend and borrow money to each other to cover their daily operations. When confidence is shaken they tend to be reluctant to lend to each other and if they do, the cost is higher – the interest rate is higher – which is what happened in autumn 2008. Big financial institutions, like pension funds, also reduced their investments in, or lending to, banks.

All these problems seriously threatened the ability of banks to carry on trading. As a result the Government had to step in to lend some banks up to £50 billion initially. It later made available a further £400 billion of tax payers' money in an attempt to get the banking system working again. This was because it was important that the banks started lending again, both to businesses and to mortgage customers. Without the ability to borrow money from their bank, many firms could be forced to cease trading.

All sources of finance have their advantages and disadvantages. You will learn more about these later in this section.

Factors that affect which sources of funds to choose

When businesses need extra funding or **capital**, they usually have a choice of several sources of funds. The following are the main factors businesses will consider when deciding which source to choose.

- **The amount required** When a business wants start-up funds or extra funding, it normally needs to justify its request by showing its business plan. The amount requested must be sensible in relation to the overall plan and Government grants often have a maximum amount available.
- **Cost** Many sources of investment require interest payments to be made or give the lender a share of future profits.
- **Risk** Normally, the higher the risk, the higher the interest payments required.
- **Permanent or temporary?** Some forms of funding are permanent, such as shares. Others, such as bank loans, are temporary and have to be repaid within an agreed time limit.
- **Influence and control** Some lenders, such as banks and venture capitalists, will want to have a say in the running of the business. In larger businesses this could mean having a seat on the Board of Directors.
- **Advice** Some sources of funding, such as The Prince's Trust, offer advice as well as low-cost loans and grants.

Talk about it

Although you still have to learn more about different sources of finance, this doesn't mean you can't think about them now! Below are two different types of business situations. Divide into small groups and discuss which source(s) of business finance each owner might be likely to choose. Then be prepared to give your reasons in each case. Compare your ideas as a class.

1 **Bill has learned about a device that would stop pet dogs from leaving their owners' garden. The device is made in Germany, but has not yet been marketed in the UK. He would have to pay £2,000 for the licence fee and the same amount again for initial stock. Bill reckons that he will need a fully equipped office, which, including a year's rent in advance, would cost another £6,000.**

2 **Tariq has a sandwich business that has been running for six years. The business has been very successful and he has £5,000 in savings from the profits. The shop next door is up for sale and he is thinking of buying it to expand his business. He reckons that he needs £15,000 to get the extended business running profitably. His uncle says that he will lend him £10,000 but would want it back in a year with 10% interest.**

Talk about it
As a class, debate what could have happened if the Government hadn't lent money to some of the banks and the system had collapsed. Discuss your ideas with your tutor.

Describe it
Capital This is money needed to start up a new business. The term is also used for money set aside or obtained for a major investment, such as an expansion programme.

Assessment tip
It is sensible to check that you understand why businesses need money to be invested in them.

Research it
Bill and Tariq are both under 30. Find out whether the Prince's Trust could help them by visiting the website (go to www.heinemann.co.uk/hotlinks). Compare your findings as a class.

Just checking
Identify two situations where a business might look for external sources of finance.

Explain the difference between temporary and permanent sources of business finance.

Understanding the range of sources of business finance

The main sources of business finance are explained in this section.

You need to spend money to make money!

Funds from the owner(s)

Many small businesses are started by people who use their own savings. Sometimes people who are made redundant use the lump sum they are paid to start out on their own. The main advantage for small business owners of using their own funds is that no interest has to be paid and the money will not need to be returned. However, there is one danger. If the business is owned by a sole trader, or a partnership with unlimited liability, then all the money could be lost if the business fails. This could even mean that the owner loses their home. If you have forgotten about this, turn back to page 20 to refresh your memory!

Selling shares

If a business has limited liability then it is normally funded by shareholders, each of whom has a 'share' in the business. In the case of a public limited company the shares are bought and sold on the stock exchange and can be owned by the general public. If one of these businesses needs to raise a substantial amount of money, it can do this by offering more shares to its existing shareholders, often at a discounted price, or make a new share issue. If the company is private then additional shares can be offered to existing shareholders or, if all the existing shareholders agree, then more potential private shareholders can be approached. Some lenders, such as venture capitalists (see page 223) may insist on being given shares in return for their investment.

Retained profits

Many businesses hope to generate a profit. This is the amount of money left after ALL costs have been paid. Assuming a business does make a profit it has to decide what to do with it. In some cases it will

Research it

In the television programme *Dragons' Den,* anyone who gives a successful pitch on a business idea, then has to decide whether or not to allow the 'dragon(s)' to own a share of their business. Watch some of the programme clips on its website and see how this works. A link is available at www.heinemann.co.uk/hotlinks

give the money to a worthy cause as with social enterprises, or it may divide the profit between the owners in the form of a dividend as is the case with public limited companies. However, many businesses will want to use some of the profit made to reinvest into the business to improve or expand it. This is called **retained profit**.

In some ways, this is an ideal source of finance since no interest has to be paid and it isn't necessary to give any control to anyone outside the business who is providing finance. A problem arises if there is not enough retained profit available to cover the amount needed.

Loans

Large businesses that need medium-term to long-term loans can approach specialised investment banks. Smaller businesses will normally go to high street banks instead. They have to decide whether they want a bank loan or an overdraft, or both!

Bank loans

One of the main activities of banks is to lend money. They lend money to businesses as well as to private individuals, in return for interest payments.

When a business asks a bank for a loan, they have to provide information about why they need the money and show proof of how they will earn enough to repay it. They do this by preparing a business plan that contains their projected future income and expenditure. In addition, the bank will often ask for security, such as a large piece of equipment or even the owner's house.

Overdrafts

A bank account holder has an overdraft when they draw more out of their account than it contains. If this happens by accident the charges are very high. For that reason anyone who thinks they will need to do this for a short time should get the agreement of the bank first. The charges are then much less. Having an overdraft is a sensible way of borrowing money for a short time as the interest is only paid on a daily basis on the amount overdrawn.

Government grants

The Government is keen to help businesses to start up and develop because they provide employment and pay taxes, as well as contributing to the economy as a whole. For this reason there are many different types of grants available to businesses. Sources of grants include the European Union, Regional Development Agencies (RDAs), local authorities and County Enterprise Boards.

A grant is a sum of money usually linked to a specific project or purpose. Often the owner has to match the sum of money given as a grant. Unlike a loan, a grant doesn't need to be repaid, which is why they are an invaluable source of funds to many businesses.

Remember it

Retained profit is the amount of money left over after all the costs have been paid and enough of the profit has been distributed to the owners/shareholders.

Talk about it

Having an overdraft used to be called 'being in the red'. Have you any idea why? Discuss your ideas as a class.

Research it

Find out more about government grants at the Business Link website (via www.heineman.co.uk/hotlinks). Clicking on 'Finance and grants' and then find the grants available in your area by searching in the 'Grants and Support Directory'. In small groups decide the type of business you would like to set up and the reasons you would like the money, then enter your postcode. Check out the sources and options available to you and compare your findings as a class.

Just checking

Name at least three possible external sources of business finance.

Suggest two advantages to a business of using retained profits to fund a new venture.

Hiring and leasing

A business needs to have 50 cars, one for each of its sales team. The cars are priced at £12,000 each so to buy new cars would cost £600,000. This is a large amount of money to find and would put pressure on the company's cash flow (see page 184), especially as the cars would be bought before anyone on the sales team had made any new sales.

Leasing a car is cheaper than buying one

Hiring and leasing are both alternatives to buying an item outright. In both cases the payments are made in instalments over an agreed period of time. From the outset the business has the use of the item (such as the car, computer or other item of equipment). The main benefits of hiring/leasing are:

- The asset(s) can be used immediately and payments are staggered which eases the cash flow situation.
- The most up-to-date technology can be used which is better than owning equipment that may quickly become obsolete.
- Some lease agreements include maintenance and emergency breakdown cover.

The main disadvantages are:

- The total amount of money paid may be greater than the actual purchase price.
- The equipment must be kept for the duration of the lease agreement, even if it is no longer needed part way through.
- There may be penalties if the user breaches the lease agreement, such as travelling more miles in a leased car than originally agreed.

Selling surplus assets

Occasionally, a business may have assets, such as equipment or buildings, which it no longer requires. Selling these can give the business a one-off source of additional income.

Remember it

Hire purchase is a special form of hiring/leasing. The main difference is that the customer becomes the owner of the item after the final payment is made.

Talk about it

A common use of leasing arrangements is when travel companies lease aircraft. Suggest good business reasons for doing this.

Research it

Choose a popular model of car and use the Internet to discover what the cost of leasing one of these cars would be over three years. Check if there are any conditions attached, such as restrictions on mileage.

Trade credit

When you buy something from a shop, you pay for the goods straight away. However, most trade between businesses is carried out on a different basis. In this case there is a delay between goods being received and payment being made. Many businesses aim to get money from customers as quickly as possible and delay paying suppliers for as long as possible! As an example, a stationery supplier receives 500 boxes of computer printer paper from a supplier on 1 June. The stationery supplier has an **agreed credit period** of two months with the computer paper supplier. If the stationery supplier can sell all the paper in one month and collect payment within the month, it has the cash available for the rest of the two-month period.

Most businesses buy things on credit

Large businesses can cause small suppliers problems by deliberately extending the time taken to pay the bills, knowing that the small business will be reluctant to complain for fear of upsetting the customer and losing the business. Because of this, the Government brought in legislation that allows interest to be charged if excessive time is taken to pay the debt.

Venture capital

Venture capital firms are businesses that specialise in investing in small and medium-sized enterprises (MSEs) that have the potential for growth. The aim of such an investment is to grow the business and withdraw the investment, or sell the business within a few years, making a profit. The following are the main features of venture capital investments:

- The venture capital company buys a share of the business or even the whole business and may receive dividends.
- It may also insist on having a seat on the board of directors and/or involvement in the day-to-day management of the business.
- It normally keeps shares for three to five years.
- Although it may take dividends, most of the return on its investment comes from selling shares or the business at the end of the investment period.
- Venture capital firms can sometimes become involved with business start-ups.

Describe it

An agreed credit period is an agreement between a supplier and a customer on the length of time to be taken between receipt of goods or services and the time when payment is made.

Research it

Find out more about Late Payment Legislation on the Business Link website (go to www.heinemann.co.uk/hotlinks). Why do you think that, even with the legislation in place, some small businesses are reluctant to pursue overdue payments?

Assessment tip

You need to understand the various sources of finance available. In the exam you may be asked to identify the most appropriate sources for the needs of the business described in the scenario and give reasons for your choice.

Research it

Investigate a venture capital business by visiting the website of Alchemy Partners. Then find out more about the government sponsored Regional Capital Venture funds by visiting the website of the UK Department for Business, Enterprise and Regulatory Reform (BERR). Links to both sites can be found at www.heinemann.co.uk/hotlinks.

Investigating business finance

Investigating sources of finance used

Businesses may need finance at any time. However, it is useful to think of two types of situation:

- When businesses start up
- When businesses have been running for some time and have a proven market and accounts to show their income and expenditure.

The first of these is the most difficult situation in which to obtain funding as there is more risk that the investment will be lost. Many entrepreneurs finance a business start-up by using savings or borrowing from family/friends. A key component when asking for funding from outside the business, such as banks, is to produce a comprehensive business plan.

Business plan

Although business plans are produced by people who want to borrow money from banks, it is a good discipline for any business to carry out from time to time. The main components of a business plan are:

- A description of the products or services offered
- An analysis of the market – number and type of customers, local or national
- Number and profile of competitors
- Forecasts of sales and income
- **Start-up** and **running costs**
- Cash-flow forecast
- Projected profits.

Investigate the role of ICT in obtaining, recording and monitoring sources of finance

In earlier sections, you have learned that ICT can assist in recording and analysing cash flow, budgets and break-even analysis. It also has an application in the area of sourcing finance.

- **Obtaining finance** An ICT based cash-flow forecast will tell a business when it may need extra funding. The Internet is a valuable source of information on sources of funding from banks, venture capitalists, government grants and 'business angels'.
- **Recording sources of finance** It is a legal requirement that businesses keep accurate records of all income and expenditure. So any source of finance should be recorded in terms of where it comes from and what the money is spent on. This information will also appear in the balance sheet.
- **Monitoring sources of finance** ICT is particularly important in relation to cash flow when the business has an overdraft. Interest on overdrafts is paid on a daily basis so it is important that the cash flow is controlled carefully so as to keep the amount borrowed to a minimum. ICT could also be used to automatically make loan payments.

Describe it

Start-up costs are the total amount of money to be spent (on equipment, premises etc.) before a business can begin trading.

Running costs is the amount of money spent to keep the business running, on things such as materials, wages, utilities bills etc.

Remember it

Reserves is the same as retained profit and is used to describe profits that are not distributed as dividends. The money can fund future developments or just act as a safety net should the business hit hard times.

Case study – Richer by name...

The way individual businesses obtain funding will depend on the specific circumstances, as well as the preferences of the owner. In some cases owners will go to great lengths to avoid having any external influence on their business. In this case they grow the business slowly by reinvesting profits. The following is an example of how a business has gone about obtaining funds. Read it carefully and then answer the questions that follow.

The story of Richer Sounds

Richer Sounds is a retail business selling hi-fi, home cinema and flat panel televisions. It was started by Julian Richer in 1978 when he used £2,000 of his own savings to start the business. An additional £20,000 of funding was obtained from the owner of the first shop he rented. This was in return for a 74% share in the business. Finally, Vic Odden allowed Julian to take over the premises without paying a deposit on the rental. Within ten months Julian had paid off the £20,000 loan from the profit he made.

For the next few years, the business grew but the path was not always smooth. At one time the business grew too quickly and there were problems with cash flow and not having enough money for the expansion. This was a temporary setback and five shops had to be closed so Julian negotiated a larger overdraft facility. A key feature of Richer Sounds finance strategy is to buy goods on 30 days' credit and sell them within 25 days.

In 2008, the profile of the business was:

- Richer Sounds owns 47 shops.
- Although it is registered as a public limited company, Julian owns all of the shares. Sometimes dividends are not paid at all.
- The business has been grown mainly through retained profit (**reserves**).
- Normally, shop premises are bought outright, rather than leased because this is cheaper in the long run.
- Some computer equipment is leased, rather than bought outright.
- The company prefers to use overdrafts rather than bank loans. This money is mainly used to purchase stock that can be sold to cover the interest payments and still make a profit.
- Julian and the management team believe in 'controlled growth', saying that their motto is 'What goes up slowly, comes down slowly'.

Now work in small groups to answer the following questions.

1 Why do you think Julian Richer chose to use his own savings and a loan from a business acquaintance to fund the initial start-up?

2 (a) Why do you think Vic Odden was prepared to risk £20,000 of his own money in the business, and (b) why did he ask for a large share in it?

3 Why did Julian buy back Vic's share so quickly when he wanted to expand the business?

4 What does being a public limited company mean?

5 Why does Julian still own 100% of the shares when he could make money by selling them on the stock exchange?

6 (a) What could have happened if Julian had been prepared to borrow money to expand the business more quickly?
(b) Where could the money have come from?

7 (a) What was done to obtain funding when the business hit hard times? (b) What other options might the business have used?

8 What is the benefit of selling goods within the supplier's credit period?

9 What are the advantages and disadvantages of buying shop premises rather than leasing or renting them?

10 Why might it be better to lease computer equipment rather than buying it?

11 Why might the business prefer overdrafts to bank loans?

12 Suggest how Richer Sounds can use ICT to monitor its finances.

Compare all your answers as a class.

Just checking

Name at least three topics which would be included in a business plan.

Assessment tip

Final accounts (profit and loss accounts, and balance sheets) are described in Unit 2. In the exam for Unit 4, you need to understand the purpose of these and how they are used in financial planning.

Remember it

Overtrading occurs when businesses try to expand too quickly and find that they have not enough money to pay suppliers. It is a common reason for insolvency.

Describe it

Scenarios are thoughts about possible future situations. If you dream about what you would do if you inherited a million pounds, that is a scenario. In business the same idea applies where the effects of possible future events are discussed.

Financial planning documents

As you know, all businesses must be constantly updating and studying key financial documents including the following:

- Cash-flow forecasts
- Break-even analysis information
- Forecast profit and loss accounts, and balance sheets.

  These documents are all covered in other parts of this book. It may be a good opportunity to now go back and refresh your memory on each of them.

Each of these financial documents can contribute to planning for:

- business expansion or contraction
- the cost of unexpected events
- changes in costs of the business.

Business expansion or contraction

Cash-flow forecasts Changes in the level of business activity can change the cash flow in several ways. Income normally rises when a business expands and falls when it contracts. Expenditure on items, such as stock, equipment and wages, will also change. If a business is borrowing money to expand, any additional interest payments must be allowed for. Sensible businesses build a safety margin into the forecast because the effects of change are difficult to forecast.

Break-even analysis If the fixed costs, variable costs and selling price remain the same, the break-even point will not change. The critical factor is the amount by which sales increase or decrease. Provided that the new level of sales is above the break-even point, the business should still be in profit. However, all cost and income figures could change, in which case the chart needs to be re-drawn. The business should do this for the worst case **scenario** that they think could happen, as well as the most optimistic.

Forecast profit and loss accounts, and balance sheets As with cash flow, the profit and loss account will show the changes in the income and expenditure figures. Generally, the profit and loss account should show an increased profit if the firm is expanding and a fall if it is contracting. The balance sheet should show what has happened to the money invested by shareholders from loans and retained profits. The key factor is whether or not the total amount of money invested is being used wisely.

Costs of unexpected events

Cash-flow forecasts Cash-flow forecasts cannot predict unexpected events. However they can be used to carry out 'what ... if' investigations, e.g. 'What would be the result if a major supplier wanted to increase prices by 10%?' or 'What would be the effect on our income if an important customer went bankrupt?'. Cash-flow forecasts can be produced for these situations and then the managers could plan what they would do. This is called 'contingency planning'.

Break-even analysis There are four main components in break-even analysis – fixed costs, variable costs, selling price and number of products sold. If an event causes one, or more than one, of these to change then the calculation needs to be revised. For example, a major increase in fuel price could affect the variable cost. If a competitor drastically reduces the price of their product then the business may have to do the same.

Forecast profit and loss accounts, and balance sheets. These attempt to predict what the financial state of the business will be at the end of the financial year. They are like a health check. If an unexpected event has caused a problem the accounts will reflect this. For example, if profitability has suffered this will show up in the profit figure in the profit and loss account and the reserves figure in the balance sheet. If a problem has forced the business to take out an extra loan, the amount will appear under liabilities in the balance sheet while the interest repayments will appear as expenditure in the profit and loss account.

Changes in the costs of the business

Cash-flow forecast Any changes in costs will have a direct effect on the cash flow. A reduction in costs will decrease cash outflows while an increase will do the opposite. The business will be concerned with the forecast bank balance, especially if it shows a potential negative figure.

Break-even analysis There are two costs used in a break-even calculation – fixed and variable. An increase in either would mean that the business will have to sell more products just to break-even. On the other hand, a reduction in either would lower the break-even point.

Forecast profit and loss accounts, and balance sheets Costs appear on the expenditure side of the profit and loss account. An increase in costs could mean that less profit would appear in this account. A reduction in costs should result in higher profit. Either way, a change in profit affects the reserves figure in the balance sheet.

Research it

Business plans always contain a section on financial forecasts. You can watch an educational video about business plans on YouTube (go to www.heinemann.co.uk/hotlinks). Check the information that should be contained in a business plan and the financial forecasts that are needed. Write a summary of what you learn – you will find it comes in useful for the activity on page 228

Just checking

Name the three main types of documents used in financial planning.

Identify the two main changes there would be to a cash-flow forecast if a business plans to expand.

Apply it

You have just inherited £500,000 from a distant relative you hardly knew. You are in the middle of deciding how to spend it when you get a phone call from your cousin. He is a keen photographer and wants to set up in business as a professional, with his own studio and facilities to do portraits, weddings and commercial projects. He needs capital and has asked you to lend him £300,000. He wants to see you soon to talk about the idea.

Work in small groups to decide your answers to the following questions.

1 **What information will you want to know about his proposed business?**

2 **What financial planning documents will you want to see, and why? Justify your choices by identifying how each document will help you to make a decision.**

3 **How accurate should his forecasts be, and why?**

4 **Research successful photographic businesses online and use this information to produce a short list of relevant questions you could ask about his future plans and prospects.**

5 **What factors would influence your decision whether to invest in his business or not?**

6 **What conditions would you make if you decided to lend him some of your money, and why?**

Compare your ideas as a class.

How financial plans are of use to different groups of people

Various groups of people have an interest in the financial plans of a business, in terms of:

- the business as a whole
- its individual departments/functions
- its investors
- its lenders/creditors.

Each group will have different ways in which they look at the information.

The whole business

This means the senior management team, particularly the managing director, who will be interested in the performance of the business as a whole. Before the start of the financial year the senior management team will have to approve the budget. During the year they will look at the budget feedback figures, paying particular attention to major negative variances.

They will also look at the forecast profit and loss account and balance sheet since these both focus on the ultimate test of the business' performance. If the forecast profit figure is not satisfactory, they will have to look more deeply at the situation to find out the reasons. Are sales worse than originally predicted? If so, why?

Its departments/functions

All functional areas will be interested in the feedback they receive on their own budget. They will be expected to give explanations for any large negative variances and to take corrective action if possible. The departments that are particularly interested in their budget feedback are:

- **Finance** The main purpose of this department is to check on the financial performance of the business and to give feedback to other departments on budget performance and other aspects. For example, finance may liaise with marketing about a customer who is late in paying. It will also monitor cash flow and assist in break-even calculations by providing income and expenditure figures.

- **ICT** This department could liaise with finance to provide and maintain appropriate software to keep records and produce financial forecasts, such as cash flow and budgets.

- **Production** This is normally the biggest spending department in terms of capital costs, materials and wages. Because of this it has the biggest budget and therefore the biggest influence on profitability.

- **Marketing and sales** The main task of this function is to sell as many products as possible. They must be aware of break-even calculations so that they can make decisions on prices. They may also link with finance to deal with customers who are behind with their payments. This would help to improve cash flow.

- **Other departments** such as HR, Administration and Customer Service will have budgets and will also have a general interest in the business' financial performance.

Its investors

These could be senior managers, venture capitalists, friends of the owner or, in the case of a public limited company, the shareholders who bought shares on the stock market. Their main interest is the amount of money they receive in dividend payments for the money they have invested. They are also interested in the long-term prospects of the business. If prospects are good then share prices should increase. Most of this information is found in the profit and loss account, and balance sheet.

Its lenders/creditors

Lenders are organisations, such as banks, which lend money to a business in return for interest payments. They want to be sure that the business can keep up the payments and that their capital can be repaid at the end of the agreed period. For repayment of interest, they would look at the cash-flow forecast, the credit period taken from the profit and loss account, and the amount of cash in the reserves section of the balance sheet.

Trade creditors would also look at the credit period taken by analysing the profit and loss account as well as the projected cash-flow forecast.

The role of ICT in financial planning

You have already learned that ICT can assist the analysis of cash flow, produce budget reports and carry out break-even analysis. It can also be used to assist financial planning in general. Apart from those aspects already mentioned, the following features can be considered:

- Financial statements can be updated daily.
- Access to information is instantaneous.
- A number of people can have fast access to information and there can be restrictions as to who has access to which type of information.
- Several types of reports can be generated as well as those already described.
- Stock levels can be monitored.

Assessment tip

Anyone who is asked to lend money to a business is keenly interested in its past, present and future performance. If you are asked about this in the exam, you will find it easier if you put yourself in the position of the person being asked to invest in the business!

Research it

For a more in-depth analysis of the capabilities of ICT systems to assist financial analysis, visit Winters Chartered Accountants website and locate section 10.3 'Choosing an accountancy package'. A link to the site is available at www.heinemann.co.uk/hotlinks.

Take it further

Take the part of your cousin, the photographer, and decide how you could best present your case to borrow the money!

Just checking

Why would a business' financial plans would be of interest to its investors?

Identify which type of financial plan would be of most interest to a production manager, giving reasons for your answer.

Unit 4 Make the Grade

This unit is assessed by a one hour exam that is set and marked externally by Edexcel. Exams are a way of assessing what you have learned and your understanding of the subject. You will not only be assessed on your knowledge of business, but crucially on your skills: your ability to apply your knowledge and demonstration of the ability to analyse and evaluate. When you have passed your exams and successfully completed your internal assessments, you can be sure that you have achieved something special that will be respected by employers and educational institutions.

This section is designed to help you prepare for the Unit 4 examination. It comprises five main sections:

- Common mistakes
- Revision checklist
- Exam preparation
- Sample questions with student answers
- Practice questions

Research it

The Unit 2 Make the Grade section contains seven key revision tips to help you prepare for your examinations (see page 116). You should read these again to refresh your memory when preparing for the Unit 4 examination.

Remember it

Everyone is nervous before taking exams. However, careful planning and preparation will boost your confidence and maximise your chances of success.

Common mistakes

- Cash flow is only concerned with money actually entering or leaving a business bank account. It is not concerned with invoices that have not yet been paid or cheques that have not been paid into the bank.

- Confusing cash-flow with profit – they are not the same thing.
- Confusing cash-flow statements with cash-flow forecasts. A cash-flow statement records what has actually happened while a cash-flow forecast states what the business *thinks* will happen.
- Not understanding that the words 'receipts' and 'inflows' mean the same thing – money going into a business.
- Similarly, 'outflows' and 'payments' both mean money leaving a business.
- 'Budgeting' refers to the process of producing a budget that shows planned future expenditure. The process of budgetary control happens after a period of time when money has been spent and comparisons can be made between the planned and actual figures.
- On a break-even graph, the total cost line starts where the fixed cost line meets the vertical axis, *not* at the zero point.

Revision checklist

To pass your examination you need both knowledge and skills. This means that you have to understand what you have learned, apply your knowledge in a variety of contexts and use this to make judgements and present appropriate conclusions. This should sound familiar because it relates to the assessment objectives you learned about in Make the Grade for Unit 2 (see page 116). These are exactly the same for Unit 4.

Below is a checklist which summarises the topics you need to know for your Unit 4 examination. On page 233 you will find hints and tips on how to apply this knowledge appropriately in the examination itself.

You might find it a bit over-whelming to read through this list of topics all at once! Instead, use it as a checklist when you are revising each section to make sure you don't miss anything out.

1 Investigating business cash-flow forecasts

You will need to be able to define and understand the following key terms:

- cash flow
- inflows (or receipts)
- outflows (or payments)
- liquidity
- bank balance.

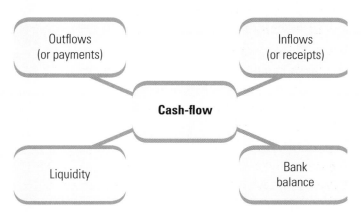

In addition you need to be able to complete a cash-flow statement/forecast that looks like the one shown below. Be prepared to produce the chart from memory.

2010	Month 1 (£)	Month 2 (£)	Month 3 (£)
Total receipts			
Total payments			
Net inflow/outflow			
Opening balance			
Closing balance			

Finally, you may be asked to explain why the closing balance is the most important figure on the statement. You may be given one or more closing balance figures and asked for an opinion on it/them.

2 Investigating business budgets

You will need to be able to define and understand the following key terms:

- budgeting
- budgetary control

- variance
- adverse variance
- favourable variance
- motivation of employees.

You will also need to know about each of the following types of budget:

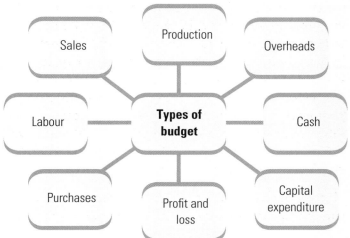

In the examination you could be asked to complete a budget statement similar to the one shown below. Included in this you may have to calculate figures before you enter them, for example 200 meals prepared at a cost of £2.20 each equals a total expenditure of £440.

Production budget	Budgeted expenditure June (£)	Actual expenditure June (£)	Variance June (£)
Nuts			
Bolts			
Metal plates			
Brackets			
Electricity			

In addition to adding the budgeted and actual expenditure figures and calculating the variance figures, you could be asked to comment on the variance figures and state what managerial action may be required.

3 Investigating break-even analysis in business

For this topic, you need to know the meaning of the following terms:

- fixed costs
- variable costs
- sales revenue
- break-even point
- profit
- loss
- margin of safety.

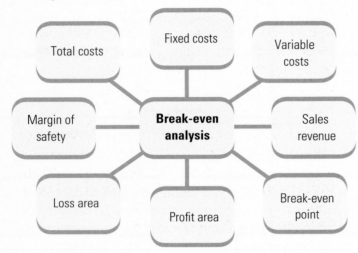

In addition you may be asked to complete a break-even chart and label all of the features: costs and sales revenue, number of products sold, as well as all of the items listed above. You may want to refresh your memory by looking at the chart on page 210.

Alternatively, you may be asked to use the formula method of calculating break-even. If this is the case, you will be given the formula to use on the figures provided for you. The formula is shown below. Study it carefully to make sure that you know how to use it.

$$\text{Break-even point} = \frac{\text{Fixed costs}}{\text{Selling price per unit less Variable cost per unit}}$$

If you are asked to use the formula, be sure to show all of your workings, so that if you make a mistake with the calculations at any point, you can still be given some credit for applying the formula properly.

You may also be asked to comment on how businesses could use break-even analysis, for example to assess a proposed new product or the impact of changing the sales price. Finally, you could be asked to say what the limitations are of this technique, for example the fact that cost and revenue figures are estimates, which could be wrong.

4 Investigating sources of business finance and financial planning

For this topic, you need to know about the following potential sources of finance for businesses:

- funding from owner(s)
- selling shares
- retained profits
- loans
- government grants
- hiring and leasing
- selling surplus assets
- trade credit
- venture capital.

In the examination you may be asked to comment on the advantages and disadvantages of each potential source of funding. In particular, you could be asked to suggest the best choice of funding source in a given scenario. In this instance you would be asked to give reasons for your suggestions.

You may also be asked to summarise the uses of cash-flow forecasts, break-even analysis and forecast final accounts when businesses are making plans for the future. This could involve applying your understanding of the different approaches to a particular situation, such as business expansion or contraction, the cost of unexpected events or changes in business costs.

Finally, you may be asked to explain how financial plans could be of use to the whole business, its departments/functions, its investors and lenders/creditors.

Exam preparation

This section is designed to help you get the most out of your time during the exam.

Research it

There are two topics in previous Make the Grade sections that you should read in relation to this section: Understanding the task (page 63) and Examiner's guide to the exam (page 118). The Examiner's guide to the exam tells you how you will be assessed in the examination. It is important you refresh your memory about the style of the exam, the assessment objectives and what the examiner is looking for. All these are the same for both the Unit 2 and Unit 4 examinations.

The whole of the exam paper will be based on a scenario. This scenario will relate to a real business. You do not have to memorise the details but the background information provided at the beginning of the paper will be needed to help you to answer the questions and to apply your knowledge to a particular case.

Applying your knowledge isn't always easy:

- You may think you know a topic well but then struggle to apply it to a given situation.
- The question may seem confusing at first.
- You may not be able to decide what to write in response.

The sample questions with student answers (see page 234–5) should help you. You might also find the following hints and tips useful too.

Multiple choice questions

- The exam may start with multiple choice questions. Don't rush to answer the first one too quickly. Give yourself time to settle down.
- Read the questions carefully, two or three times if needed. You may think of an answer before you read the choices, but then read each choice to see if your answer is there.
- *Always* read each of the options to make certain that you are correct. Think carefully about whether each possible answer could be right or not.
- If you have no idea which answer is right, start by eliminating those you know to be wrong, until you are left with only two. Then 'test' each one by thinking carefully whether it could be right or not. Pay particular attention to how each option is worded, as this may give you a clue. If you still don't know the answer, you have two choices: you can leave the answer blank and come back to it later (but whatever you do, don't forget – put a note somewhere to remind yourself) or you can take an educated guess. This is far better than not answering the question, which will never get a mark!

Short-answer questions and calculations

- Read each question very carefully, doing so several times if you are still nervous or if there are several figures involved.
- You may be asked to insert figures into a standard document (such as a cash-flow summary). Always check that you have put the figures in the right place before you do any calculations.
- If you are given space for your workings then *use* it.
- Check your calculations several times.
- If you have to provide a definition, brief description or explanation, think carefully about the information you are being asked to provide. Remember that it should be related to the scenario that has been given to you.

Extended answer questions

- You are expected to provide more information in response to these questions. The clue is in the number of marks allocated to the question and, usually, the number of lines you have available to write on.
- Remember that the more marks allocated to a question, the more you are being asked to demonstrate your skills of applying your knowledge, analysing and evaluating. Re-read the command words on page 63 to make sure you understand what they mean.
- You may be asked to justify yourself or give reasons for your answer. This means giving additional information so that the examiner knows why you made a particular decision. Make sure you give a detailed answer to these type of questions – the examiner can't read your mind!

All questions

- If you cannot decide whether a comment, conclusion or judgement is appropriate then it is still sensible to include it. You will never get marks deducted for writing something that is not correct. You cannot gain marks though if you leave out something that is important!

- If you write something and then have second thoughts, do not cross it out unless you are sure that you can replace it with something better.

- Read through all your work afterwards to check it makes sense and you haven't left anything out.
- If you get to the end of the paper with time to spare, use it to go back over your answers to see if anything can be improved.

Sample questions with student answers

Student Activity: Blackmoor Fitness Ltd

Blackmoor Fitness is a health and fitness club that is located in an out-of-town shopping centre. It is owned by Hanif and Nikki who started the business three years ago using their own savings and a bank loan. To date, they have been able to pay off most of the loan. Here is an extract from their publicity leaflet.

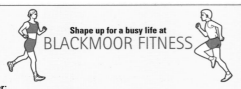

Shape up for a busy life at
BLACKMOOR FITNESS

We offer:
- A fully equipped gym with expert staff who can help you devise a personal plan to improve your fitness.
- An activities room where you can join classes in dance, aerobics, Pilates, yoga, circuit and many more.
- A specialist shop where you can browse our extensive stock of sportswear and sports equipment, as well as health drinks, vitamins and beauty products.

Visit, phone or browse our website to find out more:
- 7 Healey Place ST5 3FB
- 01234 567890
- www.blackmoorfitness.co.uk

Q1 The break-even point occurs when which of the following statements is true:

☐ The margin of safety is large
☐ The bank balance is zero
☐ Total costs are equal to total sales income
☐ Sales revenue is better than last year   (1 mark)

Alicia answers:
☑ Total costs are equal to total sales income

Comments on Alicia's answer:

This is the correct answer. When answering a question like this read it carefully and, if you are not sure of the answer, pick the one that you feel is closest. One mark is available for this question so, in this case, Alicia gained one mark. Remember that when you answer a multiple choice question you should know why the other suggested answers are wrong. In this case:

☐ *The margin of safety is large – This is incorrect because the margin of safety is the level of sales above the break-even point.*

☐ *The bank balance is zero – This is also incorrect. The bank balance is a cash-flow issue and break-even analysis is not concerned with the amount of money in the bank.*

☐ *Sales revenue is better than last year – This is also wrong. Although break-even is concerned with sales revenue, it is not concerned with comparing one year with the next.*

Q2 Hanif is looking at the financial situation of the business. He writes down the following information for the Blackmoor Centre for the next three months:

Month	Receipts (£)	Payments (£)
October	25,791	23,147
November	26,188	27,891
December	24,017	22,864

Hanif then uses this information to forecast the net inflows or outflows and bank balances for the centre. Complete the cash-flow forecast below for Blackmoor Fitness.   (3 marks)

Alicia answers (shown in blue):

Cash-flow forecast for Blackmoor Fitness Ltd, October–December 2009

2009	October (£)	November (£)	December (£)
Total receipts	25,791	26,188	24,017
Total payments	23,147	27,891	22,864
Net inflow/outflow	2,644	−1,703	1,153
Opening balance	560	3,204	1,511
Closing balance	3,204	1,501	2,664

Comments on Alicia's answer:

All of the numbers Alicia has provided have been entered correctly and all of the calculations are correct. Unfortunately, there is one small error: the closing balance for November (£1,501) has not been copied correctly into the opening balance figure for December (£1,511). This is a shame because otherwise it is a good answer. Always check figures and calculations carefully after your initial attempt.

Q3 Nikki and Hanif want to expand their business by opening up another centre in a nearby town. Hanif has been in touch with a venture capitalist who is interested in investing in Blackmoor. Nikki wants to know more about how this would work in practice.
Identify two ways in which a venture capitalist could help Nikki and Hanif to expand the business successfully. (2 marks)

Then suggest two possible disadvantages of obtaining finance from a venture capitalist. (2 marks)

Alicia answers:

A venture capitalist will invest money into the business which means they will have enough money to open another centre. A venture capitalist is normally someone with lots of business experience, so they will be able to give Nikki and Hanif valuable advice about the expansion.

The venture capitalist may want to tell them exactly how they should run every aspect of the business. Nikki and Hanif may not agree with this but will have no choice, which could cause problems and disagreements. The venture capitalist may also want to take all of the profits.

Comments on Alicia's answer:

Alicia's response to the first part is good and would gain her the full two marks for the question. Unfortunately, her response to the disadvantages section is not totally accurate. Certainly the venture capitalist would want a say in how the business is run, which could potentially cause problems, but it is unusual for them to want all of the profit. They would normally want a share of it. Alicia would only gain one mark here.

Apply it

Practice questions

Have a go at answering the following questions about Blackmoor Fitness Ltd.

1(a) In cash-flow forecasting, the opening balance for a month is:

☐ Always zero

☐ Total income minus total receipts for that month

☐ The break-even point

☐ The closing bank balance for the previous month

(1 mark)

1(b) Trade credit occurs when:

☐ A business makes a loan to another business

☐ There is an agreed delay between goods being delivered and payment being made

☐ A bank lends money to a business

☐ A customer pays cash when they collect goods

(1 mark)

2 The closing bank balance for Blackmoor Fitness for the months from June to September inclusive were as follows:

£3,530, £4,620, £5,980, £6,790

(a) Do the figures show Blackmoor Fitness is a successful business or not? Give a reason for your answer. (2 marks)

(b) Nikki and Hanif decide to buy a new exercise machine that costs £4,500. What is the earliest month they could have done this? Give the reason for your choice. (2 marks)

(c) Sportswear Ltd is a major supplier of clothing to Blackmoor Fitness' shop. Briefly explain why Sportswear Ltd might be interested in Blackmoor's cash-flow statement. (2 marks)

3 At present, there is no budgetary control system at Blackmoor Fitness. Hanif and Nikki have been advised by their accountant that it would be a good idea to introduce this. They decide to set up separate budgets for the gym, the activities room and the shop.

(a) Give two reasons why the accountant gave Nikki and Hanif this advice. (2 marks)

(b) Suggest two items that could appear in the budget for the gym. (2 marks)

(c) The following figures relate to the shop budget for September.

Staff wages £3,000
Goods purchased £7,000
Cleaning £500
Electricity £300

At the end of the month, the actual figures were £3,400, £8,000, £400 and £400 respectively. Use these figures to construct a budget table and calculate the variances and the totals for each column. (3 marks)

(d) The accountant tells Nikki that the budget shows some adverse variances. Explain what effect these might have on the business if they are allowed to continue. (3 marks)

4 Nikki is thinking about refurbishing the gym by taking out a bank loan. She hopes that the improvements will attract more members. The membership fee is £20 per month. She writes down some figures that will help her decide whether this venture will be worthwhile. She knows that the changes to the gym will increase her variable cost since the new equipment will use more resources, including hourly paid part-time staff.

Monthly loan repayment: £1,200
Extra variable cost: £10 per member

Use the table below to help you construct a break-even chart, which will tell Nikki how many new members she will need to attract to break-even.

Number of new members	0	100	200
Total additional membership fees			
Variable costs			
Fixed costs			
Total costs			

Now construct a break-even chart labelling the axes, the break-even point, profit area and loss area.   (6 marks)

5   Nikki and Hanif are thinking of opening a second fitness centre about ten miles from the one they already own. They think they will need £25,000 to set it up, which will pay for deposit on the rental, building conversion and equipment. They are keen to avoid a situation where other people could insist on having a say on how they run their business. Blackmoor Fitness has made healthy profits so far, but this has gone towards paying Nikki and Hanif's salaries and the rest has been reinvested in the business. Nikki owns a house that she inherited from her grandfather which is worth £100,000. Hanif writes a list of possible sources of money:

Selling shares
Using retained profits
Bank loans
Venture capital

(a) From the above list, suggest one source of capital that should meet the owners' needs, giving reasons for your choice.   (3 marks)

(b) For each of the sources of capital you consider to be unsuitable, give one reason why you think this is so.   (3 marks)

Glossary

Agreed credit period	An agreement between a supplier and a customer on the length of time to be taken between receipt of goods or services and payment.
Adverse variances	When expenditure is greater than planned.
Aims	The long-term goals a business wants to achieve.
Balance sheet	A document that shows a business' financial position at a single point in time.
Billion	A thousand million.
Break-even	The point at which the income from selling an item covers the cost of supplying it. There is no loss but there is no profit either.
Budget	A plan that identifies, estimates and itemises future spending.
Budget holder	The manager responsible for trying to ensure that expenditure is kept within the budget.
Business plan	A document that is a prediction of a business' overall potential performance. Often used when a business is starting up in order to secure loans/investment.
Capital	Money needed to start up a new business. The term is also used for money set aside or obtained for a major investment, such as an expansion programme.
Capital expenditure	When a large amount of money is spent on an item (e.g. a machine or a building extension) which will last a long time.
Carbon footprint	The impact of an activity on the environment as a measure of the amount of greenhouse gases it produces.
Cashback	On a credit card this means money that is given to the credit card holder for a specific amount spent.
Cash flow	The movement of money into and out of a business.
Cash-flow statement	The amount of money coming into a business, the amount being paid out and the difference between the two.
Chip and PIN	Where a credit or debit card has a digital chip within it which holds information about the card holder or their business.
Churn rate	A measure of the customers lost by a business over a period of time.
Clearing	The time between paying money into an account and the money being available.
Commodity	Basic items that are mined, extracted or farmed that go into making most other goods.
Core business activity	The activity that is most important to a business or where the business has most experience and is usually the most profitable.
Costs	Payments made from a business towards bills, the manufacture of products etc.
Cost-benefit	Comparing the costs of something against its benefits.

Credit	On a financial document, money that has been added. To be given credit means to agree to pay later.
Creditor	A business or individual who is owed money.
Credit payment	When a business pays money into a customer's account rather than taking it out.
Curriculum Vitae (CV)	A document that summarises a job applicant's background, qualifications, experience and interests.
Customer	Individuals or organisations who buy goods and services.
Customer facing	Staff who deal directly with customers.
Debit	On a financial document, money that is owed.
Debtor	A business or individual who owes money.
Diversify	Where a business carries out new activities.
Economies of scale	The financial benefits of operating on a large scale which lead to lower cost per unit produced.
Employee	An individual who carries out work for an employer.
Employment contract	A legal agreement between an employer and an employee, setting out the terms on which one agrees to employ the other. It also details the responsibilities of both the employer and the employee to each other.
Ethical business	A business that doesn't take unfair advantage of vulnerable groups of people or lie or cheat to increase its profits.
Expenditure	The money paid out by a business.
External environment	Things that are outside the control of a business, such as laws, technology and the wider economy.
Favourable variances	When expenditure is less than planned.
Financial discipline	Controlling business expenditure to the levels required by the budget.
Financial records	Documents that show the business transactions that take place on a day to day basis.
Fixed costs	Costs that do not depend on the amount of goods produced or sold.
Fraud	A crime that involves money.
Functional area	Areas into which businesses can be organised, e.g. sales or finance.
HMRC	Her Majesty's Revenue and Customs is the government department that collects tax payments such as income tax, corporation tax and VAT.
Income	The money a business receives from customers and other sources such as bank interest.
Interest rate	The charge made by banks in the UK for borrowing money. The rate is determined by how much banks have to pay in interest if they want to borrow from the Bank of England.

Glossary

Job description	A document that sets out the key responsibilities and tasks involved in performing a particular job.
Limited liability	Where a shareholder is only responsible for the amount of money they agreed to invest in a business.
Line manager	The manager directly above an employee on an organisation chart.
Liquidity	A measure of how much cash a business has available to pay what it owes.
Loss	When the expenditure of a business is greater than income over a period of time.
Market research	The use of different methods to try and find out what consumer needs are and what response consumers give to the products and services retailers sell.
Market segment	A part of the market for a particular product.
Market share	The proportion of total sales for a product or service obtained by one brand or company.
Motivation	An incentive that inspires managers to work hard and attempt to achieve the goals and aims of a business.
Non-executive director	Someone who does not run a business on a day to day basis but monitors how it is doing.
Objectives	Specific steps taken by a business to achieve a goal.
Organisation structure	The way a business is organised internally to enable employees to carry out their job roles and communicate with each other.
Person specification	A document that details the personal qualities an individual will need to perform a particular job.
PIN	Personal Identification Number – a four-digit number used with a credit or debit card which should only be known by the card holder.
Primary sector	Businesses that extract raw materials from the ground or land so they can be made into something new.
Profit	The money that is left over when all the business costs have been deducted from the sales revenue.
Profitability	A measure of how much profit a business makes for a given amount of time.
Profitable business	A business that earns more than it spends.
Profit and loss account	A document that shows the revenues and costs of a business for a given amount of time, usually a year.
Quality	In manufacturing terms, producing a product that is fit to sell.
Ratios	Calculations used to work out measurements of liquidity and profitability. A ratio is simply one number divided by another.
Receivership	When a company is taken over by a receiver. A receiver takes control of companies that are about to go bankrupt and sorts out their financial arrangements.
Recession	When for two quarters (a quarter is three months) in a row the value of all the goods sold in an economy falls. Also called 'negative economic growth'.

Recruitment	The process of identifying the need for a new employee, defining the job, attracting candidates and selecting those best suited for the job.
Reserves	Profits that are not distributed as dividends but used to fund future funds or acts as a safety net.
Revenue	Income coming into a business from sales, a grant, leasing of premises, interest on money in the bank etc.
Running costs	The costs that a business pays regularly.
Sample	A collection of 'units' (e.g. people or businesses) from a population of interest.
Scenario planning	When the effects of possible future events are discussed.
Scrapped	Where products that are produced during the manufacturing process are not up to standard and have to be scrapped or repaired (re-worked).
Screening	A means of deciding which applicants should go forward to the later stages of the recruitment process.
Seasonal market	A variation in sales levels at different times in the year.
Secondary sector	Businesses that take raw materials and make them into products.
Shortlist	A list produced by an employer of the best applicants for a job.
Span of control	The number of subordinates a manager has to control.
Stakeholder	Groups of people with an interest in a business.
Start-up costs	The costs a business has to cover when it is first set up.
Subordinate	A person directly below another on an organisation chart for whom they are directly responsible.
Targets	Set to check achievement. They are usually specific and measurable.
Tertiary sector	Businesses that provide services.
Training	The process through which an employee acquires the right sorts of knowledge and skills needed to do their job well.
Unlimited liability	Where the owner of a business is personally responsible for the debts of the business.
Variable costs	Costs that change in proportion to the level of production.
Variance	The difference between the planned and actual amount in a budget.
'What…if' thinking	Where businesses look to the future to identify possible problems and opportunities, i.e. 'What would happen if we reduced costs by 10%?'

Index

Photos

The authors and publisher would like to thank the following individuals and organisations for permission to reproduce photographs:

p10, Gregory Wronga/Alamy; p12 (top), Tony Attille; p12 (bottom), Anthony Carysforth; p14, Courtesy of Apple; p15, Bowland Wild Boar Park; p20, Courtesy of Monsoon; p26, Iain Masterton/Alamy; p28, Michael Krasowitz/Photographers Choice/ Getty Images; p31, Pearson Education Ltd/Devon Obugenga Shaw; p32, Courtesy of Republic; p35, Jupitar Images/Creatas/Alamy; p39, Courtesy of Cummins Turbo Technologies Ltd; p46, Paul Ellis/AFP/Getty Images; p49, Photodisc/Getty Images; p50, Courtesy of Innocent; p51, With thanks to Lort Smith Animal Hospital North Melbourne, Victoria, 2003/ Lindsay Edwards Photography; p52, Vue Cinema; p53, Daniel Berehulak/Getty Images; p54, Siemens; p56, Pearson Education Ltd/Lord and Leverett; p59, Sophia Evans/The Guardian News and Media Ltd 2008; p68, Image Source/Getty Images; p75, Courtesy of Deutsche Post AG; p80 (top), Sven Schrader/ Stone/Getty Images; p80 (bottom), Rex Features; p82, Altrendo RR/Getty Images; p88, Suzie Gibbons/GAP Photos/Getty Images; p89, Stewart Cohen/DreamPictures/Digital Vision/Getty Images; p98, Peter Macdiarmid/Getty Images; p99 (top), Colin Underhill/ Alamy; p99 (bottom), Eye Ubiquitous/Rex Features; p103, Inmagine/Alamy; p112, Hufton & Crow/View Pictures/Rex Features; p114 (top), Pearson Education Ltd/Peter Evans; p114 (bottom), CM Superhighway Ltd; p122, Nick Cunard/Rex Features; p125, Oli Scarff/Getty Images; p127, Whittaker Photography/Pink Ladies Ltd; p128, Courtesy of Trunki; p130, Courtesy of David Lloyd Leisure; p150, Ariel Skelley/The Image Bank/ Getty Images; p156, Courtesy of Nestlé; p158 (left), Dorset Cereals; p158 (right), Courtesy of Innocent; p160, OK! Magazine; p162, Invicta Kent Media/Rex Features; p165, Courtesy of Lush Fresh Handmade Cosmetics Ltd; p166, Red Bull; p174, Dan Kitwood/Getty Images; p183, Mike Clark/AFP/Getty Images; p185, Alistair Berg/Digital Vision/Getty Images; p189, Courtesy of Cadbury; p190, Mark Boulton/Alamy; p197, Courtesy of Harry Ramsden; p203, Lakruwam Wanniarachchi/AFP/Getty Images; p209, Kevin Britland/Alamy; p213, Cate Gillon/Getty Images; p215, Rex Features; p217, Ariel Skelley/Blend Images/Getty Images; p218, Chris Ratcliffe/Rex Features; p220, Peter Dazeley/Stone/Getty Images; p222, FOTOG/Tetra Images/Getty Images; p223, Anderson Ross/Iconica/Getty Images; p225, Richer Sounds plc.